The Carrifran Wildwood Story

Ecological Restoration from the Grass Roots

Myrtle and Philip Ashmole

with members of the Wildwood Group

Carrifran Wildwood is an initiative of the Wildwood Group of Borders Forest Trust
in association with the John Muir Trust

Published in Scotland by
Borders Forest Trust
Monteviot Nurseries
Ancrum
Jedburgh
TD8 6TU

Copyright
© Borders Forest Trust 2009

Supported by Scottish Natural Heritage

A catalogue record for this book is available from the British Library.

ISBN 978-0-9534346-4-0

Printed by:
Bell & Bain, Glasgow

Layout assistance: Cathryn Hill

Photographs: Philip Ashmole except where acknowledged

Illustrations:
Chris Rose (painting)
John Busby (birds)
Darren Woodhead (mammals)
Bill Goodburn (landscapes)
Liz Douglas (painting)
Myrtle Ashmole (maps)
Neil Bennett (cartoons)
Kate Charlesworth and
Stuart Adair (colour
illustrations)

www.carrifran.org.uk
www.bordersforesttrust.org

"Acts of creation are ordinarily reserved for gods and poets, but humbler folk may circumvent this restriction if they know how. To plant a pine, for example, one need be neither god nor poet; one need only own a good shovel. By virtue of this curious loophole in the rules, any clodhopper may say: Let there be a tree—and there will be one. If his back be strong and his shovel sharp, there may eventually be ten thousand. And in the seventh year he may lean upon his shovel, and look upon his trees, and find them good."

Aldo Leopold (1948) 'A Sand County Almanac.'

Foreword

This book marks the 10th anniversary of the purchase of Carrifran, a good time for celebration and for taking stock, even though the concept had its origins years earlier. Already there is a wonderful story to tell. The valley used to be just one of thousands throughout the Borders and the Highlands, smooth bare hillsides sloping up to the high tops, some crags even on the lower slopes, thin soils, screes and signs of erosion. In some valleys there is nothing but a pathetic scattering of trees, often stunted, clinging on beside the burns where the slopes are steepest and sheep cannot reach. In others arbitrary straight-edged patches of sitka spruce break up the landscape.

It is striking that most people seem to overlook the scars and have come to regard the valleys as natural. Of course they are almost entirely un-natural, in the sense that without millennia of human activity almost all our lower hills and valleys running high up towards the tops would be thickly forested. The bare landscape now forms part of what Frank Fraser Darling called 'a wet desert'. His harsh words reflected his despair over thoughtless human activity through the centuries, which has led to the degradation of the land and the huge loss of the diversity of plants and animals which once lived here. This is part of the 'world of wounds' to which Aldo Leopold refers in the Box on page 9, implying that scientists are only too aware of the wounds unnoticed by other people. However, Leopold is wrong to blame science. The blame should fall on society – all of us who have failed to recognise the wounds or have preferred to ignore them.

There is good news, for slowly recognition is coming and over the past few decades there has been a healthy growth of the environmental movement. As part of this, Borders Forest Trust (BFT) was formed, recognizing how far the Borders had become deforested and the value of encouraging local communities to become involved in reforesting and developing old and new woodlands as a major resource for use and for enjoyment. Here they could look to much of continental Europe where local woodlands are a treasured resource, actively encouraged and protected. Agriculture and forestry have always been together there; here we have so often lost this link. BFT is flourishing and adds not just woodlands but real cultural and community benefits.

Carrifran Wildwood is part of BFT, but the Wildwood Group retains its distinct character. This book is a remarkable account of a great adventure, I wouldn't wish to describe it in any other terms. The adventure began with the vision of a few people who were prepared to work enormously hard to achieve something which many people before them have regarded as an impossible dream. The vision was to recreate the original landscape of a large Borders valley, to bring back the ecosystem which would have met the first humans returning, perhaps eight or nine thousand years ago when trees had recolonized Scotland following the retreat of the ice.

The Carrifran project has several unique features. Firstly there is the magnificent, almost arrogant *totality* of its concept – to create from scratch a large and complete wildwood in a bare and degraded valley, to re-establish its original flora and, once established sufficiently, to leave it almost completely alone, with minimal intervention, no harvesting and no special attempt to pull in visitors. I reflect on this totality because it must have been very demanding of the tolerance and forbearance of local people, of planners and statutory bodies like Scottish Natural Heritage and the Forestry Commission and of charitable trusts. A lot of persistent persuasion will have been involved and this story is set out here in a fascinating way.

Secondly, there is the science, for this is not just another tree-planting exercise, it attempts to replicate what was there before. The Carrifran group has been meticulous in getting accurate information on the original flora, from peat cores, from geology, from the remnants which still remained. Trees have been grown from local seed. If oaks are to be planted high up and there are no such local trees, then acorns are gathered from the nearest high oak forests, and so on. As a result much important biological knowledge is coming from Carrifran as it develops and this will be invaluable to those undertaking similar projects. Of course there will have to be some compromises, nature will still require some help as trees return to the bare land, but gradually the human hand will be withdrawing. Already the natural offspring of the first planted trees are themselves growing up.

The third unique feature of Carrifran is perhaps the most important of all, for if human hands are to withdraw the human spirit pours in ever more strongly as this unusual book illustrates. The story of the purchase of the valley is in itself all the evidence one could ask for – has the term 'public ownership' ever had a more marvelously literal meaning – many hundreds contributed and the number never ceases to grow. The diverse stories of how volunteers have worked from the start all show how Carrifran has involved people and become part of their lives.

I have certainly not been an active volunteer, but just keeping in touch with progress has been very important for me. Important to know that in one tiny fragment of the planet we are going to withdraw just to look on and learn as the natural life support systems operate. We urgently need such examples if we are ever to restore some balance between humanity and the Earth that supports us. I have been honoured to be asked at times to speak about Carrifran. I am pleased to recall that in some of the first fund-raising publicity, I described this project in exactly the right way and a way which has become abundantly true for many people. I said, 'It will be an *inspiration!*'

Being asked to write a foreword for this remarkable book which brings together so many voices around a shared endeavour, gives me an opportunity to do something which, even if they were not editors and contributors, they cannot do – to dedicate this 10th year volume to Philip and Myrtle Ashmole. Without their vision, their sustained hard work and the way they have inspired others to take part, Carrifran Wildwood would not have begun. Recently I walked with them up the valley among the sizeable trees on some of the lower slopes and we heard chaffinch, blackcap and willow warblers singing – woodland birds again living in the formerly bare Borders glen. I kept a thought to myself as I stood there with the Ashmoles, *'Si monumentum requiris, circumspice.'*

Aubrey Manning

Preface

In 1993 a group of friends conceived the idea of bringing back natural vegetation to an entire valley in southern Scotland: to restore the kind of wild forest that would have existed there 6000 years ago. This book is an account of the gestation and early life of the reborn forest. Although we are the main authors, there are substantial sections and many smaller contributions by other members of the Wildwood Group. The book is written primarily for the thousands of people who have helped to create Carrifran Wildwood, by generously donating their money, working as volunteers in the background or dirtying their hands and boots in the valley and on the hills around it. These people are spread over Britain and even overseas; most of them have never visited Carrifran. They are, however, all participants in a co-operative enterprise that we hope will demonstrate the power of ordinary people to enhance the parts of the world in which they live. Grass roots tend to be largely hidden, and this account may help to expose their anatomy, showing how the project has depended on volunteers and has at the same time enriched their lives.

A theme that recurs in the personal contributions to the book – either explicitly or between the lines – is that it was the scale and ambition of the vision that led people to get involved. This perception matches our own experience. We were all sure that we should think big, aiming to create a living entity that would both pay some of our dues to the wild animals and plants that have suffered at the hands of humans, and make an impact on the minds of those who came to know about it. It is our fondest hope that this account of the early years of the Carrifran Wildwood project may encourage visionary, practical people around the world to embark on equally ambitious projects of ecological restoration.

Conservation of surviving wild places must be a priority, but where these have almost disappeared, there is a need to complement it with restoration. In ecologically degraded areas there is a compelling case for re-creation – as far as this is possible – of some examples of fully-functioning natural ecosystems. These can provide refuges for native wildlife, and can also provide inspiration and healing for people. As the conservationist John Muir wrote, a century ago: *"Thousands of tired, nerve-shaken, over-civilized people are beginning to find out that going to the mountains is going home; that wildness is a necessity."*

In southern Scotland some may ask: *What changed a richly forested countryside into the denuded one that we see today?* This was not the sudden catastrophic forest destruction that we now witness in so many parts of the world. For many millennia change must have been almost imperceptible, with only hints of the influence of Neolithic farmers in the increasing prevalence of open-ground plants and perhaps in an increased occurrence of fire. Only in the past fifteen hundred years is there evidence for more intensive land use and rapid decline of woodland, probably caused mainly by sheep, goats and cattle. At present, there is nowhere to wander in southern Scotland in an extensive, diverse and unkempt woodland of native trees, and nowhere to hear the heartbeat of an ecosystem that once was the home of lynx, wildcats and wolves, eagles and elk, martens, polecats, beavers and bears.

It is easy to ask: *Does this matter?* The members of the Wildwood Group believe that it does, and have therefore set about trying to reverse the process of destruction in a single treeless valley in the Moffat Hills. So far, the work has occupied fifteen years. We hope that over the coming centuries, our successors may reap the full reward.

So much has already been written about Carrifran, in reports, grant applications, minutes, newsletters etc, that what we have written here – even when it is in the first person – often relies heavily on the writings of others. Since the book is primarily by two of us, the use of the word 'we' was inevitable. However, the same word is used when referring to the Wildwood Group in general, and later to the Steering Group. We hope the distinction will be clear from the context and apologise if it occasionally is not. We are also aware that others would have recorded things from different points of view. If we have left out things that they feel should have been included, or have included things that they would have preferred to see omitted, we can only apologise.

Myrtle and Philip Ashmole
Peebles, Scotland, July 2009

Acknowledgements

Our first acknowledgement must be to the hunter who abandoned his bow 6000 years ago and became a leading figure in our publicity and fundraising. Among those still with us, we would like to thank the many people who have contributed to the book, especially those who wrote sections of Chapters 5, 6 and 9 – Michael Matthews, Ann Goodburn, Fi Martynoga, Hugh Chalmers, Richard Tipping, Stuart Adair, David Long, Crinan Alexander and Neville Morgan. In addition we thank the geologists Derek Robeson, Elizabeth Pickett and Steve Hannah on whose work we have drawn, John Savory who organised the information on birds, and also the authors of the numerous 'boxes'. We are sure that many other people would have been willing to record their memories of helping to create the Wildwood, and we hope they will forgive us if they did not have the opportunity.

We also thank the artists who so generously agreed to contribute illustrations and Jim Crumley for his poem. Most other contributors or helpers are mentioned in the main text or in the boxes. We also wish to thank all the other individuals who have provided information or read and commented on sections of the text, especially Crinan Alexander who proof-read the book at a late stage. We owe a special debt to Cathryn Hill, student graphic designer, who volunteered her services and worked on the layout of the book over many months, exhibiting extraordinary skill and patience.

Finally, it is a pleasure to thank Scottish Natural Heritage, who have provided major support for this publication and whose staff have been unfailingly supportive over the years.

Mission Statement of the Wildwood Group

The Wildwood project aims to re-create, in the Southern Uplands of Scotland, an extensive tract of mainly forested wilderness with most of the rich diversity of native species present in the area before human activities became dominant. The woodland will not be exploited commercially and the impact of humans will be carefully managed. Access will be open to all, and it is hoped that the Wildwood will be used throughout the next millennium as an inspiration and an educational resource.

Contents

1. The idea of ecological restoration

Ecological restoration as a complement to conservation—bringing back biodiversity and functioning ecosystems—preference for natural over technological approaches—building on what survives—value of pioneer and keystone species—role of large predators—danger of alien invaders— mimicking natural patterns—avoidance of tidying up—a helping hand where necessary—gradually reducing management—relaxing with natural outcomes—working with love and respect for nature—vision coupled with practicality.

* * * * *

In the long shadows of the final years of the 20th century, with the prognosis for the third millennium uncertain, the Wildwood Group decided to accept the challenge of biologist and conservationist Edward O Wilson, who wrote in 1992:

> *"We should not knowingly allow any species or race to go extinct. And let us go beyond mere salvage to begin the restoration of natural environments, in order to enlarge wild populations and staunch the haemorrhaging of biological wealth. There can be no purpose more enspiriting than to begin the age of restoration, reweaving the wondrous diversity of life that still surrounds us."*

The idea of ecological restoration began to gain strength in the 1980s when far-sighted naturalists – increasingly aware that in almost all parts of the planet, ecosystems evolved over many millions of years were being rapidly degraded by human activity – concluded that systematic action was needed to heal some of the wounds of the earth.

These modern pioneers share with earlier generations of conservationists the appreciation of the functional beauty of the natural world that John Muir expressed when he wrote in 1901: *"None of Nature's landscapes are ugly so long as they are wild."* However, arriving later and seeing the greater extent of the damage caused by humans, they realise that in

"One of the penalties of an ecological education is that one lives alone in a world of wounds. Much of the damage inflicted on land is quite invisible to laymen. An ecologist must either harden his shell and make believe that the consequences of science are none of his business, or he must be the doctor who sees the marks of death in a community that believes itself well and does not want to be told otherwize."
Aldo Leopold (1993) 'Round River.'

An island, like this one in Mull, or a high rock, can protect a few trees from deer, cattle, sheep and goats
Photo below: Hugh Chalmers

some areas the losses have already been so great that conservation of surviving fragments must be accompanied by more drastic intervention. Their ambitious goal is to repair degraded ecosystems.

A primary aim is the restoration of biodiversity, the richness of life. This richness is expressed at many levels; it encompasses the varied ecosystems in different climatic zones and the habitats within them, along with the multitude of species that live there and the diversity within each species. As biodiversity is restored, so is ecosystem function – the natural cycling of energy, water and nutrients through the system, which is caused by the interaction of species with each other and with their physical environment.

Some years ago the Scottish organisation *Trees for Life* set out a number of principles that can form the basis for initiatives in ecological restoration, and many of their publications refer to these ideas. The following brief account owes much to them. It focuses especially on the re-creation of forests in landscapes denuded by human activity.

One of the most fundamental ideas is that in trying to re-create a natural system, one should as far as possible reinvigorate and mimic natural processes rather than using technological approaches. Such approaches have sometimes caused the problems in the first place.

So, for example, in restoring forests, one should be wary of the use of fertilisers and herbicides, and eschew mechanical processes that leave the land scarred, such as deep ploughing or mounding before planting trees.

Where possible, ecological restoration projects should strive to protect, enlarge and reconnect the surviving fragments of natural systems. Expansion from scattered woodland fragments is therefore preferable to planting in a totally denuded landscape. However, small fragments of natural systems are usually poor in species, since over long periods they inexorably lose diversity through chance events; they thus come to lack much of the richness that was once present in the more extensive primeval habitats. If surviving fragments can be reconnected, the movements of individuals or of genes (in pollen, spores or widely dispersing seeds) can restore some species to places where they were lacking and increase the genetic diversity of populations that have become inbred. Even then, there may be a lack of the rarer, more specialised and more sedentary members of the original communities, so these may have to be brought in from afar. Only in extreme cases, where almost no trace of the original habitat is left, is it necessary to lay new foundations and import all components from healthy surviving examples of the relevant ecosystem.

Some species may be of special importance as pioneers. In Scotland, trees such as juniper, birch, aspen and some willows are able to cope with skeletal soils and high exposure, and as they grow they can improve the soil and provide shelter for more demanding species, which may later supplant them by shading. Other plants and animals are considered 'keystone species' because they exert a major influence on the composition and dynamics of the communities in which they live. The European beaver is such a species, and its removal, followed by extensive drainage of the land, has eliminated almost all our natural wetlands and decimated the plants and animals associated with them.

Large predators also play a key role, since without them the mammalian herbivores, for instance red or roe deer, may reach such high densities that forests cannot regenerate and gradually disappear. Predators such as lynx and wolves once ensured that deer were fewer and patchier in their distribution, allowing episodes of natural regeneration in local areas. Where reinstatement of predators is not a practical option at present, culling of herbivores may be needed to achieve habitat restoration.

If we are aiming to restore a natural system we may need to control or remove invasive alien species that can have devastating effects. Natural ecosystems are products of long-term evolutionary interactions among the component species, so assemblages that survive have achieved a

Aldo Leopold on wolves

One of the key qualities of Aldo Leopold, who with John Muir was one of the fathers of the conservation movement in North America, was his ability to change his views as a result of personal experience. In 'A Sand County Almanac' he described an encounter with an old wolf and her grown cubs:

"In those days we had never heard of passing up a chance to kill a wolf. In a second we were pumping lead into the pack.... We reached the old wolf in time to watch a fierce green fire dying in her eyes..... I was young then, and full of trigger-itch; I thought that because fewer wolves meant more deer, that no wolves would mean hunters' paradise. But after seeing the green fire die, I sensed that neither the wolf nor the mountain agreed with such a view. Since then I have lived to see state after state extirpate its wolves. I have watched the face of many a newly wolfless mountain, and seen the south-facing slopes wrinkle with a maze of new deer trails. I have seen every edible bush and seedling browsed, first to anaemic desuetude, and then to death. I have seen every edible tree defoliated to the height of a saddlehorn. Such a mountain looks as if someone had given God a new pruning shears, and forbidden Him all other exercise".

Trees for Life

The vision of Trees for Life "… is to restore a wild forest, which is there for its own sake, as a home for wildlife and to fulfil the ecological functions necessary for the well being of the land itself."

Moved by the plight of the ancient Caledonian forest in the Highlands of Scotland, Trees for Life began work in 1989 to help it to regenerate and expand again. They initially concentrated on Glen Affric, the largest area of relatively undisturbed forest left in Scotland, but now work throughout a region of over 2,370 sq km in the north-central Highlands, within which they envision restoring a natural wild forest to about 1,500 sq km. In the longer term, they also advocate the return of the missing wildlife species, as these are essential parts of the forest ecosystem.

Like the Wildwood Group, Trees for Life are not aiming to regenerate a forest which will be used comercially, although they recognise the need for this in Scotland. They envision their work to restore the Caledonian Forest as not only helping to bring the land here back to a state of health and balance, but also having global relevance, as a model for similar projects in other countries.

dynamic equilibrium. Alien species, in contrast, often bring new threats. Each case requires urgent study and robust decision making, since some problems can be easily nipped in the bud, while vain attempts to combat others may squander scarce resources.

It will take many decades for restored woodland to achieve a degree of naturalness, but care at the outset can speed the process. Here are a few 'shoulds'. Tree species have adapted to a variety of soil types, aspect and moisture regimes, so in restoring native woodlands one should try to match each species to its preferred conditions. In this way the natural variation within the site will be reflected in the diversity of the developing woodland. Planting should vary in density and the degree of clumping, attempting to mimic the pattern of naturally established seedlings and avoiding even spacing and straight lines. Once the trees and shrubs are in place, natural competition should be tolerated, allowing self-thinning and the death of suppressed trees, as well as accumulation of deadwood, a key ecological resource. Dead branches and trunks and rotting stumps provide a stage on which a large cast of species can enact an ecological play. Fungal species aid in the process of decomposition and the recycling of nutrients, and hundreds of kinds of insects and other invertebrates live in the decaying wood. These then form prey for animals such as woodpeckers and badgers, while holes in dead trees and branches provide nesting and roosting sites for squirrels, bats and many kinds of birds.

Deadwood communities can be given a good start in a forest restoration project. In the normal planting we can include elm trees that will probably die young from Dutch elm disease, and there may be a case for importing logs with a cargo of fungi and invertebrates. However, some species require a continuous supply of particular kinds of wood or particular stages of decay, so deadwood resources are particularly hard to restore. A somewhat easier task is the bringing in of some of those woodland plants that are unlikely to arrive naturally due to low dispersal ability, thus helping the development of a diverse ground flora in the restored woodland.

In general, however, we should resist the urge to micro-manage, once the system is up and running. As *Trees for Life* pointed out, if we can remove the destructive factors that have caused the damage, nature can be relied on to do most of the work of restoration. In ecological restoration projects there will usually be a gradual reduction in the scope and intensity of management, as natural processes gain momentum.

It is to be expected that as the nature of the land changes, some species that thrived in the man-made or transitional habitats will suffer. For instance, butterflies typical of open ground may decline as woodland develops. Such loss should be tolerated, since the philosophy of ecological restoration differs subtly from that of conservation. Those engaged in the former prefer to work on a landscape scale to re-create a natural ecosystem with the species that belong there; if other species disappear, so be it. In contrast, managers of conservation sites are often responsible for the preservation of particular rare species, which may require continuing intensive intervention. Many projects, of course, have dual aims.

A frequent comment by those who are sceptical of ecological restoration runs somewhat as follows: *"But you can't put the clock back; the world has changed since the disappearance of the pristine habitats that you aim to restore."* There is much truth in this, but we do not think it should inhibit us from attempting restoration. Our restored ecosystem will not precisely match the original, but we have faith that it can be a rich and properly functioning entity, aiding understanding of what has been lost, providing services such as mitigation of floods and absorption of carbon dioxide, and offering both a home to a host of native species and tranquillity and inspiration to those who walk in it.

In the denuded hills of southern Scotland the case for ecological restoration is as clear as anywhere. Relict fragments of native woodland – with some of the associated plants, fungi and animals – survive in precipitous ravines and on cliffs, providing a glimpse of our lost

"A well farmed and thoroughly domesticated countryside and untouched, natural terrain with its vegetation and wildlife complexes intact can both be deeply satisfying. But an inherently infertile region devastated by deforestation and repeated burning, largely depopulated and then opened to heavy and uncontrolled sheep grazing is a distressing sight to anyone with some appreciation of ecological principles."
D. McVean and J. Lockie (1969) 'Ecology and Land use in Upland Scotland.'

With a bit of help, Carrifran could be like this again

biological wealth. Conserving them is a priority, but with a little vision we can glimpse a more exciting possibility, broad swathes of restored and almost natural forested wilderness, rich in biodiversity and large enough to allow our successors to experience something akin to the primeval environment of the region in which they live.

We are much in sympathy with the final principle listed by Trees for Life, that in attempting to restore natural systems one should work with love and respect, and in cooperation with nature. We stand in awe of the extraordinary achievements of evolution by natural selection and take delight – on a daily basis – in the complex adaptations of organisms. However, we are also convinced that in attempts at restoration, idealistic vision and respect for nature must be coupled with 'feet on the ground' practicality, and we are prepared to take tough decisions in carrying forward the work. In the Wildwood Group, distress at the manner in which the behaviour of modern humans continues to degrade our world underpins a determination to restore a small part of it to its full natural beauty and complexity.

2. Gathering momentum

Impressions of a deforested landscape—loss of Scottish woodland—Trees for Life—Peeblesshire Environment Concern—Reforesting Scotland—inspiration from others—getting things going in the Borders.

* * * * *

There is no single beginning to the story of Carrifran. Willie McGhee (Director of Borders Forest Trust) recently wrote:

> *"The Wildwood objective of re-creating a native forest is an expression of the wider realisation that in areas where natural ecosystems have almost completely disappeared, conservation of surviving relict fragments needs to be complemented by positive action to establish habitats that function without the intervention of humans."*

No one of us in the Wildwood Group came to this shared realisation in the same way. For us (Myrtle and Philip) it was quite clearly a decision in the early 1990s, although in retrospect we realised that its roots were in the previous decades. In 1996 Philip wrote:

> *"When Myrtle and I came to Scotland with our three children after a decade in the Americas, we had acquired a taste for wilderness. But as biologists, it was the ecology of wilderness that fascinated us, and in the wild places of Scotland we were dismayed to realise that we were often looking at the bare bones of ecosystems that had flourished thousands of years earlier. The landscapes were beautiful, but – in today's jargon – the biodiversity was largely lost."*

Key experiences included a visit to Shetland with Edinburgh University students in 1974, where we found pathetic remnants of the low forest that once covered much of the archipelago, clinging to cliff ledges or confined to islets too small to support even a single sheep. Later, in South Harris, we saw surviving vegetation on one such islet being set fire

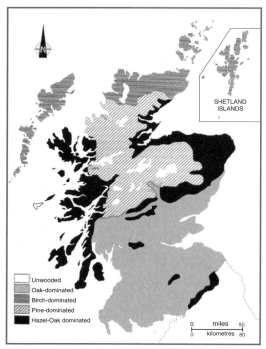

Six thousand years ago Scotland was almost entirely wooded. Courtesy Richard Tipping

Large flocks of sheep and herds of cattle, as well as the rarely mentioned goats, gradually inhibited the natural regeneration of trees and led to the development of increasingly senile woodlands

to because someone thought that 'hoodies' might nest there. In the Borders, we stumbled on a giant holly, ring-barked and killed by foresters planting alien conifers. Not only had most of the native woodlands vanished, leaving large areas of artificially maintained grassland, but great tracts of this were now being covered by regimented blocks of uniform green monoculture, and landowners were busy 'coniferising' even the tiny pockets where native trees survived.

Thinking back over that time, Fi Martynoga, a founding member of the Wildwood Group, recently wrote:

'We had always been aware of how these southern Scottish hills lacked trees. In Edinburgh, when the children were small, my husband Andy was forever growing oak, ash and elm in pots. An infant forest, all in containers, moved with us to the Borders but it was difficult to find places to plant them out. Since Andy's ambition was to plant a wood, he and I joined the embryonic Wildwood Group after the 1993 conference. When he died unexpectedly a couple of years later, it left me doubly determined to see the wildwood established.'

Ann Goodburn, who was also a part of the team from the beginning, wrote:

"When I was growing up in the Borders I loved the bareness of the hills of home and indeed they are superb. It was only later when I was a geography student at Edinburgh that I realised my hills were barren 'sheep gangs', laid bare and cropped by much munching allied to a pretty rough history of fire, foray and clearance. After the last Ice Age, some 10,000 years ago, a wonderful forest must have very gradually crept up those hills and it is a little bit of that which we would like to recreate at Carrifran. Sadly not many of the original group will live to see the Wildwood in its glory but what true tree planters ever see the climax results of their dreams? Philip and Myrtle were inspirational and I was drawn along by their incredible enthusiasm, drive and knowledge of the natural world to be a lucky small part of this adventure."

These accounts were personal reactions to the loss of the natural woodlands of Scotland and the particularly denuded state of the Southern Uplands where we live. We had eventually become aware of what was missing, but it is not easy to make the link between media accounts of the modern destruction of tropical rainforests and the loss of our own natural forest so many centuries ago. It takes the work of archaeologists and historians, laboriously documenting what was once here, to help us understand the changes. The map by Richard Tipping of the extent of woodland types in Scotland some 6000 years ago gives a general picture based on pollen evidence. It makes clear the extraordinary extent of the loss over the last six millennia.

A few ecologists argue that complex natural factors – rather than human activities – are mainly responsible for forest loss in the Highlands and the Western Isles, but everyone agrees that humans and their associated grazing animals have played the major role in the Southern Uplands. In this area, pastoralism became significant thousands of years ago and forest clearance accelerated in the Dark Ages, but the beginning of the end for the natural woodlands of the Scottish Borderlands came with the monastic expansion in the 12th century. The large and well-documented flocks of sheep and herds of cattle, as well as the rarely mentioned goats, gradually inhibited the natural regeneration of trees and led to the development of increasingly senile woodlands.

In the following centuries, warfare often involved scorched earth policies and the felling of many trees, but as pointed out by Chris Badenoch – who for many years led the Nature Conservancy and then Scottish Natural Heritage in the Borders – the lawlessness of families and internecine strife may have had equally serious impact on forests, and any attempt at enclosure and regeneration or replanting was doomed by action of one's neighbours. There were efforts to conserve woods, but the area in the western Borders known as the Ettrick Forest seems to have been largely denuded by the 16th century. Recently, it was estimated that in the Borders as a whole, only around one four-hundredth (0.25%) of the land carried ancient semi-natural woodland.

During the last three decades many people have become aware of how much of our natural heritage has been lost, and have begun to focus on what can be done about it. By the end of the 1980s there was already a palpable grass-roots ferment of ideas relating both to the restoration of land in the Highlands and to its use and ownership by people. Although it was the large number of talented people involved that actually made things happen, two figures in particular caught our attention. Alan Watson created Trees for Life in 1981. His determination to make a difference, both in the Northwest Highlands and around the world, has been a continuing inspiration to many people, including the members of the Wildwood Group.

Around the same time Bernard Planterose, while working as a warden for the RSPB, was offered a choice of location for his summer work and chose a small island off Wester Ross, thus starting a chain of

The Borders context

Long before the conference on Restoring Borders Woodland, systematic habitat survey for Sites of Special Scientific Interest had shown that the amount of ancient semi-natural woods in the Borders was pitifully small. Most woods were long and thin – open to strong sunlight, winter exposure and drying winds. No single wood was in excess of 20 hectares. Ettrick & Lauderdale and Berwickshire had some 0.25% of their land surface in ancient woodland over 2 ha in extent, Roxburgh somewhat less and Tweeddale a meagre 0.17%. To the west, Clydesdale had 0.6% and Nithsdale/Annandale only slightly more. Woodland fragments in the steep cleuchs and gullies added significantly to the total and to the typical woodland species complement, but still left long distances with little or no connection between the proper woodland: no bridges and corridors for genetic exchange. Something had to be done if the genetic and ecological resources were to be saved. Land at the time was too valuable within Borders Region and the vision of Peeblesshire Environmental Concern seized the opportunity in nearby Moffatdale: Carrifran became the focus. It was clearly defined, physically 'contained', had some ancient woody fragments and gave an excellent range of altitude. Wildwood became.

Chris Badenoch

Reforesting Scotland

Reforesting Scotland was formed in June 1991 when the founding Directors set up the organisation as an extension of the highly successful journal 'The Tree Planter's Guide to the Galaxy', which was launched in the summer of 1989. The originators of the journal were Bernard and Emma Planterose, Ron Greer and Martin Howard, soon joined by Donald McPhillimy and Andy Wightman. It continues under the more prosaic name 'Reforesting Scotland', and together with the organisation of the same name, is an independent and respected outlet for new ideas and perspectives on reforestation and associated social, cultural, economic, spiritual, ecological and international issues.

The vision of Reforesting Scotland is the "creation of a well-forested and productive landscape as well as a culture which values the contribution that trees and woods bring to our lives." The group has helped bring about a transformation in the way we, as a nation, view Scotland's forest resource and the level to which communities have become involved in managing their local woodlands.

events that led to him and his wife Emma featuring in a 1991 Time Magazine story on the still unfamiliar concept of ecological restoration. In the following year, looking back on the previous decade, he wrote:

"If there are turning points or milestones in life then this was certainly one for me. I moved up to Isle Martin at the mouth of Loch Broom in the spring of 1981 and, in a sense, have never left. I met my wife, Emma, while working there, saw my first child born there, planted my first tree there. What more is there to life?"

Bernard was one of the originators of the journal that started in 1989 under the name 'The Tree Planters Guide to the Galaxy', and also one of the founders of Reforesting Scotland, which has done so much to foster interest in native woodlands.

It was also in the 1980s that changes in attitude first became apparent in the forestry establishment. A desire to provide benefits to the public by offering opportunities for recreation in forests may have led to increased interest in broadleaved – mainly native – trees, and thence to the idea of protecting and even planting native woodlands.

Meanwhile in Peebles a group called Peeblesshire Environment Concern (PEC) had been set up in 1986 by Ann Goodburn, Fi Martynoga, Myrtle and other friends. The objective was to alert people to many of the environmental issues that are now, nearly quarter of a century later, discussed in the media on a daily basis.

Philip had been excited by the idea of ecological restoration, but was convinced that it could only work if done on a large scale. In July 1992 he made a written submission to the Regional Chairman of the newly formed Scottish Natural Heritage, suggesting that they should organise a major initiative for ecological enhancement of the River Tweed catchment, promoting the piece-by-piece development of a network of riparian and upland woodland by co-operating landowners. The initial response was friendly, but nothing happened. It seemed clear that effective action in the south of Scotland would need to come from the grass-roots.

For Philip and Myrtle, it was the first annual gathering of Reforesting Scotland in the same autumn that changed passive unease into a determination to get involved in restoring native woodland. About eighty people attended the meeting at Kindrogan Field Studies Centre in Perthshire, and we gained a strong impression that nearly all of them were dirty-hands tree planters.

During the weekend we learned about a series of inspiring initiatives by individuals and small groups of people from all over Scotland. Bernard and Emma Planterose explained how they were growing trees for Isle Martin, Alan Watson described the travails of Trees

A sea change in the Forestry Commission

Developments in the Forestry Commission near the end of the 20th century provide a remarkable example of the speed with which changes in public attitudes can be reflected in bureaucratic organisations and in the targeting of government support.

One of the last manifestations of the old regime came in 1985, when A.A. Rowan of the Forestry Commission started the lead contribution to a symposium on Trees and Wildlife in the Scottish Uplands as follows:

"If anyone had reviewed the status of British upland forests in 1885, he would have found little to write about; the fundamental feature of these forests today is that they exist. The restoration of forest cover to a substantial part of the uplands must be one of the most dramatic land use changes experienced in these islands."

The restored forests referred to were the swathes of non-native conifers that now cover so much of Scotland. Rowan described the Commission's response to the Government policy of forest expansion in the decades following World War II, but – in spite of his name – the only hints of an interest in native woodlands were a mention of a 'guideline' aim of a proportion of broadleaves in upland forests and a comment that:

"The first, colonizing, post glacial forest gave way to the forests which were exploited by man up to and beyond mediaeval times, and of which only semi-natural remnants are left."

Less than a decade later, R.T. Bradley, Head of the Forestry Authority, began his foreword to FC Bulletin 112 (1994) on Creating New Native Woodlands with the words:

"The proportion of native trees and shrubs planted within woodlands of all kinds has increased dramatically over the last few years and there has also been a growing interest in establishing new native woodlands, composed entirely of native trees and shrubs suited to the site. There are probably two principal motivations: firstly the desire to expand the remnants of our semi-natural woods and secondly the more general aim of reversing past losses of native species in the wider countryside."

The Commission had widened its focus from the simple aim of timber production to take account of the strengthening public interest in social and environmental aspects of forestry. The change has led to the funding by the taxpayer of thousands of acres of new native woodland, including that at Carrifran. When the Scottish Forestry Strategy was published at the start of the new millennium it stated:

"The vision is that Scotland will be renowned as a land of fine trees, woods and forests which strengthen the economy, which enrich the natural environment, and which people enjoy and value."

It all happened in 15 years.

The denuded uplands of the Borders are plastered with conifer plantations

Reforesting Scotland visited Glen Garry where Ron Greer had established tiny groups of waterside trees, carrying tools and trees on his bicycle or on the bus

for Life in working with the Forestry Commission in Glen Affric, Alan Drever talked about community woodlands, Edward Milner showed part of his Channel 4 film series Spirit of Trees, Graham Tuley described his work in developing tree tubes, and there was spirited discussion of land reform, living in the woods, the strength of Norwegian forest culture and a host of other topics.

A field trip to Loch Garry crowned the event, with Ron Greer explaining how he had hitched lifts and carried tools and bundles of trees on his bicycle, establishing tiny groups of waterside trees to improve the feeding conditions for young fish. En route, our minibus rounded a corner to find a rowan tree, covered with brilliant berries but also adorned by half a dozen feasting blackcock, reinforcing the message that loss of trees brings other losses in its wake.

The effect of all this was to galvanise us into action. Talking things over in the car on the way home, we decided that while the restoration of the Caledonian pinewoods was in good hands, the broadleaf woodlands of the Southern Uplands needed more help. It occurred to us that a high profile conference might be the way to get things moving.

We quickly decided that PEC should organise the conference, and we somewhat presumptuously called it 'Restoring Borders Woodland'.

Philip – a zoologist with little knowledge of forestry – spent much of his time in the following year working on the programme. There was much to learn about native woodland creation and about the people who mattered on the Scottish forestry scene. Andy Wightman, Development Officer for Reforesting Scotland, provided many insights on personalities and land ownership issues, and Michael Osborne, Director of the Royal Scottish Forestry Society, was a tower of strength. We were aware from the start that latent interest and concern about native woodlands were there, and as we talked to people it often seemed that we were pushing at an open door.

If the conference were to be influential – and there was no point in doing it otherwise – we had to raise credibility, since PEC was a small organisation little known outside Peebles. The first move was to ask Lt. Col. Aidan Sprot, a woodland owner and Lord Lieutenant of Tweeddale, to open the conference, and we followed this by inviting Sir Michael Strang Steel, estate owner and Forestry Commissioner, to give a vote of thanks at the end. Since landowners were the people most likely to be able to restore local woodlands, we then asked the Duke of Buccleuch, the largest landowner in the Borders, to make a presentation. Although he was unable to accept, his son Richard Dalkeith (now 10th Duke of Buccleuch) agreed to take part.

Participants and publications from the 1993 conference

Peeblesshire Environment Concern

Peeblesshire Environment Concern (PEC) is just a group of ordinary people from the Borders, who happen to live around Peebles. It is a voluntary organisation founded in 1986 when it initiated a series of evening classes in Peebles covering local and global environmental issues. A few years later it published a booklet entitled Peeblesshire Green Pages. Such publications were rare at the time, and it seems surprising, looking back from the early 21st century, that issues like air pollution, forest destruction and the need for recycling were then new to many people, although the activities of organisations such as WWF, Friends of the Earth and Greenpeace were having considerable effect.

Several years later a third lecture series for PEC under the title of 'Border Landscapes Past, Present and Possibilities' reflected the excitement generated by the Borders bid to the Millennium Forest for Scotland. This was followed by PEC's main initiative on woodlands, which was the organisation of the 'Restoring Borders Woodland' conference in November 1993.

From the beginning we were clear that we should invite individual speakers whom we wanted, rather than asking organisations to send a representative. This became critical when approaching the Forestry Commission, Scottish Natural Heritage and also some non-governmental organizations (NGOs), since we were determined to avoid getting routine statements of official policies, and instead to focus on ambitious visions for the future. Such visions were well represented on the day, with inspiring talks by leading thinkers about ecological restoration and future land use, and with input from Trees for Life, Reforesting Scotland, RSPB, WWF and the Scottish Wildlife Trust. The local focus was strengthened by contributions from staff of the Tweed Foundation and SNH, as well as the Forestry Commission.

About the same size as in 1905, the partly coniferised woodland fragment in Gameshope valley still contains a wide variety of native trees and shrubs one hundred years later

None of us in PEC had experience in organising conferences, so we didn't have the disadvantage of knowing how much work it would be. The conference was held at the Dryburgh Abbey Hotel near St Boswells, on 12th November 1993, and was followed by a day of excursions. When publicising the affair we first invited landowners and farmers, then proceeded to ask other people who had experience or influence, and finally opened it to anyone interested. We were soon fully subscribed with 120 people; even now, many years later, there are people who remind us that they were turned away, although most of them were able to come on one of the excursions. We made many good friends for the future Wildwood at that time.

Full proceedings of the conference were later published by PEC and several of the key articles were reprinted in Scottish Forestry, journal of the Royal Scottish Forestry Society. However, since publication would take time, we arranged for immediate distribution of the Restoring Borders Woodland Newsletter, written by Anna Ashmole and with funding from the Borders Regional Council. It included, under the title 'Sowing seeds for Borders Woodland', a synthesis of contributors' ideas on the future role of native woodlands in the landscape and culture of the Scottish Borders, which to a large extent outlined the future role of Borders Forest Trust, founded two years later.

It was also in this newsletter that the idea of an ambitious grass-roots ecological restoration initiative in the Southern Uplands, which Philip had outlined in response to a question at the end of the conference, first appeared in print. This idea was based on the vision – of a denuded Borders valley restored to something like its natural forested state – which had come to Philip on 29th May 1993 during a walk in Gameshope valley (coincidentally leading up to a watershed with Carrifran). Near the start of the walk he had stumbled across a fenced and partly coniferised woodland fragment and had been surprised to find that it still contained a wide variety of native trees and shrubs. Further on, he had looked down on the scrubby birch trees surviving on a tiny islet in Loch Skene, the only place where they were safe from sheep and goats. Within a few days he had written a paragraph that could still stand as a blueprint for Carrifran Wildwood:

> *"The vision is to restore the post-glacial ecology of an area large enough to enable visitors to experience the landscape as 'natural' wilderness. Ideally, there should be scope for re-creating the full spectrum of natural vegetation zones of the Borders: rich broadleaf woodland on lower ground; birch, hazel and rowan on steep slopes; willows, alder and aspen near watercourses; and a tree-line with woodland grading into montane scrub and then into upland heath. Such a scheme would be one of the most dramatic ecological restoration projects in the United Kingdom."*

A good example of birch-juniper woodland in Strathdon

Woodland that was not

Scent the distilled whisky
of the land;
scan the sheep-shorn glen;
toast the woodland that was not.
Drink:

To every willow
which never wept
with the joy of being.

To every silver birch
which never found
its crock of gold
at summer's rainbow's end.

To every rowan
which never bannered
the throneroom of an eagle,
and every eaglet
which never fledged
and never flew
from a rowan-bright nursery.

To every hazel,
oak and aspen
which never shadowed the burn
and every trout and salmon
which never lingered
in pools never shaded.

To every songbird
which never pierced
every silent May-Day dawn
and never lived to die
in the fast clutch
of every sparrowhawk
never weaned in nests
which never leaned
by tall pine trunks
which never grew
in the woodland that was not.

To every tree-creepering,
woodpeckering, owl-hootering thing
which never clawed bark
which never wrapped
all the ungrown woodland
and every roe deer and stoat,
badger and bat,
squirrel and wildcat,
four-legged this-and-that
which never stepped
into woodland clearings
across the whole unwooded hill.

To every woodland moth
and mite and moss
and tree-thirled lichen
which never sought a tiny haven here.

A health to you
wherever you prospered.
It was not here
on the hill grown empty
as a hollow tree.

Jim Crumley (1993) 'Among Mountains.'
Mainstream Publishing

3. The Search

The Millennium Forest for Scotland—gathering local support—diversity of the Borders bid—gestation of Borders Forest Trust—coping with bureaucracy—formation of the Wildwood Group—searching for the ideal site—learning about native woodlands—mirage of lottery money—formulating the Mission Statement—finding Carrifran valley—rejecting a silly price—complex negotiations—reaching a deal—pronouncing 'Carrifran' and naming the project—assessing our skills and structuring the group—just a thought.

* * * * *

Although the idea of re-creating a Wildwood was presented briefly at the Restoring Borders Woodland conference in 1993, it then went to the back of our minds, since funding such a project did not seem feasible and we (Myrtle and Philip) were planning a six month research visit to St Helena in the South Atlantic. However, no sooner had we left Scotland in late 1994 than the advent of the lottery changed everything.

The National Lottery Act was passed in 1993 and the Millennium Commission (one of the original lottery 'good causes') was charged with promoting inspiring projects to mark the start of the new millennium. It sought bids for projects which were *"unique in vision, scale, novelty, or the harnessing of new energy in the community, enlisting grass-roots support, celebrating excellence... and, above all, forming a permanent enhancement of our national heritage".*

Representatives from major environmental NGOs, including Simon Pepper of WWF Scotland and John Hunt of the RSPB, responded to this challenge by coming up with the brilliant idea of a 'Millennium Forest for Scotland', to be made up of an array of separate native woodland initiatives spread around the country. A steering group was set up, chaired by Simon Pepper, and this soon led to the formal establishment of the Millennium Forest for Scotland Trust

Alan Watson Featherstone of Trees for Life talking about an aspen plot on a trip organised by the Millennium Forest for Scotland Trust

(MFST). This was a co-ordinating organisation enabling relatively small projects to obtain lottery funding from the Millennium Commission. Barbara Kelly became Convenor and Penny Cousins and John Hunt were appointed Project Manager and Programme Manager respectively.

The Millennium Forest initiative, with its initial aim of creating or restoring a thousand square kilometres of native woodland using fifty million pounds of lottery money, caught people's imagination. Philip still remembers his excitement when he first heard of it, reading an article in *The Scotsman* reviewing ideas for celebrating the millennium, in which the journalist singled out the Millennium Forest as being a truly inspirational and appropriate project. A later campaign to gather evidence of public support, led in the Peebles area by Ann Goodburn and Fi Martynoga, gathered more than 67,000 signatures from all over Scotland. The final outcome was relatively modest, since MFST obtained only £11.3 million from the lottery, but the initiative was credited with creating or taking into positive management some 230 square kilometres of woodland, through 80 projects working on about 400 woodland sites.

After hearing about the Millennium Forest initiative, Dominic and Anna Ashmole coordinated a series of meetings – involving nearly 30 people – in Peebles during late 1994 and early 1995, to discuss the idea of combining an ecological restoration project with forest-related community living and productive forestry. The idea was that this project could form part of a wider Borders submission to MFST.

In the early weeks of 1995 the sculptor and furniture maker, the late Tim Stead, organised a series of public meetings aimed at developing this general Borders bid. Apart from founding Borders Community Woodland (BCW) Tim had cooperated in early 1994 with Eoin Cox (who was also heavily involved in BCW) to obtain funding from another source for a proposal under the title 'No Butts'. This was aimed at establishing a centre to promote community based tree planting schemes and sustainable use of woodland resources in the Borders, and it provided a springboard for the development of ideas to be put forward to MFST for lottery funding.

WORKING WITH TREES
PEOPLE & PRODUCTS

LIVING WITH TREES
ECOLOGY & EDUCATION

Creative summary of the Borders bid

Several members of PEC took part in Tim's meetings and the notes made by Ann Goodburn and Anna Ashmole vividly convey the excitement generated by the prospect of actually getting funding for projects that had previously seemed to be only remote possibilities. Scottish Natural Heritage, the Forestry Commission and Scottish Borders Enterprise were all involved, as well as various NGOs and lots of enthusiastic individuals.

Even before the first of Tim's meetings he had received suggestions for more than 20 separate initiatives, and after some culling of the less practical ones the preliminary Borders bid still comprised eight grass-roots projects covering an extraordinary range of ideas. They included the establishment of the Woodschool (a woodland centre of excellence for training, research and design), community woodlands, agro-forestry, schools initiatives, an inventory of ancient woodland, a gene bank and the 'Borders Wildwood' project.

In Scotland as a whole most Millennium Forest initiatives were straightforward and came from established NGOs and local authorities. Because of this it was understandable that MFST found it hard to cope with the multiplicity of projects from the Borders, though they evidently realised that it was a sign of a productive ferment of grass-roots ideas. They asked the initiators to get together and put in a single bid, but accepted a compromise by which the projects were grouped under two umbrellas, Living with Trees and Working with Trees, the former including the Wildwood project.

At an MFST meeting in February 1995 Eoin Cox presented the idea of the Woodschool and Anna outlined the plan for a Borders Wildwood ecological restoration project. On the same day Anna formalised the Wildwood project proposal, after taking a decision – with support from us thousands of miles away in St Helena – to keep the focus very clearly on ecological restoration and not to emphasise the woodland community possibilities that had been discussed earlier. Although in sympathy with these, we all felt that they complicated the Wildwood vision and would be best carried forward separately.

Once all the Borders proposals had been sent off everything went rather quiet. Around this time, however, Jim Knight of Borders Regional Council, who had worked with Peter Gordon of RSPB in developing some ideas for the Borders bid, made an intriguing suggestion. Instead of insisting on a single Wildwood site of around 2000 acres, Jim suggested that we should develop a partnership organisation in the south of Scotland, including a range of governmental and other bodies. This would select a much larger target area and negotiate management agreements (or leases or purchase) with landowners or tenants within it. Native woodland could then be established incrementally by buying out

Holding the fort

I became embroiled with my parents' enthusiasm for native woodland when I edited the newsletter of the 1993 conference on Restoring Borders Woodland, although perhaps I should have seen it coming when they first got me planting a tree when I was nine. After having sown seed of inspiration at the conference they disappeared off to Saint Helena. The seed quickly started sprouting, watered by the prospect of funding from the newly-launched National Lottery. My parents, however, were literally the other side of the world; there was no email and the post took eight weeks round trip. Rather than let the tender seedling die off, I discussed the ideas with others, exchanged a few faxes with Philip and Myrtle via their neighbour, and put together a proposal which captured the vision of a restored woodland wilderness. We joined forces with Borders Community Woodland to form a new trust and put together about eight well-planned funding proposals. When the lottery people said that was too many, we re-wrote the same ideas under two broad headings: Living with Trees and Working with Trees. I thought that when my parents came back from exile I would be able to hand back responsibility for their rapidly growing project, but inevitably I have stayed involved ever since.

Anna Ashmole

Borders Community Woodland

Borders Community Woodland, established in 1987 as a result of an initiative by Tim Stead, purchased its site at Wooplaw (near Lauder) with the help of major grants from WWF and the Countryside Commission for Scotland. Wooplaw was the first wholly owned community woodland in Scotland and has now become a model for initiatives elsewhere in Scotland and further afield. Tim's enthusiasm and determination, as well as his imaginative fundraising methods, have been an inspiration to a great many people, including the Wildwood Group.

sheep subsidies and bringing owners into the project as partners who were compensated for loss of grazing.

This idea had some similarity to the vision of Trees for Life, who aim to undertake 'rewilding' incrementally within a 1500 sq km area in the northwest Highlands. It also has many of the features of the 'Wild Scotland' scheme subsequently promoted by Toby Aykroyd and of the 'habitat networks' that conservationists now take so seriously. Two decades later, BFT is focusing on the restoration of the Ettrick Forest, using an incremental approach that has much in common with Jim's proposals. At the time, however, it was obvious that the core people concerned with the Wildwood idea did not want to be diverted from their simpler vision of a limited area within which ecological restoration was the primary aim.

We heard later that during this period SNH gave key support to the Borders bid, mainly through Chris Badenoch and Pip Tabor in the local office. They consulted their policy people in headquarters and received a warm response, with a clear implication that the Borders should show the way to the rest of Scotland:

> *"Can we help in the appointment of a project officer? Yes; of course we can. When can the post be established? ... The time to start was yesterday ... It is unnecessary and undesirable to wait until the Millennium forest bid gets the go ahead."*

However, the SNH letter also commented:

> *"Some of the [Borders] ideas are excellent ... Some are more "off the wall" like the idea of purchasing an estate [for the Wildwood] ... It is very unlikely that we would support a purchase by individuals without the explicit involvement of some NGO."*

There was also a comment that if grant at a rate of more than 50% of costs was offered for any project, it must be to a voluntary body. It thus became increasingly obvious that there was a need for a legally established organisation focusing on native woodlands in the Borders, to manage projects funded by the Millennium Forest for Scotland. An informal steering group developed – led by Tim Stead and soon with Philip as a member – and this was the precursor to a formal charity which was eventually named Borders Forest Trust (BFT). The steering group members formed the core of the Board of Trustees, though with the crucial addition of Rory Macleod who became the first Chairman.

The Trust was not legally established until January 1996, so the post of Woodland Co-ordinator in the Borders was initially set up under the aegis of Borders Community Woodlands, but when Willie McGhee was appointed to this post in summer 1995 he became effectively the first staff member of the embryonic BFT. A problem arose in September when MFST gave outline approval to 'Living with Trees' (including Wildwood) and 'Working with Trees', since Willie was already committed to spending several weeks in Chile during the autumn, but Carol Buist was appointed to hold the fort.

The Borders composite projects were only two out of the 45 approved in principle as components of the Millennium Forest for Scotland, and it is hard to imagine, more than a decade on, the impact made at the time by the massive bureaucratic machinery of the Millennium Commission – channelled via MFST – on the fledgling organisation that was to become BFT. The paperwork was overwhelming and the autumn steering group meetings, mostly in the offices of SNH, were dominated by reports of seemingly unreasonable deadlines and demands by the accountants that were largely incomprehensible to ordinary people. After lengthy sessions we thankfully migrated across the road to the local pub. Over a pint of beer it was easier to remember the exciting potential of the visions that might turn to reality if we could only stick with it and thus get lottery funding. In the end, it was the doggedness of the future BFT Trustees and the dedicated work of Carol and Willie that held everything together.

During these prolonged birth pangs of Borders Forest Trust in the autumn of 1995, the people most concerned with the Wildwood project were following a somewhat separate route. When – in September – we heard of the approval of the first phase of the Borders bid by the Millennium Commission, the idea of recreating a forested wilderness in the Southern Uplands suddenly seemed a realistic goal – at least to us.

However, while many people had expressed interest in the Wildwood idea over the previous two years, there was no organisation in place to carry the project forward. The news of support from the National Lottery galvanised the loose and relaxed group of friends associated with PEC into somewhat frenzied activity. On 19th October we held a meeting – attended by 27 people – to create an organisation called Borders Wildwood (forerunner of the Wildwood Group) and further meetings followed quickly.

We were mostly based around Peebles, with relatively loose links to the other people involved with the Borders bid. It was always obvious, therefore, that the Wildwood project would stand slightly apart, and during that frustrating autumn Philip seriously suggested that we should go it alone, working directly with MFST rather than through the overall Borders organisation. Fortunately, wiser counsel prevailed and it became clear that the group would operate best as a devolved entity within the future Borders Forest Trust.

Borders Forest Trust (BFT)

Borders Forest Trust is an environmental charity and membership organisation, formed in 1996 to foster the restoration, enjoyment and use of the native woodlands of the Scottish Borders. It prides itself on being 'rooted in the community' and its formation brought together several local initiatives, most notably the Woodschool, Wooplaw Community Woodland and the Wildwood Group. BFT aims to develop and manage ambitious habitat restoration projects, to help the development of community woodlands and to undertake education and arts projects, along with woodland-based economic activities. In its first 12 years BFT initiated or assisted community development of over 80 projects, organised several conferences and planted over one million native trees. It is supported by thousands of people around Britain and has generated volunteer opportunities and employment for a large number of people, as well as bringing substantial sums of public money into the local community. The Trust has organised the restoration of special floodplain habitats at Ettrick Marshes, helped to conserve many ancient woodland sites and co-operated with local landowners in establishing large areas of native woodland.

Woodschool

Woodschool grew out of a proposal by Tim Stead in 1994 promoting the use of woodland resources in the region. Eoin Cox built on this idea and became the dynamic leader of a unique organisation, established as a wholly owned subsidiary of BFT. Development funding was provided by SNH and Scottish Borders Enterprise. This became a unique collective which maximised the potential of the human and natural resources of the Scottish Borders. Combining the talent of young furniture designers and makers with the greatly undervalued low grade or waste hardwood from the area, it created a focus for a very hands-on approach to working with wood. The successor to Woodschool, Real Wood Studios, carries on with the same ethos.

From the beginning we gathered in a Peebles pub, discussing everything over bar supper and beer. Being wary of traditional organisations we elected no committee and set up no rigid structure. People chose roles that suited their style and the group evolved dynamically. Influenced by the Quakers' approach to decision making, we always avoided voting on critical issues and instead attempted to reach consensus. Sometimes, in the years that followed, this meant that decisions were deferred or sidestepped, but this rarely caused problems and it avoided the alienation (and loss of members) that can arise when a group is divided by a vote on a contentious issue.

In spite of the informal organisation, an effective group of activists quickly emerged, and we set about trying to find a site for the Wildwood. However, much of the Borders is owned by large estates and rarely, if ever, comes up for sale; as a group of amateurs hoping to buy a large swathe of land, we must have seemed idealistic and somewhat impractical. We tended to ignore the problem and went ahead in hope.

For a few weeks that autumn we were also under the naïve impression that we might soon be sent a cheque for around £400,000 of National Lottery money to go out and buy a piece of land; needless to say, we quickly realised that things don't work like that. We became aware of some of the vagaries of lottery funding on the day that Willie McGhee arrived to tell us that we had been awarded £5000 to spend on the search for land, but that the sum available was really only £2500 and that the rest had to be in the form of matching funds from other sources. We were allowed to take into account 'sweat equity' (notional money based on hours of work put in by volunteers) but the whole business was bureaucratic and contrasted strongly with the way we normally worked. We did make an effort to fill in time sheets for a few weeks, but we found it extremely difficult to define work since so much time was 'thinking time.'

Furthermore, we didn't yet need more than a fraction of the money since we were only searching for a site, but we were told that it had to be used within the next three months and couldn't be carried forward. Feeling under pressure to demonstrate our seriousness by spending the money, we telephoned a prominent land agent and asked him his hourly rate, thinking that it might be worth while to ask him to spend time investigating possibilities on our behalf. We never actually did this, but it was a valuable experience, since it made us determined to avoid getting into such a ridiculous situation again. We all wanted to spend money on woodland creation, not on expensive consultants or in any other unnecessary way, and felt pushed around by the process. This was the start of a period of four years in which almost everyone involved with the Wildwood project worked for nothing, irrespective of their normal professional expectations. We were left suitably wary of any sources of funding that came with strings attached, and with strengthened resolve never to be parties to wasteful spending of any kind.

Nonetheless, it was useful to have some funds, since it enabled our fledgling organisation to produce a little brochure to explain the Wildwood idea and to seek help in finding a site. In late October members of the group had a meeting with SNH staff at which they helped us to understand the pattern of land holdings in the western (high) part of the Borders and explained the ways in which they could support us and those in which they could not.

During the months that followed, much of our energy was spent in investigating potential sites. We studied maps and systematically assessed all the upland farms and estates, trying to work out which local landowners had land that might be suitable for the project. Our interest in buying land had been registered with estate agents throughout the Borders since the start of the year, but now we mailed brochures and accompanying personal letters to 40 relevant landowners, on the off-chance that one of them might be prepared to sell. We also had extensive but ultimately unproductive discussions with both the National Trust for Scotland and Wemyss & March Estates. At the same time we published advertisements for land and began writing articles for the local press.

Understandably, most of our approaches were ignored. However, we did get some replies and started investigating these. Small groups of members made informal visits to about ten potential sites, mainly when there was a hint that they might become available. These reconnaissance trips were useful since they sharpened our perceptions of the kind of site we needed.

We were very particular. Above all, the Wildwood had to be in a place where it would form a natural entity in the landscape, preferably the whole catchment of a burn, surrounded by hills rising to 600 m (~2000 ft) or more. We were not prepared to settle for just any patch of land, since we did not believe we would sustain the momentum and enthusiasm that had been generated unless the site was impressive. Furthermore, roads or large forestry plantations would present awkward problems and attractive buildings would put the price far out of reach.

During this period we also went on learning about establishing native woodland. As early as January 1996 we arranged for Gordon Patterson to lead a group discussion on the approach to be used in creating the Wildwood. He was the person in the Forestry Commission headquarters in Edinburgh who was most concerned with native woodlands, and he also provided valuable advice at a later stage. We also made connections with a number of other relevant organisations and people. Richard Tipping of Stirling University helped us understand the vegetational history of the Southern Uplands, Diana Gilbert of Highland Birchwoods advised on possibilities for montane scrub restoration, and a number of experienced people contributed ideas about tree establishment techniques. We also gained credibility from the fact that Adrian Newton, a member of our group, was a forest ecologist at the Institute of Ecology and Resource Management at Edinburgh University.

In spite of this evidence that we were serious in our approach, a professional forester who attended some of the early meetings told Philip privately that she felt we had no chance of achieving our goal, on the grounds that we were too idealistic and didn't have our feet on the ground. This was a timely warning, but we were convinced that a grass-roots activist group had to follow its own instincts. A decade on, and now herself managing a major restoration project, we think she would admit that she underestimated us.

In the meantime, however, as we and the other people in the Borders continued to labour under bureaucratic demands from MFST, we gradually came to realise that they were under similar pressures from the Millennium Commission. The MFST Guidance Notes for writing project plans were produced in draft only on 27th November 1995, although applicants were given a deadline of the end of the year for submission of the full plans. During December, Willie McGhee and his colleague Alex Smith scrambled to put some flesh on the bones of all the other projects that had been approved in outline by MFST, and Philip vividly remembers going to the office of their consultancy to lend a hand with the final drafting, one evening between Christmas and New Year, with the deadline looming.

For our project, however, there was a more fundamental problem: we had nowhere to create the Wildwood. We tried to gain time by pleading with MFST for approval of the Wildwood as a concept, pending location of a suitable site, and when this failed we built an application around a 'phantom site' – a valley that we knew had been on the market some time before. We had not managed to make contact with the absentee owners, but although we strongly suspected that it was not currently for sale, we submitted the plan anyhow, hoping that we might find somewhere that really was available before the window of opportunity closed.

This plan was promptly rejected, but our hopes of lottery funding for land purchase briefly revived later in 1996 when MFST made a final – and ultimately unsuccessful – bid for funds from the Millennium Commission. We were offered a farm in the Moorfoot Hills – marred by a bisecting minor road – only to have the offer withdrawn five days before we were due to submit the application for funding to MFST, because of complications relating to inheritance tax that the owner had overlooked. This was a blessing in disguise, since the site would always have been second best. The experience stiffened our determination to avoid compromise and to go all out for a prime site.

In spite of the bumpy ride, we owed MFST a major debt, since the momentum gained during the year when lottery funding seemed possible proved sufficient to make us determined to create a Wildwood anyhow. And in the end MFST did help, though not with land purchase.

In order to keep up our morale during this difficult period, members of the group visited other native woodland initiatives around Scotland. One was to the Royal Scottish Forestry Society's project at Cashel on the shores of Loch Lomond, which we envied since they had managed to get major MFST funding for land purchase, by virtue of having a site already available at the time of the application deadline.

Perhaps the most inspiring trip, by nine group members, was to Creag Meagaidh National Nature Reserve, the last major site bought for the country by the Nature Conservancy, later managed by its successor Scottish Natural Heritage. After the trip Fi Martynoga recorded:

Creag Meagaidh was of great interest to us as it was the largest scale area of ecological restoration in Scotland

> *"It was of great interest to us as it is the largest scale area of ecological restoration in Scotland. It is managed by SNH and Dick Balharry was our guide. He described the policy in that area – where there are intact fragments of native woodland – of not fencing and relying on the topography on this steep hillside to limit grazing of sheep. The deer are culled severely by professional marksmen, which has led to questions in the House! However Dick Balharry is adamant that stalking is not profitable. 1000 deer are now 100 and the venison is sold to finance the work. There is now mature birch forest which was planted at the time of the first world war and seeds from this are germinating as is rowan and soon juniper, hazel and oak. Bracken infests but there is non-intervention as it is thought to act as a nursesmaid to saplings and then dies out. There is a very SMALL car park (NB) and therefore few visitors at a time who tend to keep to the path which is made of double railway sleepers so the impact is minimal."*

On this visit we were so preoccupied talking to Dick Balharry – whose dedication to ecological restoration was truly inspiring – that we didn't walk far, and an important insight was gained later by Anna Ashmole, who made a separate visit and was struck by the absence of

A late winter satellite view shows Carrifran in the centre of 'white grass' uplands of Southern Scotland and also the extensive plantation forestry

significant tree regeneration further into the glen, although there were lots of rowan saplings held down to heather height by deer browsing. It was apparent that the main deer culling effort was relatively low down, and that on this unfenced site the deer still had free access to the more remote and higher parts. The lesson was that if we were to establish native woodland in a naked valley, we would have to ensure that browsing animals were kept out or rigorously controlled. This knowledge encouraged us to hold our nerve during the feral goat controversy several years later.

Back in the Borders, none of the sites that we investigated turned out to be ideal – either the price was exorbitant or the site was unexciting or both. We felt we were on the cusp – with a chance of the project going forward, but prepared for disappointment. Did we get despondent? Our guess is that some of the group were more or less relegating the project to just a good dream.

Nevertheless, during the period when we were involved in apparently fruitless negotiations over a number of potential sites, we decided to set about formulating a clear statement of our aims. The creation of a Wildwood would take a century or more, and although we knew that the project had a clear central vision, we needed to ensure that this vision was kept firmly in view as the decades passed, when the originators were no longer involved. The agreed wording was:

> *"The Borders Wildwood project aims to re-create in the Southern Uplands an extensive tract of mainly forested wilderness, with most of the rich diversity of native species that was present in the area before human activities became dominant. The woodland will not be exploited commercially and the impact of people will be kept to a minimum. Access to the Wildwood will be open to all, and we hope that it will be used throughout the next millennium as an inspirational and educational resource."*

Although there were minor alterations later (partly because Carrifran is in Dumfries & Galloway, not the Scottish Borders) this Mission Statement has been the guiding light of the project ever since. It reflects a conviction that although conservation of surviving natural habitats and wildlife is essential, there are situations where more drastic action is required: lost ecosystems need rebuilding from the bottom up.

It was in mid 1996 that Carrifran became an exciting possibility. Philip had looked down on this valley three years previously, on the day when the idea of creating a Wildwood was conceived, and the site was again in our minds at the time that the Wildwood Group was formed. We had not approached the owner during our search in late 1995, partly because Capplegill Farm (which included Carrifran) was almost entirely in Dumfries & Galloway and we were looking for a site in the Borders, but also because we heard that the farmer had bought it only in 1994 and it seemed most unlikely that he would think of selling. However, fate then took a hand. Fi Martynoga, who never missed a chance to talk of plans for the Wildwood, takes up the story:

"In summer 1996, almost a year into the search for a suitable site, we were growing disheartened. I remember going for a walk with a neighbour, an Oxford professor of Biochemistry who spends his holidays in a bothy near where I live. I was explaining our problem when he turned to look at me: 'My cousin has just bought a big farm near Moffat. He would sell you some land' he averred. I didn't have high hopes. But when we saw from the map that the most perfect valley, Carrifran, was included in that farm, Philip and Myrtle were excited, so we asked my friend to contact his cousin on our behalf. The answer was encouraging and we soon opened negotiations."

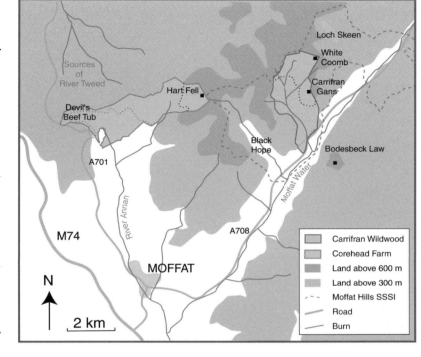

Position of Carrifran

While we were waiting to hear whether John Barker – the owner of Carrifran – was prepared to talk to us, we (Philip and Myrtle) visited the valley and were instantly convinced that we would never find a better Wildwood site. It was almost entirely denuded, but it was the right size (about six square kilometres), had the feeling of being a natural unit in the landscape and was surrounded by impressive crags rising to summits that were among the highest in the south of Scotland, giving an almost Highland feel.

When we received encouraging news from Fi's friend, Philip plucked up the courage to phone John Barker and was startled to be offered an appointment for the following afternoon, 2nd August 1996. A quick call to Bill Goodburn (the lawyer in our group) secured his agreement to come and provide moral support and Philip spent the next morning in the Registry of Sasines finding out how much Barker had paid for the farm (of which Carrifran was less than half).

When we arrived we were treated to tea and scones by Wendy Barker, and John immediately made it clear that he was a businessman

Carrifran valley: we were lucky to have friends with a microlite!
Photo: Pete and Viv Reynolds, Capreolus Wildlife Consultancy

and would only consider selling Carrifran if it was going to be very well worth his while. Bill then drove us up to the sheepstell near the road and we looked out over the glen, explained to John that we needed the entire catchment of the Carrifran Burn and asked him what he would take for it. The response was instant – a million pounds. Since we knew that he had paid much less than a million for the entire farm, this was clearly a try-on, and we said that we would look for somewhere else. But we left the door ajar for further discussion.

As it happened, there was one upland farm in the Borders that came close to matching Carrifran in suitability. We had made a site visit on 25th July and towards the end of August Philip went to see the owner, but after consultation with family members he decided not to sell. The only other door in sight was thus firmly closed.

In the autumn a new approach to John Barker seemed to convince him that we were serious. He expressed interest in our project, agreed not to sell to anyone else, and suggested a price of £550,000. At only a little over half his original price, this was good enough progress to convince us that we stood a chance of getting a deal. In mid November we held a key meeting of the Wildwood Group.

We now had to face the fact that our only chance of getting a good Wildwood site within a reasonable time depended on paying much more than the agricultural value of the land. At the time, Scottish landowners were under the spotlight and many group members felt uneasy at the idea of paying over the odds for land. In the end, however, after viewing slides of Carrifran and discussing its characteristics, everyone accepted the argument that in 50 years time the important thing would be that the Wildwood had been created, not that we had paid a somewhat exorbitant price. The minutes of the meeting are eloquent "DO WE GO FOR IT? – unanimously YES!"

The hard bargaining then commenced. We were very fortunate to have a lawyer, a land agent and a business consultant associated with the Wildwood Group, each bringing their various skills and all prepared to work on the volunteer basis that had by now become the norm. When they went with Philip to meet John Barker and his lawyer in Annan in October 1997 to finalise the deal, the fact that all four of our negotiators were professional people working for nothing quite clearly played a part in getting the best terms possible.

Autumn in Holly Gill

The previous eleven months had seen a series of meetings between John Barker and various combinations of our negotiators. The skeleton of an acceptable deal had emerged in late November 1996 when our land agent Colin Strang Steel and Philip met with John Barker and his agent. Subsequently, Ian Carr was primarily responsible for getting a substantial reduction in the price by agreeing that for several years after

The lonely rowan beside Carrifran Burn now has nearly half a million trees for company!

the final purchase the farmer could graze his sheep – and collect the relevant subsidies — on the parts of the valley where we were not yet planting. This was manageable for us, since we could not contemplate planting the whole valley at the same time, but the arrangement did necessitate the erection of various temporary and quite expensive fences.

As we inched towards a deal, John Barker suddenly said that he wanted to retain the slopes above Rispie Lairs, on the eastern face of Saddle Yoke. We were appalled by this and determined not to give way, but Ian and Philip agreed to walk over the land with John to work out a compromise. During the day we conceded a small area at the head of the burn above Priest Gill which is out of sight from almost everywhere in the valley, but we stood firm on the important slope. The business then took an entertaining turn as we walked south towards Peat Hill, placing canes to mark the future western boundary line, since we found that John was continually veering to the left (towards Carrifran valley) while we were pushing the line to the right, attempting to gain ground; whenever we were due to place a cane, a compromise had to be reached.

The negotiations were frustrating at times and we were somewhat exhausted when a deal was eventually reached. Our minutes of May 1997 state: *"Anyone really wanting the full details of all the frustrations of the last few weeks should ring Philip"* (and that was before the end). John Barker may have had similar feelings, since we were told later that he had said *"they kept bullying me"*; but he also admitted *"I like the thought that I have played some small part in helping to turn the valley into something that will be quite unique."* In November 1997 all was finally agreed, and we were in a position to complete the purchase two years later, if we could raise a third of a million pounds by that time.

During the year of negotiations we had also focused on organising ourselves to cope with the tasks ahead. First, we needed a name for the project. The working title had been 'Borders Wildwood' but Carrifran was not in the Scottish Borders – at least in local authority terms. A brainstorm session led to a decision – after rejection of several more cumbersome names – to call the project 'Carrifran Wildwood' and to refer to ourselves simply as 'The Wildwood Group'. This left the door open to Wildwood initiatives on other sites in the future, and the two-word project title had the virtue of brevity (reducing the temptation to use an acronym) and conveyed both the location and the nature of the vision.

Some of us had worries about the pronunciation – should it be CaRIFren, Criffren, CarriFRAN or CarrIfren (the latter used by the neighbouring farmer). It seems that the Welsh sounding CarriFRAN (seat of ravens) is not used locally and across the road the cottage gate had an old sign with the spelling Carriferan. This seemed insoluble, but not a reason for using a different name for the project, so we accepted that people would always ask and that probably we would each give a different answer.

With the name settled, we needed to devise some structure for the project. We were still simply a group of about 40 enthusiastic people who met infrequently in a Peebles pub. However, when we began to think about skills, it became clear that we had a remarkable range. There were ecologists, educators, an archaeologist, zoologists, botanists, foresters, artists, a sculptor, a landscape architect, a lawyer, a business consultant, a nurse, a land agent, organic gardeners, writers and above all dreamers.

There was now a lot of work ahead and we needed to know who was able and willing to give up the necessary time, so Myrtle sent a questionnaire to everyone in the Wildwood Group asking who would be

> ### Just a thought
>
> When we found Carrifran, it was immediately evident that it was ideal for our project; it was an entire watershed within reasonable reach of those of us who lived in or near Peebles, and it was available for purchase. However two other attributes came as complete surprises to us. We had never heard of the Rotten Bottom Bow, and we had no idea that the pollen record was the best for any upland site in Britain (see Chapter 6). The story of the hunter and his bow have been a significant help to us in fundraising and the pollen record invaluable in planning the restoration. It is tempting to ponder on these 'co-incidences' and whether we found Carrifran or whether the hunter was searching for us when he shot an arrow from his bow.

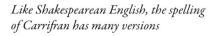

Like Shakespearean English, the spelling of Carrifran has many versions

"The Lowlands of Scotland had once undoubtedly an equal portion of woods with other countries… But I believe few regions have been denuded like this, where many centuries must have passed in waste without the least thought of future supply."

Samuel Johnson (1775) 'A Journey through the Western Isles.'

interested in fundraising, publicity, article writing, ecological planning, planting trees, or seed collecting and propagation. The answers were interesting. All but one said they would plant trees, a large number were interested in ecological planning, but only about four said they were prepared to become involved in fundraising.

Armed with this information, we soon assembled several active sub-groups, each with a convenor. Philip adopted a co-ordinating role and Myrtle tried to keep things organised. Michael Matthews, who had been running Tweeddale Countryside Volunteers (TCV) for some years, shifted its focus gradually towards the Wildwood project and easily recruited seed collectors; furthermore, he organised about a dozen small back garden nurseries to grow trees for planting at Carrifran (see Chapter 9).

An Ecological Planning Group gradually gathered about 25 members under Adrian Newton's leadership. Its first significant activity was organising a conference at the Royal Botanic Garden Edinburgh in November 1997, which laid the groundwork for planning ecological restoration at Carrifran (see Chapter 7).

It was more difficult to assemble an adequate group to take forward the key business of fundraising for the purchase of the site and organising the associated publicity (see Chapter 4). This group had very fluid membership and was led initially by Ian Carr and later by Fi Martynoga. It proved to be highly effective.

The decision to try to buy Carrifran even though there was no prospect of help from the National Lottery, coupled with recognition of the skills within the group, gave us all renewed confidence. This led to a conviction that we should maintain control of the project as it developed, seeking advice from experts and funding from outside bodies, but do the planning and take the key decisions ourselves.

4. Raising the money for purchase

No hope of lottery money for purchase—novice fundraisers—consulting WWF—relationship with the John Muir Trust—support from Chris Bonington and others—advice against trying to raise funds from industry— approaching charitable trusts—Chris Rose's painting—establishing Founderships—designing the website and fundraising brochure—the longbow and the launch—distributing the brochure—early supporters— writing letters and articles for publication—fundraising art exhibitions.

* * * * *

In November 1996, when we first realised that a deal to buy Carrifran was conceivable, we had begun investigating whether there might yet be some chance of help with land purchase from the National Lottery. Deadlines for Millennium Forest applications had already passed but the Heritage Lottery Fund seemed worth trying. However, as we talked to lottery officials it became apparent that a difficulty would arise because we knew that John Barker would never sell unless we offered a price well above the agricultural value, while all lottery bodies work to official valuation – 10% over valuation being about the maximum considered.

Colin Strang Steel and Philip paid a visit to the District Valuer in Dumfries, to see if he would be likely to take account of the high 'heritage' value of the site, which in our view made the agricultural value unrealistically low. However, the valuer was blunt. He said, in effect *"Where's the competition? You want the site badly, but no-one else does, so I can only give it an agricultural value."* This was depressing, since although we naturally had no wish to pay more than the agricultural value (around £180,000) we knew that we could not make a deal close to that figure and that a higher price would probably bar us from lottery support. With no other course to pursue, we went back to John Barker and began the long task of getting the best deal that we possibly could, as described in Chapter 3.

The John Muir Trust (JMT)

The John Muir Trust is one of the country's leading guardians of wild land and wildlife. As a prominent membership organisation it carries out its charitable role through the ownership of land, the promotion of education and volunteer conservation activities. Established in 1983, JMT owns and manages estates on Skye, Knoydart, Assynt, Lochaber and Perthshire. The iconic peaks of Ben Nevis, Schiehallion and many of the southern Cuillins of Skye are protected by the Trust. In addition to owned properties JMT works in partnership with many other communities in the management of estates across Scotland. Although the Trust currently owns land only in Scotland, it is very much a national and international body. The environmental John Muir Award promotes awareness and responsibility for wild places across the United Kingdom. Overseas, the John Muir Trust has strong links with the Sierra Club in the United States which also celebrates the work, spirit and legacy of Dunbar-born John Muir.

At the same time, early in 1997, the hard work of fundraising began. The strategy for the purchase was to ask John Barker for a two-year option on Carrifran, fixing the price and ensuring that the deal would go through if we could raise the money in time. The two-year limit was self-imposed, since none of us felt that we would be able to keep up our enthusiasm for fundraising without a target date. At the start, the tiny group of volunteer fundraisers got together, twisted a few arms to pull in extra people whom we felt we needed, and had a brainstorm session. The April 1997 minutes (written by a core member of the group) record that *"the ideas flowed as follows – some good, some nuts!"* They certainly got us thinking.

Because none of us had done fundraising before, we had no preconceived ideas about how to set about it, but had to think through the approaches that we felt might work. We knew that apart from the lottery, the government, or the European Union, none of which seemed likely to help, there were three main potential sources of funds: industry, charitable trusts and the general public. We really had no idea what proportion of our funding could be expected to come from each of these. Someone suggested about a third each, which seemed reasonable, but it turned out to be wildly wrong.

We did talk to experienced people. For instance, some of us went and spent a day in Aberfeldy with helpful staff members of WWF Scotland. They advised us to try to present a furry animal image, which we decided to avoid, but they convinced us of the importance of an effective logo. We therefore invited suggestions for logo designs from members of the group. After a good deal of discussion, Fi arranged for a wood engraver friend, Paul Kershaw, to create one for us. It is his beautiful lettering that we now use on all our correspondence and publicity material.

At this time Borders Forest Trust (BFT) – the registered charity that would be formally responsible for the whole Carrifran project – was only just over a year old and we worried that potential donors might need reassurance about the long term security of the site, since the project was based on a vision for future decades and centuries. One solution was some sort of partnership with a more established environmental charity. Most of the obvious ones seemed likely to turn into dominant partners, starving our grass-roots, but the idea of an association with the John Muir Trust (JMT) was more attractive.

As early as March 1995, when Anna was putting together the initial Wildwood proposal for the Millennium Forest for Scotland, she had raised with JMT the possibility of them acting as a kind of backstop, to take custody of the Wildwood land (which of course was unidentified at the time) if the project got into financial difficulty. They could not commit themselves at short notice, but in 1997, with a real prospect of a deal on Carrifran, Philip obtained the approval of BFT Trustees for a new approach to JMT.

We proposed an association between Borders Forest Trust and the John Muir Trust, involving an initial phase in which JMT provided moral support in fundraising and planning for the Wildwood, to be followed by a more formal partnership after the site was bought, which would provide backup security in the long-term. JMT representatives were to have the right to participate in Wildwood Group meetings and to be heard at BFT Trustee meetings.

Trustees of the John Muir Trust discuss the possibilities of woodland restoration at Carrifran with Wildwood Group members

In July 1997 the late Andrew Raven, JMT Director of Land Management, came to visit Carrifran and walked over the site with some of us. He was clearly impressed by the valley and by the professionalism of the group, which was heartening. Two days later Myrtle and Philip went to Perth to meet JMT Director Nigel Hawkins, to glean ideas for fundraising and to discuss the proposals for an association.

The Trustees of the John Muir Trust approved the link with BFT later in the month. Crucially, this enabled us to use the wording 'In association with the John Muir Trust' on our fundraising brochure. We also had an opportunity to write about the project in the JMT Journal and to enclose our brochure with an issue of the journal. When the time came, we took a party of Wildwood volunteers into Edinburgh to help stuff the 6000 envelopes for the mailing. Many JMT members quickly sent substantial donations, giving the fundraising a crucial early boost. Philip later gave talks about the project at several local meetings of JMT members. Although legal complications prevented the development of a more formal partnership after the land purchase, we were able to maintain a warm ongoing relationship and JMT volunteers often turn up at Carrifran.

We also realised at this stage that we could raise the credibility of the project by gaining support from public figures. Sir Chris Bonington and his wife walked over Carrifran with us and gave an enthusiastic endorsement. Zoologist and broadcaster Aubrey Manning, an old friend, was unfailingly supportive, and both author Richard Mabey and Nigel Hawkins of JMT gave us warm statements that we used in our publicity.

Another idea was to try to get an indication of our likely success with industry by talking to one of the few successful businessmen whom we knew personally. We invited him and his wife to dinner, and afterwards began explaining our situation. Philip was amused to note that the conversation suddenly became much more relaxed when he made it clear that we were not leading up to a request for major funding from him, but merely wanted an opinion as to whether companies were likely to make substantial contributions. His answer was clear: we shouldn't expect more than the odd thousand. Large-scale sponsorship could not be expected for a project where there would be little dramatic action and where progress would be measured by the rate of growth of trees over a period of many decades.

We explored with a couple of people the possibility of corporate fundraising on a commission basis, but their initial attempts came to nothing and we didn't pursue this avenue, although a friend did arrange a donation from a company with which he was associated, which apparently had a bad conscience about the pollution that it had caused. In general, we couldn't raise much enthusiasm for approaching commercial organisations, and although we may have missed out on a few company donations that we could have got, our energy was better spent elsewhere. Furthermore, since we didn't put days of work into applications to companies that would usually say no, we rarely suffered morale-sapping rejections.

Charitable trusts were a different matter. We got off at a good start with an approach to KZT. Here we were dealing with people who knew us and who shared many of our own concerns and enthusiasms, so we were comfortable asking for their support. They gave us £3000 to pay for the initial fundraising brochure and provided more help when we needed new editions; much later, they made a donation to help in the establishment of treeline woodland.

The application to KZT provided a model for approaches to other trusts, whose names we culled mainly from lists of donors to similar environmental projects. We soon learned that any sort of personal contact made a big difference, and that some trusts would become long-term supporters of the Wildwood. In

After Chris and Wendy Bonington visited Carrifran, Chris said: "To have a complete valley re-forested would be a joy in itself but also a wonderful example of what could be achieved over a much wider area."

the end, we were to raise about one fifth of the money for land purchase from this source.

Meanwhile, a special event showed us how exciting fundraising could be. Long before we had a formal deal on Carrifran – and apparently out of the blue – we were contacted by the renowned bird artist Chris Rose, a local resident, who said that he would like to paint a picture for us. After discussion of the most appropriate subject, Chris painted a magnificent picture of a peregrine on Raven Craig at the head of the valley. Auctioned at the gallery in Suffolk where he often exhibited, it raised £5000 for the project, as well as eventually providing a similar sum from the sale of impressive prints made from the picture.

This wonderful gesture had a palpable effect on our campaign. It showed us – and all those who heard about it – that this was a project capable of touching a deep chord in people who cared about the world they lived in. It also convinced us that donations from individual members of the public were likely to provide the core of our funds. However, we realised that we would never get the large sum we needed by depending on typical methods of grass-roots fundraising, through local raffles, jumble sales and coffee mornings. We had to reach out to a wider community of interest, engaging people from far outside the area.

'Carrifran Lookout.' Chris Rose, a local resident and accomplished wildlife artist, said that he would like to paint a picture to help us raise funds

Mirage of a government land purchase grant

A year after the door had closed on potential land purchase money from the lottery, when we had settled on a price for Carrifran, an unexpected opening arose in relation to Scottish Natural Heritage (SNH). We learned that a major land purchase by conservation bodies in the Highlands, to which SNH had planned to contribute, had just fallen through, leaving an embarrassing budget underspend as the end of the financial year approached. We met with some very senior people and were told that a grant up to 50% of the value of Carrifran might be possible. We pointed out that the valuation would probably be an insuperable stumbling block, but SNH decided to go ahead and duly obtained a valuation at the agricultural value. They insisted that we should try to persuade John Barker to accept a deal at this price. It was only two thirds of what we had agreed, but he would get the money quickly. Not surprisingly, he said "I would rather put a pistol to my head" and that was the end of the matter. We didn't feel bad about this since we had never really expected it to work. Furthermore, there was a silver lining, since SNH ultimately paid the salary of our Project Officer, and would probably not have been able to do this if they had alredy helped us to buy the site.

We also had to bring in much larger donations than a small local group could normally expect.

After extensive discussion we settled on a scheme by which people could become Founders of Carrifran Wildwood by sponsoring a half-hectare or hectare with gifts of £250 or £500 (or more). We made no status distinction between the two amounts, reasoning that less well-off people who gave the smaller amount deserved just as much credit as those for whom it might be easy to give more. In the event, about 55% of Founderships (sometimes established by two or more people) were based on the smaller sum while about 45% were for donations of £500 or more. Some members of the group had misgivings about this emphasis on large sums, but we did of course make it clear that gifts of any amount would be warmly welcomed.

At the beginning there were some wild ideas about having an interactive website where you could choose your hectare, but Ann Goodburn's commonsense quickly intervened. Apart from the technical and administrative load that this would have imposed, there was an obvious danger that attractive parts of the valley would be snapped up quickly, leading to a loss of momentum as time went on. More fundamentally, we realised that we wanted contributors to feel that they were participants in a communal project, not focusing on their own particular patch.

In 1997 fundraising by means of websites was relatively new, but we were aware that the Isle of Eigg appeal had made good use of theirs. Our first site was designed by Dominic Ashmole and hosted at no cost by Scotweb through the generosity of Nick Fiddes. We had no direct measure of the part it played, but we suspect that it provided a key element of credibility for people considering becoming Founders, as well as providing attractive images of Carrifran valley.

Early in 1998, when we had already put a lot of effort into planning the fundraising but had not really got it going, we were distracted by what seemed initially to be a chance to get major government support for the land purchase (see Box on the left). A period of frenetic activity ensued, but it all came to nothing and we had to get back to the business of raising the money ourselves. We were actually more comfortable this way, as we felt more in control.

It was obvious from the start that an arresting and beautiful brochure would be prerequisite for fundraising success. Producing it was a communal effort and we spent many months studying other people's leaflets and pushing text drafts to and fro among members of the Fundraising Group, while we struggled to convey both the excitement of an ambitious goal and our determination to tackle the job in a realistic and practical way. We realised that we had to strike a positive note, and toned down early versions that emphasised the destructive role of sheep. Impressive photographs were crucial, and we were lucky to have David Geddes – a talented landscape photographer – as a member of the group. He captured an image of the valley that formed the centrepiece of the brochure (and also of the website). We were initially worried by a lack of technical design expertise within the group, but Maiken Erstad, recently graduated in graphic design from Glasgow University,

Dan Jones displays his find of the Rotten Bottom bow at a local archaeological dig Photo: Courtesy of the late D. Jones

continued the tradition of professionals working on the project for nothing and showed extraordinary patience in the face of our fussiness over the smallest details of the brochure.

When we had a draft printout we took it to half a dozen people with no prior knowledge of the project and asked them to scrutinise it in detail. Almost all of them saw ways in which it could be improved. However, they did not see the final folding arrangement and as a result nobody noticed one significant problem. When finally printed, the brochure was folded in such a way that the casual opener could miss the main inside pages, with the photo of the whole valley and details of our plans for the site. We often wonder how many potential donors were lost because of this. Nonetheless, the brochure was a major success and became the mainstay of our fundraising for the next two years.

We also had one special card to play. In 1990 the late Dan Jones, psychiatrist and hillwalker, had found in a peat bog at Carrifran the oldest longbow known from Britain (see Chapter 6). At about 6000 years old it was slightly earlier than the famous 'Ice-man' of the Alps. It was obvious that the ancient bow resonated with many people, so we decided to make it the centrepiece of the launch of our fundraising campaign.

We knew that Dan Jones lived locally, but then we heard that the actor Robert Hardy – a noted authority on longbows – also had a house in the Borders, so we were able to make an approach to him. He agreed to help, and in March 1998 he joined Dan Jones and the rest of us at a media event at Carrifran. Several national newspapers published photos of Robert Hardy in the valley, poised to release an arrow from a replica of the bow, although some reporters came only to a repeat

Robert Hardy, actor and longbow expert, tries the replica bow while Dan Jones looks on

Please remember

For all you folks who make a will
I hope this thought won't make
you ill
At Wildwood we don't want you
dead
But rather we'd put in your head
–
A thought:
This thought is of those wondrous
trees
Which now can billow in a breeze
But need a lot of cash and care
To keep them growing green and
fair.
An idea:
When to your lawyer you may
wend
A legacy you might intend
For Wildwood and its future
health
Safeguarded by your kindly
wealth.
So please:
If reading this may jog your mind
Such legacy would be so kind
We all would shout hip, hip,
hooray
Please come and visit any day!
Please do....

Ann Goodburn

performance that we arranged in the Royal Botanic Garden Edinburgh in the afternoon. Robert Hardy was an entertaining person to have at the site that day and several of us came away with good memories of him and his generous contribution of time, which enabled us to get ample press coverage for the launch.

We were gradually becoming aware that fundraising could be fun,

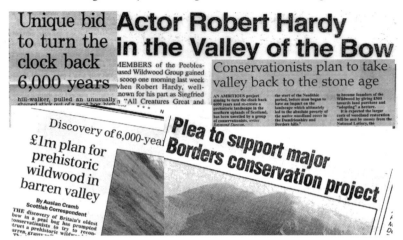

partly because – as in the case of Chris Rose and his painting – we were always getting nice surprises. A letter or fax would come through from the BFT office with news of an unexpected donation, or an envelope would arrive with a large cheque. It was also a very personal business. As soon as the brochure was printed, we (Myrtle and Philip) plucked up courage and sent copies to about 100 relatives and friends, inviting them to join us in an exciting enterprise. The response was remarkable and some of the comments enormously heartening. Ian McLeish wrote *"This is the best example yet of the sort of vision and practical forward planning that is needed all over the world".* In the first few weeks £25,000 was raised and by midsummer of 1998 were one third of the way to our target, convincing us that our instinctive approach was going to work and that we need not worry that we were not professionals.

There were several special donations at an early stage. One family, whose son had been killed in a traffic accident, had been collecting money for several years in order to buy some land near Aberdeen to establish a woodland in his memory. They never found a suitable place and when they heard about Carrifran, they decided to give the money to the Wildwood, establishing a Foundership in memory of their son. Similarly, one of Philip's postgraduate students from Edinburgh University – Peter Marsh – died young of cancer and his parents became Founders and long-term supporters of the project. A decade later, a large proportion of new donations to the Wildwood project are made in memory of people who loved trees and wildness, or in celebration of life events such as engagements, weddings, births, anniversaries and retirement.

Most of our early Founders were recruited via magazines to which they subscribed. We eventually printed 100,000 brochures and used most of them in mailings with magazines. Whenever possible the brochure went out with an issue that carried an article written by one of our core members. By the end of 1999 we had written 16 articles or letters for journals and magazines. Additional publicity came through articles and letters in newspapers, some written by us and some by reporters. Whenever we wrote about the project, we emphasised our need for donations and included details of the Foundership scheme.

A variety of organisations allowed us space in their members' newsletters; several of them, though not directly concerned with activities relevant to our project, were strikingly supportive. For instance, the Society of Friends in Edinburgh decided to donate to the Wildwood project several thousand pounds from the profits of the Society's Rainforest Café during the Edinburgh Festival.

The largest donation came out of the blue early in the campaign, when a lady who preferred anonymity telephoned the BFT office and said that she was inclined to give us £25,000 or so. Later, we received a couple of other donations of comparable size, and a significant number of people gave £1000. However, the vast bulk of the money came from

We were becoming aware that fundraising could be fun — Peebles Folk Club busking for Carrifran

Exhibitions

'Wildwood' is an evocative word. Early in the fundraising campaign we asked artists to respond to it. Several of them came on a site visit to experience the spectacular open space which was then Carrifran then was and to take in what our proposal to reinstate woodland really meant. Back in their studios, painters, sculptors and print makers created beautiful works. They went on display in the Tweeddale Museum and Art Gallery in Peebles under the title 'Wild Wood'. The exhibition drew unusually large numbers and succeeded in making a profit, giving the Carrifran Wildwood nearly a thousand pounds as well as a good deal of publicity. It was an effective, and enjoyable, way of raising the project's local profile. The year before, when plans for the valley were in their infancy, the Wildwood Group had been one of the recipients of funds from a different exhibition. This was specifically a charity show, held in the house and grounds of a supporter. Amongst painters and sculptors, several wood workers from Woodschool took part, as well as other furniture makers, giving the show a woody theme. The idea was repeated with more or less the same caste of artists but in a different venue in 1999.

Fi Martynoga

Memories from the office

I don't think that many people at the start really believed it would be possible – to raise more than a third of a million pounds from donations to buy the valley. What is truly amazing is that it was possible. Almost every day for nearly two years we received donations in the post to the BFT office. People gave small amounts and large amounts, and repeated amounts, and the total raised slowly crept up. Donations were made in memory of loved ones, and in celebration of new children, for birthdays, and weddings and for individuals themselves. I can still remember some of the names of the donors, people I'll probably never meet, who are all connected to an extraordinary place. And it's amazing now to drive past the valley and see the trees growing, and think back to those hundreds of people who took a risk and made it possible.

Samantha Smith

Founderships of £250 and £500. By Millennium Day we had over 500 Founders, and hundreds of other people had responded to our appeal with lesser amounts. When we finished the fundraising for the land, four fifths of the money had come from private individuals, widely scattered around Britain and with some from overseas.

The Wildwood Group had always included people involved with the arts, and in 1998 and 1999 there were several art exhibitions promoting the Wildwood. Fi Martynoga set up an exhibition in the Chambers Institute in Peebles, where local painters and sculptors showed work relating to trees. At about this time she ran a workshop in Moffat Academy, the nearest school to Carrifran, and the children's work was included in the Peebles show. Group members also organised exhibitions on tree themes in Kailzie, Traquair, Peebles and Moffat, all in aid of the Wildwood. Apart from the sales, these were excellent opportunities to let local people know what we were doing. Additional local support came from the Peebles Folk Club, who collected for Carrifran by busking in Peebles High Street.

Although the fundraising effort was entirely by volunteers, we had wonderful backup from Samantha Smith in the BFT office. Donations had to be made to the Trust, and the cheques and banking were all handled there. However, Philip sent personal thank-you letters to all Founders, and it is clear that this direct contact between supporters and the people responsible for the project is one of the factors that has encouraged so many people to make repeat donations over the years.

We never really doubted that we would be able to raise the funds we needed, though outside observers probably thought us wildly optimistic. In the event, we started very strongly and continued with a steady inflow of money at about the rate we needed to ensure that we reached our target in time. As the deadline of November 1999 approached, it seemed that it would be close-run thing, so we made tentative arrangements for short-term loans in case of a minor shortfall. However, a final surge of donations made these unnecessary, and in the end we overshot the target and were able to purchase an extra piece of land in a key position just to the south of the valley entrance (see Chapter 8).

5. Learning about Moffatdale

By members of the Wildwood Group

Appreciating a different landscape and working with different people—woodland history—prehistoric people and animals—early historic records—Covenanters and Border Reivers—extreme weather events—early farming.

* * * * *

Focus on a different area

As we began to focus on Carrifran as the place where we would carry forward the vision of a restored Wildwood, we had to reorientate ourselves in both geographical and bureaucratic terms. Moffatdale, within which Carrifran lies, is part of the Scottish Borderlands in terms of its human history. It is not within the catchment of the river Tweed, which dominates the landscape of the administrative Scottish Borders, and only the hills around head of the valley can be considered as part of the historical Ettrick Forest. Moffat Water joins the River Annan and drains into the Solway and the Irish Sea rather than the North Sea, and when crossing the county boundary from the east at Birkhill it is often only too obvious that the climate of Moffatdale has the distinctive character of western Scotland.

The more immediate impact of the change in our geographical focus related to the organisations that we had to deal with. Over the years we had built up a close relationship with the staff of Scottish Natural Heritage (SNH) in the Borders, but now we would be dealing with the Dumfries office. We also had to get to know the people who worked for the Forestry Commission in southwest Scotland, and to deal with the planners in Dumfries and Galloway Council.

Less obvious at first was a social dislocation, which came to the fore when we faced the issue of the feral goats (see Chapters 8 and 9). Our group was founded in Peebles and all of us had roots – some deep and some relatively shallow – in the Borders, while in Moffat we sometimes found ourselves viewed as outsiders. Nonetheless, it was with

Descriptive words with various origins

Celtic

craig:	*a rock, cairn or heap*
pol:	*a pool or stream*
mod:	*an enclosure*
hope:	*a small enclosed upland valley*
linn:	*a deep and narrow gorge; a waterfall; a pool below a waterfall*

Anglo-saxon

law/top/dod/knowe or head:	*a hill*
croft:	*an enclosed cropped land*
park:	*an enclosed field*
burn:	*a brook, stream*
shaw:	*a small, especially natural, wood*

Scandinavian

beck:	*a burn*
gill:	*ravine or glen*
dale:	*valley*
scaur:	*a sheer rock, precipice; a steep eroded hill*
rig:	*a ridge of high ground, a long narrow hill*
grain:	*a branch of a stream, river*

excitement that we began to learn about Moffatdale, past and present, and to appreciate its dramatic scenery, continually reminding us of the glacial history of the area.

Surviving ancient woodlands
Michael Matthews

From Medieval times until the middle of the 20th century there had been a gradual decline in the extent of ancient native woodlands that once covered the hills and valleys to the east of Moffat. The old names Birkhill (birk = birch) at the head of the valley, and Birkie Cleuch which runs up behind the house there, imply that the upper part of Moffatdale was wooded in the past. Furthermore, the poet James Hogg, writing around the end of the 18th century, mentions that the hills of Bowerhope, beside St Mary's Loch just to the east *"were, like much of that country, formerly covered with wood."*

Most of the historical information comes from General Roy's detailed military map of 1750. Of the deciduous woodlands that still exist in Moffatdale, it is hard to establish what is genuinely ancient woodland and what is long-established semi-natural woodland. Many woods have a continuous woodland history since Roy's time, but there is no way of knowing whether some of the trees (particularly those of economic value such as oak) were planted rather than descended from primeval stock. The Roy map of 1755-60 shows no trees in Carrifran, although a few are indicated in Black Hope (the next valley to the west) and also on islets in the Moffat Water. By the time that the first Ordnance Survey maps were published in the 1850s, the hills were almost entirely denuded by grazing and burning.

The largest of the surviving ancient woods in the area is Craigieburn, four miles south of Carrifran and embedded in a large Forestry Commission plantation. It is now about 35 hectares in extent but in Roy's time it was larger and extended a mile further to the north. This is doubtless the natural wood described in the Statistical Account of 1791 as being *"about 50 acres in extent; consisting of oak, ash, birch, alder etc."* It is significant in being the only place in Moffatdale with a sizeable natural woodland containing oak (although its modern composition is a poor guide to that of pristine woodlands in the area, since oakwoods have often been 'weeded' by woodsmen over many centuries.) There are a few oaks in a small ancient wood at Roundstonefoot, but as there are also non-native beeches there, they may have been planted.

A few smaller woods low down along Moffatdale are also historically documented and recognised as being ancient, but the non-

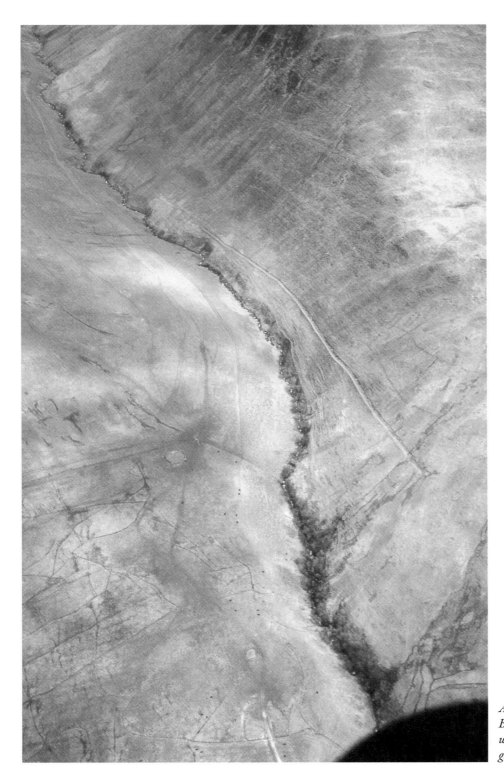

Aerial view of Selcoth Burn revealing both woodland relicts and glimpses of land use history

native beech and conifers are also present in some of them, so one cannot rule out planting even of native species. Of greater interest are the linear woodland fragments, mainly too small to appear on any map, that can be found – with a little effort – in the steep-sided cleuchs (ravines) by which the hill burns flow down towards the Moffat Water. An excellent example is the one on the Selcoth Burn, which has its lower end enclosed by the small conifer plantation just above the farm at 200 m altitude. It straggles up the burn in a narrow and intermittent strip for more than a kilometre and reaches over 300 m. This is undoubtedly ancient woodland, with no sign of planting.

The presence or absence of trees in these cleuchs depends entirely on the nature of the banks. Trees can survive only where saplings can become established out of reach of grazing stock and deer. In the upper parts of burns such as this, where the slope has eased, small rocky outcrops provide cliffy retreats for individual trees, with rowan and eared willow often the last to peter

Where burns are not deeply cut, trees can survive only in scarce rocky places out of reach of herbivores. Where the burns are deeply incised, substantial woodland stands can develop on the cliffs and steep slopes, protected from sheep, goats and deer

out. However, there are sometimes surprises even at high levels; one of the highest bushes on the Selcoth Burn is a hazel, and there is a large clump of bird cherry far up along the Bodesbeck Burn and another in a gorge at Carrifran. This species also occurs at the limit of the woodland in the Spoon Burn, where it is accompanied by guelder rose, a very scarce species in the area. Lower down, where the burns are often deeply incised and form impressive cascades, extremely steep slopes and cliffs provide larger refuges where real woodland can develop; these places are occasionally fenced to prevent loss of stock.

On the Selcoth Burn this woodland is dominated by ash and hazel, with rowan, downy birch and montane goat willow also present, as well as occasional hawthorn, holly and rose; honeysuckle is common and ivy can be found in a few places. Wych elm seems not to be present there, but occurs in several other cleuchs; blackthorn and alder also turn up sporadically in some of these, although the latter species is normally only low down and close to the floor of the main valley.

The populations of trees and shrubs in these widely separated cleuchs are – in the current ecologists' jargon – clear examples of 'metapopulations', often with small numbers and at high risk of local extinction due to mischance, especially falling off the insecure water-saturated cliffs to which they cling. A species lost from one cleuch may recolonise from another, but in competition for a vacated space on a cliff, the odds will be stacked in favour of species that are already abundant and those that have good dispersal mechanisms. The effect is inevitably a gradual loss of rare and poorly dispersing species from the smaller sites, and increasing dominance – especially high up the burns – by a few species such as the bird-dispersed rowan.

A wych elm forms part of a narrow strip of ancient woodland on the Polmoody Burn squeezed between two walls of plantation conifers

Near the head of Moffatdale there is a hint that the character of the natural woodlands was once subtly different. For example, Raking Gill, a precipitous cleuch on the southeast side of the valley between the Grey Mare's Tail and Birkhill, rises from about 300 m at road level to the watershed with the Ettrick valley at over 600 m. The steep slopes lower down carry a fine stand of aspen, but the higher stretches have a beautiful community characterised by the silver-leaved montane goat willow, along with rowan and downy birch.

The three latter species, along with aspen and some smaller willows and especially juniper, may have been the main elements in a band of boreal treeline woodland along the upper fringe of the

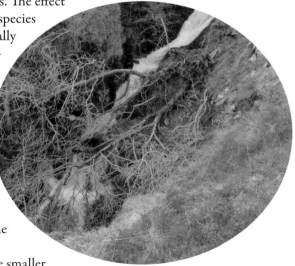

Trees in steep-sided cleuchs are always in danger of falling off

55

woodlands, dominated by oak, ash and hazel, which seem once to have occupied the lower parts of the hills in the Southern Uplands. Although we have found no junipers in Moffatdale, the 1834 Statistical Account for the parish of Moffat mentions that *"a few plants of juniper exist"* and in the area of St Mary's Loch, just over the watershed, we have found a few scattered bushes and one more substantial stand fairly high up on Bowerhope, which is significant in the light of the comment by James Hogg quoted above.

The only substantial plantation in the area before the second half of the 20th century is Crofthead Wood, now a mature oakwood of about 8 ha, which was replanted on the site of an ancient wood referred to in the Statistical Account of 1791 with the acid comment *"belonging to His Grace the Duke of Queensberry ... lately cut down, and being left unenclosed is lost to the proprietor and to the public".* Otherwise there was little change in the landscape until the second half of the 20th century, when the appearance of the Southern Uplands was rapidly changed by blanket afforestation with conifers. The Forestry Commision led the way, but private investors followed eagerly, stimulated by seductive tax avoidance schemes. The conifers included scots pine, japanese larch, douglas fir, norway spruce and serbian spruce, but in the later years sitka spruce was by far the most commonly planted species.

Prehistoric people

Fi Martynoga

Six thousand years ago, and perhaps for six thousand years before that, people were already present in the Southern Uplands, but there were not many of them. They probably appeared as small bands of nomadic hunters, following the salmon migrating up the rivers and burns to shallower waters, where the fish were easy to catch. They surely hunted the four-footed game – aurochs, elk, wild boar and red deer – and the ducks, geese, snipe, woodcock and many more that lived in woods, marshes and along the watercourses.

Finds of stone tools and worked flints are scattered but tend to occur near rivers and lochs. Greater concentrations are sometimes found at the junction of rivers. Since the Carrifran valley is distant from any such junction, and its own burn is tiny, it was probably not a prime hunting site. It is likely that the Moffat Water, below the mouth of the valley, was fished seasonally, and that the hills above were occasional hunting grounds.

This makes the find of the Rotten Bottom bow (see Chapter 6) the more remarkable. Its dating to approximately six thousand years ago

---

The View from White Coomb

"If the day be clear, you will get such a view as you have seldom got before. Round and round and round, hills, hills, hills, billowing away north, south, east and west – "too plain to be grand, too ample and beautiful to be commonplace," as dear old Dr John Brown so aptly said. Broadlaw and Cramalt Craig, the two highest summits in all the Border country, are almost within calling distance. How near the hills come to you when you are upon the tops! Tinto, Queensberry, Ettrick Pen; Hartfell, too, just beside you. The Eildons stand clear out to the east. The Dunion, Ruberslaw, Penchrise, Skelfhill, and the Maidenpaps are yonder watching the passes over the English border, just as they watched the forayers long ago. You can even catch the faint blue outline of the Cheviots, and – if you are specially favoured – you will get a glimpse of some of the Cumberland peaks, with the shimmer of the Solway between."

C.R.B McGilchrist (1905) 'Birkhill: A Reminiscence.'

Left: The pristine woodland at high levels probably looked something like this part of Raking Gill, a steep cleuch a few miles from Carrifran

places it on the cusp of the new era of settled agriculture. Analysis of pollen from the Upper Annandale area suggests that pre-agricultural maintenance of clearings had already been going on for some time by then. The core samples from Rotten Bottom itself suggest vegetation changes, indicative of increased grazing, from approximately the time that the bow found its way into the bog.

People in historic times
Ann Goodburn

Moving on to historic times, Moffatdale in the 6th and 7th centuries was part of the Celtic Kingdom of Rheged. Then for two centuries it was a colony of Anglian Northumbria (the cultivation terraces at Cappelgill – now usually spelled Capplegill – are supposed to date from this time). In the 10th and 11th centuries the area was prey to the Vikings and Gaelic-speaking Irish. By the 13th century it was part of the mediaeval Scottish Kingdom. The earliest legal document of Moffatdale records the grant of the *"whole lands of Polmoodie"* to Sir James Douglas - the *'Black Douglas'* by Robert the Bruce. The Douglases and later the Johnstones are the most important families in the history of Moffatdale.

By the 12th century there is evidence of 'pannage' of swine in forested areas, both in the Borders and further west in the Southern Uplands. However, sheep farming had been introduced into southern Scotland by the great Cistercian Abbeys founded during the reign of David I (1084-1153) and during the 13th and 14th centuries monastic farming, using large numbers of sheep as well as cattle, became the dominant land use. At the peak of the wool trade in 1372, over 9000 sacks were exported from Scotland, leading to an estimated population of over two million sheep, of which a high proportion were probably in the Borderlands.

Over the same period the frequent military incursions into Scotland by the English caused swathes of forest to be felled or burned:

> *"When the Duke of Lancaster led an aggressive force into Scotland during the reign of Richard the Second he had to employ so many men in opening up a line of march, that the strokes of 80,000 hatchets might have been heard, while at the same time the heavens were made red above with the fires by which the impeding trees were burned down!"* McDowall, W (1867) 'History of the Burgh of Dumfries.'

This should be taken with a pinch of salt, especially since another account of the same episode (which occurred in about 1385) mentions

Corbies – an encounter with reivers

Early morning on the 2nd of April 1583, a good time for crows in Tweedsmuir; the once live stock of Menzion lay drowned in the Tweed, and where the carcasses of cows, sheep and goats fetched up in the shallows there was a feast to be had. Seven miles south of the smoking ransacked steading, at the peat cuttings, a young woman, Katherine, was heading for town. She paused at the Corehead nick, scanning the Beef tub and Ericstane brae. Not scared, it was full daylight now and the band of men she had seen last night would surely be home by now. That had been a different matter, but at thirteen she had the sense to hide in the saugh-buss until they passed. Seeing nothing to worry her she skipped down the steep path into Annandale. A fast walker, she soon splashed through the ford and joined the main road. Katherine felt safer now and sheltered briefly under the thorn tree while a heavy shower of rain swept up the valley. On the point of setting forward again she realised that she had company. Two boys were making their way into town. The well-fed pony they were leading had cropped mane and tail and across its back two half filled muddy sacks tied together at the neck. The boys looked at Katherine. – What are you doing here? She thought they were no more that two years older than her, stupid but far from harmless. – I was taking meal to my brother at the peats. – Is that right. They gave one another significant looks. – Well we were at Menzion last night. Do you want a lift? Giving no answer, but jumping onto the sod dyke and springing aboard she got her lift down the road on the pony's wet back. Much later that day, the sun sinking behind the Chapel hill, Katherine spoke to her grandmother. The old woman of forty five was helping her cow to calve. Grandmother frowned when she heard about the morning's encounter. – Do you know what they said to me? Grandmother was busy. – They said 'Aren't you afraid to take a lift from us?' – And what did you say girl? I just said no, should I be? And then they said 'Well we are Moffats'. Grandmother shook her head and frowned again. After a while she said – They say the King will come our way this summer. He'll see some of these crows' nests poked down and hopefully some of them will soon be hanging on the gibbet. That's its foot, give me the rope girl.

From the family records of a local resident

The Covenanters in Moffatdale

The Covenanters chiefly remembered in the Borderlands of Scotland comprised an element of the reforming and zealous Presbyterian movement that played such a key role in Scottish life during the turbulent 17th century. These Covenanters, who had refused to accept the reinstatement of episcopal authority after the restoration of Charles II in 1660, left the established church and resorted to open-air 'conventicles' in the countryside. Ruthless persecution ensued, with small groups of Covenanters taking refuge in the hills. By 1689, when William of Orange succeeded to the throne, order was finally restored and the Presbyterian Church of Scotland established.

In his Annals of three Dumfriesshire Dales, published in 1954, W.A.J. Prevost described the use of Moffatdale by the outlawed Covenanters:

"The hills round Moffat and particularly the rough and broken country at the head of Moffat Water provided admirable cover for the wanderers. The moss hags near Loch Skene are extensive and the numerous holes, hollows and ditches to be found there can afford concealment for a large number of men. The Covenanters carved out shelters in the peat, set watches all round on suitable vantage points, and moved from one hiding place to another on the approach of unfriendly visitors. It was impossible for these men to keep themselves altogether concealed from the country people, who at great risk to themselves often supplied them with food and necessaries, and upon whom the fugitives must have depended to a great extent for their livelihood. It is said that the farmers of Chapelhope and Bodsbeck were of great assistance to these people. The farmers who gave no active help, passively assisted by affecting not to notice the loss of lambs and ewes from their stock, which the Covenanters had managed to demolish."

This recourse to obtain meat is the subject of the following fragments of an old song, included by James Hogg a century later in his notes to Mess John:

> *"Carrifran Gans they're very strait,*
> *We canna gang without a road;*
> *But tak ye the tae side, an' me the tither*
> *An' they's a' come in a Firthup dod.*
>
> *On Turnberry, an' Carrifran Gans*
> *An' out amang the Moodlaw haggs,*
> *They worried the feck o' the laird's lambs,*
> *An' eatit them raw, and buried the bags.*
>
> *Had Guemshope Castle a tongue to speak,*
> *Or mouth of flesh, that it could fathom,*
> *It wad tell o' mony a supple trick*
> *Was done at the foot o' Rotten-Boddom.*
>
> *Where Donald and his hungry men,*
> *Oft houghed them up wi' little din,*
> *An' mair intent on flesh than yarn,*
> *Bure aff the bouk, and buried the skin."*

24,000 axes, but there is no doubt that military operations caused much deforestation.

Nonetheless, in the 15th and 16th centuries some parts of the uplands were still relatively wild, uncultivated and with tracts of woodland that were the resort of outlaws or huntsmen. In Moffatdale there were wild boar and deer. On one occasion in the mid 15th century, King James the Second summoned many lords and gentlemen with their deer-hounds to the chase in Megget – the valley north of White Coomb. They *"assemblit at Edinburgh, and thairfra went with the King's grace to Meggatland, in the guhilk boundis were slain at that tyme aughteine score of deir."*

Large mammals once roamed these hills, such as this aurochs whose skull was found in the Borders in 1980
Photo: James Thomson

Some hundred years later in 1566 Queen Mary set out with Darnley for Megget, but so disappointed were they with the scarcity of game, that they held a council at Rodono and issued an ordinance *"that the deer should not be shot under the pains of law."* But already it would appear that the woodland, as well as its wild occupants, was largely cleared, and a map of the Ettrick Forest based on work of Timothy Pont in about 1608 shows only small wooded areas, including some around St Mary's Loch and in the Ettrick Valley.

Between the years of approximately 1300 and 1600 there was constant Border reiving. Tilling and agricultural pursuits were in vain because of the system of plunder and reprisal taken up by both English and Scots moss-troopers. They were from all classes from chiefs to serfs. Lawlessness prevailed and the lands were inaccessible and uncivilised. Houses were of simple construction, with walls of earth sods or wattle and roofed with thatch. These have not remained but in the mid 15th century the lairds were required to build peel towers for defence – simple square buildings with extremely thick walls and very few small windows. In Moffatdale peel towers were built at Bodesbeck, Roundstonefoot (Runstonfoot), Craigieburn and Pocornel.

After the Union of the Crowns in 1603 the area became more peaceful, but as a result the remaining ancient woodlands suffered further destruction when the country began to be farmed more intensively, with sheep being the main product. Sheep were now allowed to wander in many of the remaining patches of forest and most parts of the uplands gradually turned into sheepwalks or 'gangs' (cf. the hill name Carrifran Gans) as woodland regeneration collapsed and timber was cut. Religion took the place of reiving and the times of the Wars of the Covenant, when the Scots revolted against religious dictatorship from London, made the hills around Moffatdale famous in story as the

Gaps in the native fauna

Walking through Moffatdale a few hundred years ago, you could still have seen signs of pine marten, polecat and wildcat, species no longer found in southern Scotland but surviving elsewhere. There were also red deer until the mid 18th century. There would have been only ghosts of earlier denizens, doubtless familiar to the hunter in Rotten Bottom but subsequently lost from the whole of Britain. Elk (called moose in North America) perhaps disappeared around 4000 years ago. The skull of an aurochs unearthed in the Borders in 1980 is about 5000 years old and these wild cattle may have become extinct in Britain only just before the Roman occupation. Bear were probably lost at about the same time, but dating of lynx bone from a cave in North Yorkshire shows that this species survived to at least AD 600. Three more large mammals were lost only in the last millennium: wild boar perhaps in the 13th century, beaver in the 16th century and the wolf as recently as AD 1700. Within ten miles of Carrifran the modern map shows Wolf Cleuch and Wolf Shank, and also Bear Craig and nearby Bear Den. These grazers, tree-fellers and predators, key components of a naturally functioning ecosystem, were part of the Scottish scene. Reinstatement of some of the lost species is now on the political agenda, with beaver just arrived and lynx next in the queue.

outlawed Presbyterians took to the hills to avoid persecution. These 28 years were full of ghastly atrocities on both sides, chiefly in Galloway and Nithsdale, and culminated in the infamous 'killing time' of 1685.

The 18th century saw the agricultural revolution. In the Borderlands it involved widespread removal by landlords of rights to the use of what had previously been common land, and also clearances of cottars and the merging of groups of small tenanted farms into single large ones. The changes were less drastic in the upland areas that were already used mainly for sheep farming. In 1759 Thomas Gillespie, the farmer at Carrifran and tenant of *"Correferran and Capplegill, renewed his tenancy of both these farms on a 9 year lease at a yearly rent of £150 and £100 sterling of entry money for Correferan and £73 rent and £120 entry money for Capplegill"*. As before, Carrifran valley would agriculturally still be the haunt of sheep.

The sheep farmers or 'store-masters' as they were called were *"not much disposed to publish or make known the amount of their respective flocks; but it is supposed, that there are, in all, from 18,000 to 20,000 sheep."* Mostly they were cheviot crossed with black-face which gave better wool. In the past the sheep had been of the 'four horned kind'. Many of the dry-stane dykes in Moffatdale were built before 1800 – there was no shortage of stones! All the fencing, dyking, road making and other improvements had but one end – the more efficient production of sheep and wool for this was the main employment.

However, the area was still wild to some extent. The Statistical Account of 1791 mentions that at Loch Skeen *"There is a small island in it, where the eagles bring out their young in great safety; as the water is deep, and no boat upon the Lake"*. There were also foxes, hares, wildcats, fulmarts [polecats], otters and badgers in the Parish of Moffat. Interestingly, the account mentions that *"There are both red and black game in the parish; not much, indeed, of the latter, but they are increasing, and as the plantations get forward, it is expected, that they will become more numerous"*. The New Statistical Account of 1834 also mentions that ptarmigan are very rarely seen. This account also comments on deer, saying that *"In former times, the hart and hind were found in this parish; the last hart was killed in 1754, having long been single. The roebuck and doe were also natives, but have long since disappeared."*

At rare intervals, sheep production in the Borderlands suffered under the impact of major storms. Even allowing for the inevitable opportunities for exaggeration over time, it is clear that these were sometimes extremely severe. James Hogg – the famous self-taught writer of the area known as 'The Etttrick Shepherd' – recorded those that happened in his lifetime in the early 19th century, but also collected traditional stories and records of earlier storms in the area:

"The most dismal of all those on record is The Thirteen Drifty Days. This extraordinary storm as near as I have been able to trace must have occurred in the year 1620... It is said that for thirteen days and nights the snow drift never once abated – the ground was covered with frozen snow when it commenced and during all that time the sheep never broke their fast. The cold was intense to a degree never before remembered and about the fifth and sixth days of the storm the young sheep began to fall into a sleepy and torpid state and all that were so affected in the evening died over night. The intensity of the frost wind often cut them off when in that state quite instantaneously. About the ninth and tenth days the shepherds began to build up huge semi-circular walls of their dead in order to afford some shelter for the remainder of the living but they availed but little for about the same time they were frequently seen tearing at one another's wool with their teeth."

The final consequence of this storm was that almost nine tenths of the sheep in the area were killed, and the history of the present sheep stock can be dated from that time.

Hogg records an 18th century storm (probably on 24th January 1794) when 17 shepherds died in South Scotland, and as for the sheep:

"Many hundreds were driven into waters, burns, and ravines by the violence of the storm, where they were buried or frozen up, and these the flood carried away so that they were never seen or found by the owners at all." When the storm subsided, in one place on the Solway Firth, where the tide throws out and leaves whatsoever is carried into it by the rivers, were found *"1840 sheep, 9 black cattle, 3 horses, 2 men, 1 woman, 45 dogs, and 180 hares, besides a number of meaner animals."*

Such extreme weather events are rare in the area. The New Statistical Account of 1834, in describing the climate of Moffat, says:

"The climate and temperature of the village of Moffat may be stated most intelligibly by comparison, being neither so cold as in Edinburgh, nor so wet as in Glasgow and not so warm as in Dumfries and Annan, no haar, nor the Solway fogs."

The climate is influenced by the prevailing westerly winds and frontal patterns coming from the Atlantic, with mist, cloud and gray skies with rain being common. Rainfall appears to be well distributed throughout the year with the driest months being April, May and June. Major floods are reported periodically in the area; most extreme floods occur in early winter although severe summer floods are also known. The extent of flooding at Carrifran itself is unknown, but the general lack of alluvial deposits suggests that flooding in the valley is rare.

Springs below Dun Knowe, revealed by a light fall of snow, join the Carrifran Burn shortly before it enters Moffatdale

On the remains of the Ettrick Forest

The scenes are desert now, and bare
Where flourished once a forest fair,
When these waste glens with copse were lined,
And peopled with the hart and hind.
Yon thorn – perchance those prickly spears
Have fenced him in for three hundred years,
While fell around his green compeers –
You lonely thorn, would he could tell,
The changes in his parent dell,
Since he, so grey and stubborn now,
Waved in each breeze a sapling bough:
Would he could tell how deep the shade
A thousand mingled branches made:
How broad the shadows of the oak,
How clung the rowan to the rock.

And through the foliage show'd his head,
With narrow leaves and berries red:
What pines on every mountain sprung,
O'er every dell the birches hung,
In every breeze the aspen shook,
What alders shaded every brook:
"Here, in my shade" methinks to say,
The mighty stag at noon-tide lay:
The wolf I've seen, a fiercer game,
(The neighbouring dingle bears his name.)
With lurching step around me prowl,
And stop, against the moon to howl:
The mountain-boar, on battle set,
His tusks upon my stem did whet:
While doe, and roe, and red-deer good,
Have bounded by, through gay green wood.

From Marmion by Walter Scott

6. Carrifran – Seat of Ravens

By Members of the Wildwood Group

A walk of discovery into the glen—Site of Special Scientific Interest and Special Area of Conservation—location and topography—geology—woodland history and the pollen record—woodland relicts—ground vegetation—special plants of the area—lower plants of the valley—mammals, birds, reptiles and amphibians—beetles, butterflies and other invertebrates—the Carrifran Burn—archaeological remains.

* * * * *

Caer–y–fran ... raven's crag or fort
from Brythonic *carr* – a high rocky place and *vran* – a raven
freely translated ... **Seat of Ravens**

In 1999 Jim Gilchrist wrote in *The Scotsman* that Carrifran is:

> *"... a hidden place where the clock is about to be wound back to a time before man ever impacted on the landscape. A century from now, the bare valley will be verdant with the kind of lush, broad-leaved woodland amid which that hunter-gatherer discarded his bow, some 6,000 years ago. It has been an act of faith, the run up to this rewinding of the spool of time, the pursuit of a vision which the visionaries themselves will not live to see fulfilled."*

A chapter on the Wildwood site should perhaps begin with details of its location, climate, history, geology and other physical and historical subjects. Let that come later. First let us walk into the glen as on the July day in 1996 when we had just learned that its purchase might be possible.

We approach Carrifran on the narrow and winding A708 from Moffat, or from the direction of Selkirk, passing St Mary's Loch. Reaching the mouth of the valley, we pause and gaze towards the cliffs of Raven Craig in the distance, with the steep slopes of Peat Hill on the left and the dark mass of Carrifran Gans on the right. From here,

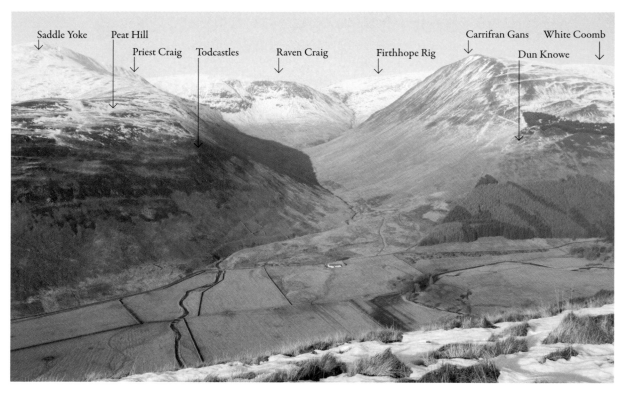

Saddle Yoke · Peat Hill · Priest Craig · Todcastles · Raven Craig · Firthhope Rig · Carrifran Gans · Dun Knowe · White Coomb

The Wildwood will extend almost to the summits of the Moffat Hills. Sadly, we can't (yet) do anything about the plantation on the right of the picture

Slopes as steep as it is possible for hillsides to be

however, the main sweep of the glen is obscured by the massive glacial deposit that blocks its mouth. We walk up across it and reach – at the highest point – a perfect round drystane sheepstell with sinuous stone 'wings' extending from it.

Suddenly the valley is before us. Its striking U-shaped profile evokes its history – during the Ice Age – as the bed of a glacier flowing from the massive hills to the north to join the larger one in Moffatdale. From this viewpoint, there is a full sense of Carrifran as a natural entity. The surrounding high ground creates a strong feeling of enclosure, with scree-strewn slopes of the kind described by Derek Ratcliffe as being *"as steep as it is possible for hillsides to be, without breaking out into actual crag"*, running up to the heather covered summits.

Leaving the stell behind, we cross a series of tiny burns flowing from high on the flushed slopes to the right, with the track stretching ahead towards the cliffs. A buzzard hangs in the updraughts over Carrifran Gans and ravens croak overhead.

Walking on past another sheepstell on the bare slope to the west of the burn, Carrifran's second secret is gradually revealed. The valley, appearing quite short when viewed from the road crossing its mouth, does not end with the cliffs that bar the way ahead, but bends to the right and rises towards Firthhope Rig and the still hidden White

66

Coomb, two of the highest hills in the south of Scotland. Here, the burn is untamed and liable to change its route in times of flood, leaving massive ridges of loose rock between the channels. Wild thyme flourishes, along with parsley fern, one of the pioneer colonists of screes. On the left is a boggy area, dotted with the white heads of cottongrass and the occasional orchid.

Half an hour into the walk, however, it is clear that all is not well with the valley. Coarse grasses and sedges, close-cropped blaeberry and bracken dominate the lower slopes, while heather has retreated towards the summits. Closer to the mouth of the valley we had glimpsed a few trees almost hidden by the low cliffs along the burn, and a solitary rowan stood out on a bluff, but the rest of the valley is stripped bare of all its natural trees and shrubs. No seedling tree has a chance unless it is out of reach of the omnipresent sheep, backed up by the feral goats, which can just be seen as groups of black and white dots high on the surrounding crags.

Holly Gill in July 1996: trees and cattle can lose their foothold when overgrazed land becomes sodden in a downpour – cow bones on the left of the picture

Entering a ravine, we find the uprooted trunks of several birches, still carrying shrivelled brown leaves, and from the riffles in the burn protrude the bones of at least one cow. Something has recently happened here, probably a spring storm saturating the steep slopes above the burn, loosening the roots of the trees and making it impossible for cattle to keep their footing.

We later took cuttings from the ancient holly stump and planted them nearby

Nearby lies the detached stump of a massive twin-trunked holly – still clinging to life – which has crashed into the burn and remains there, trapped by a large reddish rock split off from the low cliff that had protected it for hundreds of years. This ancient tree provides cogent evidence that once there was high forest in Carrifran glen.

Continuing upwards, we are mobbed by a pair of peregrines who have young in an eyrie on Raven Craig. Their

strident chattering as they swing around high above us is interspersed by the whoosh of wings as one of them stoops past in protest at our intrusion, though this will not cause harm so late in the season. Gaining height, we are rewarded by the first sight of another of Carrifran's secrets, the sinuous cascade that we later christen Firthhope Linn, which continually teases us with partial views but never permits us to see it in its entirety.

The climb up past the waterfall – the best access route to the hanging valley above – must wait for another day, but we have gone far enough to understand the scale and character of Carrifran, and to get a sense of the rich diversity of life that could be restored to it. In 1996 that vision was still a leap of faith, but one that now lay within the bounds of possibility.

During the months that followed our own first visit to Carrifran, as we inched towards a formal agreement to purchase the valley, members of the Wildwood Group tried to learn all they could about it and prepared briefing papers on various aspects of it and its surroundings and history. The sections that follow are developed from what was written then, along with information we gathered about the plants and animals that survived in the valley around the end of the last millennium.

Carrifran has long been officially recognised in terms of conservation and scenic value as a very special place. The valley forms part of the Moffat Hills Site of Special Scientific Interest, originally designated in 1956 and confirmed in 1991 as a Grade 1 Nature Conservation Review Site. The area is noted especially for its rare mountain plants, along with the fine glacial landscapes and historically significant geological features, and has now been designated as a Special Area of Conservation (SAC) under European legislation (see Box). Carrifran also lies within an Environmentally Sensitive Area (ESA) and a Regional Scenic Area under the Dumfries and Galloway Structure Plan.

Right: 2009 map with final planting details (Ordnance Survey data Crown copyright. All rights reserved. Licence no. 100034302.)

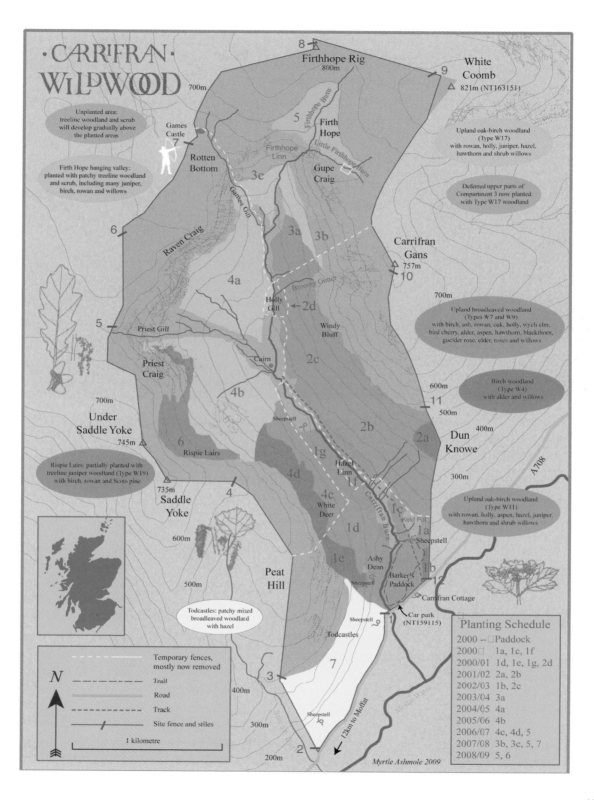

·CARRIFRAN· WILDWOOD

Firthhope Rig
800m

White Coomb
821m (NT163151)

8

9

700m

Unplanted area:
treeline woodland and scrub
will develop gradually above
the planted areas

Games Castle
7

Rotten Bottom

Firth Hope

Firthhope Linn

Little Firthhope Burn

5

Firthhope Burn

Gupe Craig

Upland oak-birch woodland
(Type W17)
with rowan, holly, juniper, hazel,
hawthorn and shrub willows

Firth Hope hanging valley:
planted with patchy treeline woodland
and scrub, including many juniper,
birch, rowan and willows

3c

Deferred upper parts of
Compartment 3 now planted
with Type W17 woodland

6

Raven Craig

Games Gill

3a

3b

Carrifran Gans
757m
10

4a

Broomy Gutter

Holly Gill

2d

700m

5

Priest Gill

Windy Bluff

Upland broadleaved woodland
(Types W7 and W9)
with birch, ash, rowan, oak, holly, wych elm,
bird cherry, alder, aspen, hawthorn, blackthorn,
guelder rose, elder, roses and willows

Priest Craig

Cairn

2c

4b

600m

Birch woodland
(Type W4)
with alder and willows

700m

Under Saddle Yoke
745m

6

Rispie Lairs

Sheepstell

2b

500m

11

Dun Knowe

2a

400m

Rispie Lairs: partially planted with
treeline juniper woodland (Type W19)
with birch, rowan and Scots pine

1g

4d

735m

Saddle Yoke

4

Hazel Linn

1f

4c

White Deer

Keld Pot

1c

300m

Upland oak-birch woodland
(Type W11)
with rowan, holly, aspen, hazel, juniper,
hawthorn and shrub willows

600m

1d

1a

Sheepstell

12

Peat Hill

1e

Ashy Dean

Barker's Paddock

1b

500m

Sheepstell

Carrifran Cottage

Todcastles: patchy mixed
broadleaved woodland
with hazel

Sheepstell

1

Car park
(NT159115)

400m

Sheepstell

Todcastles

Planting Schedule

2000 -- ☐ Paddock
2000 ☐ 1a, 1c, 1f
2000/01 1d, 1e, 1g, 2d
2001/02 2a, 2b
2002/03 1b, 2c
2003/04 3a
2004/05 4a
2005/06 4b
2006/07 4c, 4d, 5
2007/08 3b, 3c, 5, 7
2008/09 5, 6

3

300m

7

12km to Moffat

Sheepstell

2

200m

N

Temporary fences,
mostly now removed

Trail

Road

Track

Site fence and stiles

1 kilometre

Myrtle Ashmole 2009

69

Glaciers have carved Carrifran out of the plateau of the Moffat Hills: the site extends to the summits of Firthhope Rig and White Coomb (top right)
Photo: David Geddes

The geographic setting of Carrifran
Ann Goodburn

Carrifran valley lies in the Moffat Hills in the central Southern Uplands of Scotland, 55° north and 3° west, in Dumfries and Galloway Region. These hills are north-east of Moffat and east of the M74 – the road from Carlisle to Glasgow – and they form the first really impressive area of high ground seen by the traveller from England to Scotland.

Immediately the landscape is most impressive. At Capplegill farm (which included Carrifran until this was purchased by Borders Forest Trust) the first of three unusually beautiful valleys on the left is reached. This is Blackhope Glen, a sharp steep cleft into the hills which can just be seen opening up to the north from the road. The west or left-hand side of this glen is wild and rocky, with broken crags and sharp ridges. The steep north slope runs up to Hart Fell (808 m) and the east side has the beautiful narrow curve of Under Saddle Yoke (745 m) and Saddle Yoke (735 m) forming a spectacular skyline identifiable from a great distance.

Carrifran itself is a deep U-shaped glen with a total area of more than six square km, opening northwards off Moffatdale. It has penetrated less deeply into the high plateau than Blackhope Glen, but the setting is magnificent. It lies beneath a high grassy ridge that forms the spine of the Moffat Hills, rising from the Devil's Beef Tub far to the west to the summit of Hart Fell and then sweeping on to Hartfell Rig, Firthhope Rig (800 m) and White Coomb (821 m), the fourth highest hill in the south of Scotland.

Within the valley, Gupe Craig and Carrifran Gans (757 m) form a massive barrier to the east, while the dark cliffs of Raven Craig dominate the view to the northwest. Above the cliffs lies Rotten Bottom, a wide expanse of peat bog on the watershed where the ancient bow was found (see Chapter 4). It is the source of the Gameshope Burn, which flows north to Talla Reservoir, down through the valley that provided the initial inspiration for the Wildwood project.

Carrifran forms an entire watershed, amounting to about 1640 acres (665 ha). In form, it is not typical of the Southern Uplands. Carrifran Burn and its tributaries, descending into the valley in a series of long ribbon-like cascades, and its surrounding steep hills and crags, are more Highland in character than the more usual gently rounded hills of the area. It is hidden away from the ancient route-way of Moffatdale and on a wild wet wintry day, when the clouds are low over the crags, it has an austere, forbidding aspect. It is not difficult to imagine why the Covenanters of the 17th century found it a good hiding place, although hardly hospitable. When the skies are blue, the sun twinkles on the burn and the wild bedstraw and tormentil bloom, it has a serene, peaceful and timeless quality.

East of Carrifran lies a third impressive tributary valley before the watershed at Birkhill is reached. This is owned by the National Trust for Scotland and famed for its hanging valley with the cascade of the Grey Mare's Tail where the Tail Burn flows from a moraine impounded corrie loch – Loch Skene – over the cliffs for 70 metres, forming one of Britain's highest waterfalls. The National Trust land marches with Carrifran through the summits of Firthhope Rig, White Coomb and Carrifran Gans.

The climate of Carrifran is distinctly western in character. Annual rainfall statistics for 1971-2000 from Eskdalemuir (12 km to the southeast of Carrifran and at 242 m a.s.l.) show annual rainfall of just over 1600 mm. The wettest months are December, January, October and November, the driest May, April and June. The monthly averages of the daily maximum (and minimum) temperatures for the coldest month (January) are 4.7^{0}C (-0.7^{0}C) and for the warmest month (July) are 18.1^{0}C (9.2^{0}C). Airfrost is frequent from November to April. The site is windy throughout the year, with slightly higher averages from November to April than from May to October.

Farm stock at Capplegill and Carrifran

Throughout the 20th century the predominant land use at Capplegill Farm (including Carrifran) was still sheep grazing, with a little grouse shooting. In the time of Mr Haig Douglas, who farmed Capplegill from 1938 to 1972, Carrifran was split into two hirsels, 'The Gangs' and 'The West Side'; together, these carried 660 ewes and 160 hoggs (yearlings). We are fortunate to have this farmer's verbatim description of farming in the 20th century. When John Barker took over Capplegill in 1994 he initiated a different regime on the whole farm, putting on large numbers of cattle as well as maintaining high stocking with sheep. In November 1996 he had 2100 ewes plus 750 hoggs and 620 cows plus 608 calves, on the 5000 acres of Capplegill. However, there was sometimes high mortality among the cattle in bad weather, apparently as a result of beasts losing their footing on steep slopes. Also during Mr Barker's ownership cattle manure was applied to the semi-improved pasture on the moraine at the entrance to Carrifran (which we call the Paddock) and some drainage was carried out in the same area. (An interview with Haig Douglas, recorded shortly before his death, is available on www.carrifran.org.uk)

Ann Goodburn

Using acid to check for lime-rich rocks

Geology

Based on information kindly provided by Derek Robeson, Elizabeth Pickett and Steve Hannah

The rocks underlying the entire length of the Carrifran valley, now exposed in the crags and the channels of the burns, are marine shales, siltstones and sandstones usually referred to as 'greywacke'. They are part of the 'Llandovery series' of rocks, dating from a time just after the transition from the Ordovician to the Silurian Period some 438 million years ago. They were laid down as sediments around the margins of the ancient Iapetus Ocean.

At that time, the area now occupied by the Moffat Hills was situated 15 degrees south of the equator and the Iapetus Ocean lay between two large landmasses. Through the process of plate tectonics – the movement of the plates forming the crust of the earth – these landmasses gradually came together rather more than 400 million years ago, along a WSW to ENE line extending from the Solway into the Scottish Borders. The intense pressures associated with continental collision caused the layers of sedimentary rock to be drastically folded and faulted, forming the Southern Uplands that we know today.

Intriguingly, rock types similar in age and character to those of Carrifran can be found elsewhere, forming a belt from the American Appalachians, through the maritime provinces of Canada, across Ireland and Scotland and into Scandinavia. It is therefore clear that these land masses were all connected at that time and have spread apart since then, as a result of continental drift.

The huge sequences of greywacke rocks at Carrifran – many hundreds of metres thick – are relatively uniform, making it difficult to date particular outcrops accurately. Sequences are dominated by medium or thick beds of sandstones with interbedded packets of siltstone and thin-bedded sandstones, and include distinctive thick units of laminated siltstone, massive sandstone and conglomerate. Slivers of Moffat Shale – a rock type that forms the base of the greywacke sequence – run across Carrifran, one near the bottom of the valley and one near its head, and are thought to indicate faults. Geochemically, the sandstones and siltstones usually have a silica-rich cement, whereas some of the shales are bound together with calcium carbonate (calcite) giving rise locally to calcareous soils.

Some of the rocks contain fossils of graptolites – floating, marine, filter-feeding polyps – preserved as small pencil-like and sometimes serrated marks, often showing up silvery on the dark rock surface. These fossils have been used to broadly date the greywacke sequences and have played an important part in the history of geology, since the graptolites from nearby Dobs Linn at the head of Moffatdale were used to help define the Ordovician-Silurian transition.

Igneous rocks (as opposed to the sedimentary rocks that dominate the region) are represented by a thin intrusive dolerite dyke, only a few metres thick, which was injected as molten rock along a fracture line and forms a band of very hard rock running in a NW-SE band below the crags of Carrifran. It is probably about 40 million years old – and thus only a tenth of the age of the surrounding sedimentary rocks.

The Southern Uplands seem to have been entirely covered by a thick sheet of ice on several occasions in the past million years and Carrifran valley was doubtless carved progressively by glaciers during this period. The last occasion was only about 18,000 years ago and the solid bedrock is now covered in much of the valley by unconsolidated layers of sands, gravels and clays that formed towards the end of this glacial period. At this time Carrifran was occupied by ice and Moffatdale was also occupied by a large glacier. These glaciers may have met at the mouth of Carrifran and flowed southwest down the valley towards the modern day site of Moffat, but evidence from this period is fragmentary at best.

A large deposit of glacial debris has accumulated in the area known as the Paddock, adjacent to the main road and with its northern limit close to the main sheepstell at the highest point of the track. It is composed of loose sand, gravel and rock (typical of unconsolidated glacial till), which is clearly visible in the large erosion scar formed by the Carrifran Burn immediately to the west of the sheepstell. The deposit probably dates from the end of the last major glacial rather than from the subsequent and relatively minor Loch Lomond Stadial (see below).

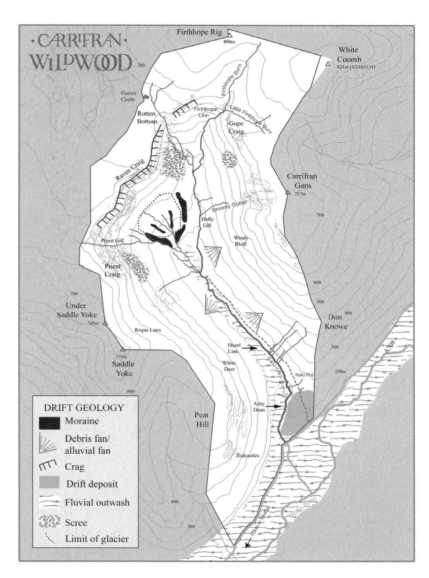

Drift Geology (Ordnance Survey data Crown copyright. All rights reserved. Licence no. 100034302.)

The deposit has been interpreted as a terminal moraine, but this is now in doubt and future studies may confirm a suspicion that it was formed by a build-up of debris in an area of relatively low pressure between the converging glaciers in Carrifran and Moffatdale.

Although the ice had melted entirely around 14,000 years ago, it later re-occupied part of the Carrifran valley for a short while. Between 12,900 and 11,500 years ago, the Younger Dryas cold period (known as the Loch Lomond Stadial in the UK) caused ice to occupy the upland areas of Scotland. This ice was most strongly developed in the Highlands but it also occupied the Southern Uplands, and some of the most prominent evidence for this is to be found in the area of Loch Skene. Furthermore, there is evidence that a small glacier occupied the northern end of Carrifran. Just below Rotten Bottom, at the base of Raven Craig, are moraines in a semi-circular pattern. One set lies within the other, possibly suggesting some recession and stagnation of ice growth during this time. In addition to this, the amount of scree directly above the moraines is far less than that just outside them to the north. Given that scree is formed periglacially – during glacial conditions but outside the ice limits – this is further evidence that the site was occupied by a small glacier.

Analysis of the deposits below Raven Craig suggests that during the Loch Lomond Stadial a glacier maintained itself here above about 310 m, a contour that runs just above the cairn near the confluence of Firthhope Burn and Priest Gill. However, the origin of this glacier below Raven Craig is still open to speculation. It may have formed *in situ* at the head of the valley and remained fairly small, or it may possibly have been a 'reconstituted glacier', a glacier which has broken off a larger one but has since sustained itself. In the latter case, the most likely source would be Rotten Bottom, assuming this was covered by ice. This is possible since Gameshope valley – running north from the watershed at Rotten Bottom – is known to have been occupied by ice during the Loch Lomond Stadial.

At present Carrifran valley shows evidence of 'paraglacial development', with landforms influenced by previous glacial activity. These come in the form of some rockfall debris, debris cones and small alluvial fans, both now covered by vegetation. Given their position at the centre of the valley they are products of the last major glacial period and consist of moving drift and other glacial debris. Debris cones would have resulted from hillslope failure, while alluvial fans formed through fluvial action.

Left: The burn has cut round the edge of a major glacial deposit (centre) formed at the junction of Carrifran and Moffatdale

Colt's-foot thrives on the unstable glacial debris of the erosion scar

Left: The dull light of early spring shows up the heather-capped moraines

The peat core from Rotten Bottom – a unique record of a changing environment
Philip Ashmole and Richard Tipping

In 1990 the Rotten Bottom Bow was discovered in the blanket peat high on the plateau above Carrifran valley (see Archaeology section). As a result of this find the National Trust for Scotland (which owns the nearby Grey Mare's Tail) had the inspired idea of approaching Bulmers Strongbow Cider for sponsorship for coring the peat, in order to study the preserved pollen grains and so throw light on the history of vegetation in the hills. Receiving a generous donation, the Trust commissioned Richard Tipping to undertake the work. He made a reconnaissance visit to Rotten Bottom in a snowstorm in January 1994, with Alison Sheridan of the National Museums of Scotland. However, the peat was frozen to a considerable depth and it was only in late April that a core was finally taken (at NT 145145, altitude 620 m a.s.l.) after a careful search for the place where the peat was thickest and thus probably oldest.

The peat was sampled by digging a pit by hand into one of the peat haggs, down to 320 cm, creating a vertical wall more than ten feet high. Seven large tins, each 50 cm long, were then hammered in sideways to sample all layers of the peat and give a continuous record. Samples from different depths in the core and also from the earliest layers of peat in other parts of Rotten Bottom were sent to a laboratory for radiocarbon dating, paid for by a special grant of £19,000. These

Artist Liz Douglas was inspired by the story of the pollen from Rotten Bottom

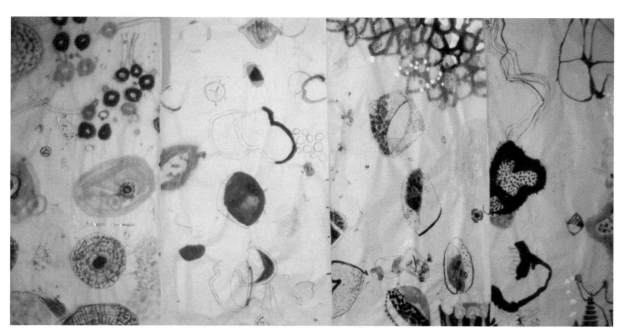

dated samples provided a way of assessing, firstly, the rate of accumulation of the peat and thus the age of any part of the core, and secondly, the time at which peat first started to form elsewhere on the plateau. Various other characteristics of the peat were also assessed, such as the degree to which it was decayed, in an attempt to chart changes in climate and other factors influencing peat growth.

For the pollen analysis itself, over 90 half-centimetre slices of peat were taken from different levels in the core.

Without goats and sheep, the exposed peat may yet again support vegetation

Pollen is generally well preserved in acid peat bogs and microscopic examination reveals a wide diversity of form in the pollen grains of different plant species, thus permitting identification. It is thus possible to obtain a series of 'snapshots' of the changing plant communities at a site, by identifying and counting hundreds of pollen grains (and spores of lower plants) in each sample of peat from different depths in the core. Not all plant species can be separated, and the analysis has to take into account the biology of the different plants (for instance, which species are insect-pollinated and tend to produce relatively little pollen, and which produce large quantities of pollen adapted for dispersal in the wind) and of the nature of the site (for instance altitude, aspect and exposure).

Richard Tipping pointed out in his report that:

> *"The peat represents almost the entirety of the present interglacial, the Holocene, and with peat accumulation more-or-less constant, at around 30-31 years per cm, this provides a quite magnificent palaeoecological record, and undoubtedly the most highly resolved analysis from any upland locality in the country."*

The results provide information about the vegetation on the plateau from just after the end of the last Ice Age, 10,300 years ago, until the present. The Rotten Bottom pollen record has yet to be fully published, but information from the site has been used in several publications. We are lucky also to have two additional pollen records (though covering shorter periods) from within 5 km north of Carrifran, one at Talla Moss close to the Meggat Stone at 400 m and one (based on a student project

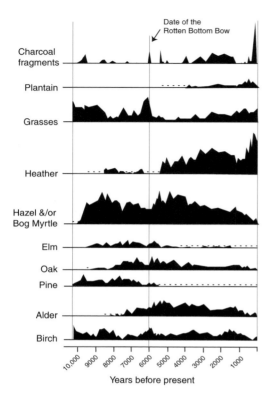

Date of the
Rotten Bottom Bow

Charcoal
fragments

Plantain

Grasses

Heather

Hazel &/or
Bog Myrtle

Elm

Oak

Pine

Alder

Birch

10,000 9000 8000 7000 6000 5000 4000 3000 2000 1000

Years before present

Sketch showing variations in relative abundance (percentage based) of pollen of selected plants and plant groups, and of charcoal fragments, in peat from Rotten Bottom over the last ten thousand years (the profile for birch is approximate)

at Stirling University) in Crunklie Moss in the Gameshope valley at more than 500 m. These two sequences shed light on differences in the plant communities in different situations in the hills.

Peat usually forms when waterlogging lowers the rate of microbial decay, thus leading to accumulation of dead plant material. From inception, peat usually holds enough water to be self-sustaining. Peat formation on Rotten Bottom started around 10,300 years ago, and it is possible that before this, glacier ice still occupied the plateau. At first the peat accumulated only close to where it is now deepest, over a small depression in the rock surface. For the next three thousand years there was little spread of peat to other parts of Rotten Bottom, but about 7200 years ago the peat began to spread laterally. By the time that the longbow was discarded, around 6000 years ago, even the slopes 150 m from the deepest peat and substantially uphill were also covered by blanket peat.

The pollen in the Rotten Bottom core shows that birch was already in the area at the start of the sequence, having spread into the Moffat Hills before 10,300 years ago, while hazel colonised a few hundred years later. Hazel and perhaps also birch may have grown on the plateau in this period. Juniper was probably also growing here even before its first appearance in the pollen record 10,000 years ago, since it is one of the earliest colonists of land exposed by glacial retreat. Pine arrived in the general area soon afterwards, perhaps spreading east across Galloway from sources in Ireland, but seems to have grown only in especially cool, shaded spots in the Moffat Hills, including the steep-sided north-facing Gameshope valley. Elm may have come next, at about 9000 years ago, followed closely by oak. Alder became abundant around 6800 years ago, doubtless colonising poorly-drained areas and perhaps largely ousting Scots pine, but is not likely to have grown at the high altitude of Rotten Bottom.

The next two thousand years saw the period broadly described as the 'climatic optimum', which may also have seen the strongest development of native woodlands in Scotland. At lower altitudes in and near Carrifran there was well developed mixed woodland including much oak, ash, alder and elm, along with rowan, hawthorn, aspen, holly and cherry (doubtless bird cherry, but perhaps also gean). On the plateau, birch, oak and perhaps alder may have joined the hazel which was already there, but juniper may have been shaded out at an earlier stage – except in the most exposed places – by hazel and other trees. Elm may possibly also have grown as high as this, while the local presence of willows is attested both by the pollen from this insect-pollinated plant and by bands of preserved willow wood in the peat from 7400 and 6600 years ago.

Just before the time when the bow was discarded conditions seem to have become particularly wet as well as warm. The peat surface was apparently grassy and would not have been gullied as it is now, but would have presented a smooth surface, broken only by open pools in which bogbean grew. Trees may have become scarce on the plateau at this time, but they recovered quickly and may have reached their greatest abundance around 5400 years ago.

Starting suddenly at this time, however, there was also a massive increase in heather (*Calluna*) which evidently became abundant on the plateau and maintained this abundance right through to the present. Intriguingly, the increase in heather occurred thousands of years after the spread of blanket peat within Rotten Bottom (and probably elsewhere in the area). The record shows that for most of the first half of the period during which peat accumulated in Rotten Bottom, its surface was occupied by grasses and

The Carrifran march fence snakes across Rotten Bottom and up over Firthhope Rig; the bow was found near the centre of the picture
Photo: Hugh Chalmers

sedges, with heather playing a variable but generally minor role before 5400 years ago. The sudden increase in heather (at least on Rotten Bottom) is not easy to explain. However, data on the condition of the pollen indicate that this was in the middle of a relatively dry period, which probably favoured heather at the expense of grasses and sedges. It may also be significant that the rise in heather pollen was immediately preceded by a massive but brief increase in charcoal fragments in the peat, clearly indicating fire in the area, which might have promoted drying out of the peat surface.

The peak in tree abundance on Rotten Bottom around 5400 years ago was followed by a hint of local decline in the major tree species (hazel, alder, oak and birch) at the time that heather increased, but the trees seem to have continued to maintain a presence until around 3700 years ago. Thereafter, however, trees were probably largely absent from Rotten Bottom except perhaps briefly around 1800 years ago.

The rise in heather on Rotten Bottom 5400 years ago seems not be mirrored in the short term by a decline in trees in the wider area around. Elm apparently became very scarce around this time (as it did throughout Britain) but hazel, alder, oak and birch continued to provide

✱ The common names of plants and animals

While it is a delight to have contributions to this chapter from several Wildwood Group members, it brings with it editorial problems. Botanists and zoologists diverge in their customs of naming plants and animals, both in books and scientific publications. We have avoided using too many Latin names in the text, although a good many more are in the index. We also decided to use lower case ie: goat, not Goat – wren, not Wren – heather, not Heather – oak, not Oak. However, Crinan Alexander, who wrote 'Some interesting plants at Carrifran' said "I would be very angry!" if we did not use capital letters for the common names of plants, in accordance with contemporary botanical practice. We are sympathetic to Crinan's position as a botanist and agree that the use of capitals avoids ambiguity where the first part of the name is adjectival, for instance in Dwarf Willow or Wild Thyme. Rather than anger a good friend we have compromised! In three sections of this chapter – 'Woodland relics', 'Open-ground vegetation' and 'Some interesting plants' – we have used capitals. Oh dear, what do we do in the index?

almost constant proportions of the total pollen input to Rotten Bottom for about 1500 years. Pollen evidence is lacking for rowan and aspen, but they were doubtless also present in the area.

About 4000 years ago heather pollen became even more abundant in Rotten Bottom. This may reflect the spread of heather in the general area, since its increase is complemented by a slow, long-term decline in hazel pollen, perhaps indicating some replacement of hazel by heather. Intriguingly, these changes were accompanied by a somewhat increased prevalence of fire. Since heather is both flammable and tolerant of fire, its presence may have increased the incidence of fires, but fires may also have favoured its spread – and that of *Sphagnum* and some grasses – at the expense of other plants. However, the pollen input from trees other than hazel shows little change until a sudden collapse around the start of the last millennium. It therefore appears that extensive woodlands with hazel, alder, birch and oak survived until that time, close enough to Rotten Bottom to provide a steady inflow of windblown pollen.

There is no evidence as to whether the fires were caused naturally by lightning, or by humans. The longbow indicates that people visited Rotten Bottom in pursuit of game, but whether they used the plateau in others ways is unknown. It is intriguing that from about 5700 years ago onwards, the pollen of ribwort plantain is occasionally recorded in Rotten Bottom. This is a perennial herb of open and often disturbed ground, so the pollen may indicate the presence in the general area of domestic grazing animals, or of open spaces created by clearance of woodland, perhaps at much lower levels. About 1300 years ago there is an increase in pollen of this plantain, along with that of other plants typical of disturbed ground. This suggests an increase in the intensity of pastoralism after a long period during which pressures from humans seem to have remained fairly stable.

The pollen record suggests that in the ensuing centuries, most of the trees were eliminated from the Carrifran area, presumably as a result of the massive increase in sheep stocks in early Medieval times. Intensive grazing has also now led to the retreat of heather uphill in many parts of the Southern Uplands; where this has happened, the heather is replaced by a sward of coarse grasses and sedges.

Woodland relics at Carrifran ✱
Stuart Adair and Philip Ashmole

Although the natural tree cover of Carrifran was destroyed many centuries ago, a few small stands of trees and shrubs, as well as some widely scattered individual survivors, were present in 1996. Virtually all the remaining trees were confined to the few places inaccessible to grazing and browsing animals. Centuries of intensive pastoral use of the land had prevented natural regeneration except in these inaccessible places, as well as restricting the development of tall herb communities and promoting both the expansion of grassland at the expense of heath communities and the degradation of blanket bog on higher areas. Bracken had become invasive on some of the lower and drier slopes, where it dominated the heath and grassland communities.

As mentioned above, the effects of grazing are detectable in the Rotten Bottom pollen record from more than a millennium ago. This type of woodland destruction is not usually a sudden affair, but occurs over a period of centuries. Under intensive grazing, seeds germinating within or around any existing woodland do give rise to seedlings, but sheep, goats or deer quickly eat them. If this regime continues, the woodland becomes senile and gradually dies, meanwhile changing in composition because of the widely differing palatability and lifespans of the various woody species.

In places that lack crags and gorges, hungry sheep and goats can eliminate every last tree and shrub, as testified by the naked landscapes of the Tweedsmuir, Moffat and Lowther Hills. If there are inaccessible places, however, small groups of trees may survive indefinitely, each space vacated by a dying tree being filled by one or a few of the thousands of aspiring seedlings generated by nearby survivors. Seedlings establishing themselves away from the protecting crags may survive for many years, but can never emerge – except on a very temporary basis – from the dense sward near ground level.

At Carrifran, the relict stands of trees were frozen in time. The first edition of the

Some people said that trees would have trouble growing on the steep slopes (the wounds on the tree trunk were probably caused by goats)

The culprits in Hazel Linn in 1996

Ashy Dean: much of the Carrifran Burn will look like this one day

Holly Gill occasionally looks like this
Photo: Hugh Chalmers

Ordnance Survey map, published in 1859, shows groups of trees in the same places – and only the same places – where we found them in summer 1996. Later that year, Philip saw a herd of goats slowly making their way along a stretch of the burn where some trees survived on low cliffs, and watched as every branch that had grown enough during the summer season to bring it within reach of a hungry mouth was firmly pruned.

Nonetheless, the relict stands – none of them extensive enough to be classified as woodland proper – collectively show surprising diversity. They comprise three main stands as well as individual trees and tiny clumps of shrubs isolated in more or less inaccessible places in various parts of the valley. The largest trees, which are Ash, form an attenuated woodland strip along both sides of the steep-sided but not quite cliffy ravine of Ashy Dean, where Carrifran Burn edges its way round the western tip of the massive glacial deposit barring the southern end of the glen. Various other woody species are also present in this strip, with Ash and Rowan saplings especially frequent.

The second largest stand, Hazel Linn, is a similar strip along the precipitous banks of Carrifran Burn 500 m further north. We enclosed it in a deer fence between 2000 and 2008, so as to ensure that any seedlings regenerating naturally got away to a good start; in practice

there were some Rowan and a few Hazel. This fenced area also provided the basis for comparing the growth of planted trees fully protected from deer with that of trees planted in the rest of the valley. Hazel Linn had the best group of surviving Hazels at Carrifran, as well as a few Ash, several Downy Birch and Goat Willow, Rowan, Hawthorn and Dog Rose, with Honeysuckle on the rocks, Eared Willow near water level and a single clump of Ivy just upstream.

The third significant stand is Holly Gill, bordering Firthhope Burn two km into the valley. Here there is a group of scrubby trees and shrubs on a substantial cliff, including Rowan, Downy Birch and a single Silver Birch, willows, Burnet Rose, Dog Rose and an Ash which at 340 m a.s.l. is the highest surviving in the valley. At the top of the cliff are some larger birches and Rowans, with more in craggy places nearby. There is a clump of Bird Cherry (hagberry) in a gorge a little higher up the burn, and one on Raven Craig.

All three stands consist of very small, linear clumps characterized by low, scrubby growth and the scarcity of large mature trees. Most of the growth consists of small (< 5m) pole-stage trees, spindly saplings and low scrubby bushes, with occasional older and larger specimens. The latter, although small in stature, are readily identified by their greater girth and better formed crowns. The stands are subject to regular damage, wrought by severe winter floods, heavy browsing and natural decay. This results in much irregular and contorted regrowth. The new growth often resembles poorly cut coppice stools, with young, uneven, wispy shoots and stunted bushes emerging from clearly much older and larger boles and stumps.

Natural regeneration, other than that from regrowth, is very scarce. This is due mainly to grazing and browsing pressure combined with the lack of local seed sources. However, where heavy flooding has caused erosion and exposed bare ground, or where gaps have opened up due to the mortality of older stems, tree seedlings can become quite abundant, particularly those of Rowan, willows and Ash, although the latter rarely become established even where protected.

Species diversity among the tree and shrub flora here is fairly limited, with a total of eleven species found within the three main stands and a further five species – including Bird Cherry, Holly and three species of shrubby willow – occurring as scattered individuals throughout the glen. The most abundant species overall, including seedlings, saplings and mature stems, are Rowan, Downy Birch, Ash and Eared Willow, the latter easily overlooked due to its generally diminutive stature and prostrate growth-form. Silver Birch is very rare, appearing only once as a very stunted specimen on a dry sandy ledge in Holly Gill, although it may well have been overlooked elsewhere due to difficult access. Hazel,

Bird Cherry and Rowan in the highest woodland fragment in the valley

The stands are subject to regular damage, wrought by severe winter floods

The importance of woodland relicts for lower plants

Diversity among lower plants such as mosses and liverworts, and also of lichens, is often quite high in small areas of relict woodland, which provide shading and support for epiphytes (plants which grow on other plants, especially trees). The importance of these refugia cannot be overstated in woodland restoration, because even though the Carrifran project brings in trees and shrubs, it is not feasible to bring in all the lower plants. The woodland relicts are vital since they provide places from which spores from these lower plants – and some associated invertebrates – can disperse, thus allowing them to become established in the rest of the valley as the woodland develops.

David Long

Hawthorn and Goat Willow (sauch) are fairly common, generally forming a rather indistinct understory beneath the Rowan, Downy Birch and Ash. Grey Willow is limited to one or two wispy specimens in Holly Gill, although as with Silver Birch, it may have been overlooked. Small shrubs are relatively scarce here with only a sparse scattering of Dog Rose, Raspberry, Bramble and Stone Bramble, the latter marking out more limey rocks. Honeysuckle can be seen occasionally sprawling over rocks and trees, and there are two or three clumps of Ivy. Despite one cleugh bearing the name 'Broomy Gutter', both Gorse (whin) and Broom were absent from the glen in the 1990s.

The field and ground layers in the woodland relicts at Carrifran vary according to differences in soil and shade. On shady ledges, a group of plants typical of upland oak-birch and ash-elm woodlands takes precedence. Among these are several ferns including Male-fern, Broad Buckler-fern, Hard-fern, Lady-fern (laidie brechan), and Lemon-scented Fern, the latter two in damper situations. Very occasionally in shadier sites, Common Polypody is found. Grasses make an important contribution to the field layer, especially Wavy Hair-grass, Yorkshire Fog and its near relative, Creeping Soft-grass. Wood-rushes, especially Great Wood-rush, are also fairly common.

Among the flowering plants, especially under heavier shade, herbs typical of broad-leaved woodland with a closed canopy can become quite abundant. These include familiar woodland herbs such as Wood-sorrel (suckie sourocks), Common Dog-violet, Primrose, Wild Strawberry, Barren Strawberry, Foxglove (bluidy fingers), Tormentil, Wood Crane's-bill and Herb-robert, as well as Broad-leaved Willowherb and Red Campion. In damper spots on deeper soils Wood Anemone, Wood Avens, Bugle, Opposite-leaved Golden Saxifrage, the tiny red-eyes of Sanicle, Lesser Celandine and Creeping Buttercup add to the variety. In drier places on sandy soils, Wood Sage is very common. Mosses and liverworts make a significant contribution to the flora of woodland fragments, often forming thick, luxuriant mats over soils, rocks, trees and rotting wood.

On wet ledges, cliffs and low-lying, flood-prone margins, a group of plants typical of wet flushes, river margins and wet ash-alder woodlands predominate. The most prominent and consistent of these are Meadowsweet, Marsh Hawk's-beard and the stiff, sharp-edged, finger-cutting blades of Tufted Hair-grass. More occasional, in moist cavities and on dripping wet cliffs and boulders, are Lady's Mantle, Water Avens, Water Forget-me-not, Marsh Thistle, Common Comfrey, Soft Rush, Wild Angelica, Common Valerian, Wavy Bitter-cress, Cuckooflower, Water Mint, Marsh Willowherb and Greater Bird's-foot Trefoil.

The open-ground vegetation of Carrifran *
Stuart Adair

The vegetation in most parts of Carrifran at the time of purchase was dominated by various open, short-cropped communities – mainly fine-leaved grassland – very typical of long-grazed and/or burned habitats within the British uplands. Some of the higher altitude communities in the glen, however, are of very restricted occurrence south of the Highlands and are the main reason the site has been included in the Moffat Hills Special Area of Conservation.

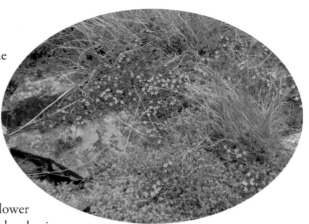

Wild Thyme and Woolly Fringe-moss

The most widespread type of grassland in the lower and middle parts of the valley is bent-fescue grassland, the classic grassland of open sheep walk. Typical of these low, tight swards are grasses such as Common Bent, Brown Bent (on parched soils), Velvet Bent (in damper spots), Sheep's Fescue and Sweet Vernal-grass together with the small brightly coloured flowers of Tormentil, Heath Bedstraw and Heath Speedwell. Where the soils are more limey, plants such as Meadow Oat-grass, the appropriately named Quaking-grass, Fairy-flax, Eyebright, Lady's Bedstraw, Scottish Bluebell (harebell) and Wild Thyme can become quite abundant, giving the vegetation a colourful mixture of blues, purples, pinks and yellows.

Where the soils become wetter and slightly waterlogged, in low lying depressions and hollows and along the margins of springs and flushes, grassland grades to rush-pasture, a community dominated by rushes (threshes), usually either Soft-rush or Sharp-flowered rush, and the sprawling Common Marsh-bedstraw. Other plants are fairly scarce and include the grasses Velvet Bent and Yorkshire Fog (windle strae) At higher altitudes over wetter peaty mineral soils, the tough wiry leaved tussocks of Matt-grass and Heath-rush dominate the turf, often accompanied by the lank tufts of Green-ribbed Sedge and patches of the tall, deep-green moss *Polytrichum commune*. These swards are easily recognised at considerable distances in winter due to their yellowy-white colour, which arises from the dense thatch of dead Mat-grass leaves and also accounts for the plant's old name of white bent. On mineral soils or shallow peats at higher altitudes with northerly aspects, where snow lies late into the spring, these species are joined by plants such as Stiff Sedge and stunted sprigs of Blaeberry.

The windswept summits of White Coomb and Carrifran Gans are dominated by the distinctive, severely wind-clipped and low growing vegetation known as moss-heath. This community is marked out by the diminutive flower stalks of the appropriately named Stiff Sedge, standing up erect against even the most severe gales, amid a carpet of Woolly

Deergrass

Tall herbaceous plants on a ledge on Raven Craig survive only because they are inaccessible to goats (and photographers—this is a telephoto shot)

Fringe-moss (*Racomitrium lanuginosum*) and fine-leaved grasses. In the extreme conditions encountered here, Sheep's-fescue is often replaced by Viviparous Sheeps-fescue, recognisable by its habit of producing many small plantlets instead of flowering panicles.

Heather moor occurs throughout the valley at moderate and higher altitudes. Most of this heathland is very typical of the Southern Uplands, being relatively dry and dominated by either Heather (ling, *Calluna*) or Blaeberry. On steep slopes over freely draining drier soils at moderate altitudes ling shares the ground with Bell Heather, easily spotted by its bright purple colour in late summer, the bright yellow flowers of Tormentil and various fine-leaved grasses. Over similar but generally slightly wetter soils at higher altitudes the Bell Heather is replaced by Blaeberry which accompanies the Heather and various mosses such as *Hypnum jutlandicum* and *Scleropodium purum* to form the most widespread type of heathland found in the glen. On steeper slopes in the upper parts of the glen (>600 m) these communities give way to heath dominated by Blaeberry together with scattered wispy tussocks of Wavy Hair-grass, the latter species marked out by its shimmering reddish-white panicles, over a carpet of various mosses such as *Hylocomium splendens and Pleurozium schreberi;* Cowberry occurs occasionally in these stands.

Blanket bog covers a considerable proportion of the higher plateaus at Carrifran, especially around Rotten Bottom and Games Castle and the head of Little Firthhope Burn. The bogs are dominated by an uneven, shaggy canopy of Heather and mixtures of other sub-shrubs including Cross-leaved Heath and Crowberry (crawberry), the rusty-orange tussocks of Deergrass and the white cotton buds of Hare's-tail Cottongrass (known to old shepherds as draw moss) which mark out the bogs at a considerable distance in early summer. The ground beneath these species is carpeted by various mosses, the most abundant of which is *Sphagnum capillifolium* subsp. *rubellum*.

Several bog pool communities occur within the blanket bog. These communities are, for the most part, dominated by Common Cottongrass and several species of bog-moss (*Sphagnum*) including the bedraggled-looking S. *cuspidatum*, somewhat cruelly known as drowned kittens! The Round-leaved Sundew, which catches tiny insects, can become quite abundant around the fringes of these pools. Where the peat thins out and becomes drier, the blanket bog grades to wet-heath and mires dominated by Purple Moor-grass or blaw grass (Galloway broad bent), so called because of the habit of the tall, dense tussocks to blow, cornfield-like, in the wind in high summer. These are generally species-poor communities often consisting of virtually pure stands of either Deergrass or Purple Moor-grass, with just the colourful spikes of Bog Asphodel and a scattering of small herbs such as Heath Milkwort, Lousewort and Tormentil for company.

Bracken (brechan, less commonly rannoch) dominates the lower slopes of Peat Hill and Dun Knowe, picking out the deeper soils on moderate slopes. Beneath the canopy of Bracken fronds there is usually a scattering of small herbs including Tormentil, Creeping Soft-grass, Sweet-vernal Grass, Common Dog-violet, Climbing Corydalis and occasionally Bluebell (Wild Hyacinth) on the otherwise bare ground. Over screes and loose boulders the appropriately named Parsley Fern can be very abundant, usually accompanied by mosses such *Racomitrium lanuginosum, Campylopus flexuosus* and *Polytrichum formosum*, with little tufts of fine-leaved grasses in gaps between the boulders.

On sheltered inaccessible ledges and cliffs various species-rich tall-herb communities flourish. Typical of these situations are plants sensitive to grazing, including Meadowsweet (Queen o' the meidie), the densely packed rusty-green tussocks of Great Wood-rush, Water Avens, Wild Angelica and Common Valerian, Lady's Mantle, Sea Campion, Golden-rod and the frayed pink flowers of Ragged Robin. These are often accompanied by various alpines such as the succulent Roseroot, Mountain Sorrel

Sea Campion, once confined to crags, can now also be found on shingle along the Carrifran Burn

Bog Asphodel

Alpine Foxtail in a flush in Firth Hope

with its kidney-shaped leaves and the delicate Alpine Meadow-rue.

Small spring-fed mires are widespread throughout the glen in small hollows within other, larger communities and below springs, flushes and seepage lines. These communities have an abundance of small grass-like sedges, along with rushes, rough herbs such as Marsh Thistle (bog thristle) small herbs such as Marsh Violet and Devil's-bit Scabious (bluebunnets) and various mosses including the deep-green *Polytrichum commune* and several species of *Sphagnum*. The Heath Spotted-orchid is occasionally found in these mires, easily recognised by the purple-black blotches on its waxy, lanceolate leaves. Another very distinctive, if fairly restricted, mire type found in areas irrigated by limey waters is home to the pale yellow leaves of the carnivorous Common Butterwort. This type of mire is often includes small patches of bare wet peaty soil on short, steep slopes, often with nothing more than a scattering of small sedges, especially Flea-sedge, accompanying the Common Butterwort.

The springs, flushes and rills of Carrifran offer some of the most beautiful, rich and interesting vegetation to be found within the Moffat Hills. Spring heads, especially in Firth Hope, are marked out by colourful suites of mosses and liverworts such as the fresh green cushions of *Philonotis fontana*, the golden-green *Dicranella palustris*, the orange-purple tinged *Sphagnum denticulatum* and the reddish liverwort *Scapania undulata*. These are accompanied by a wide variety of small herbs including the distinctive Starry Saxifrage, the tiny white flowered and often submerged mats of Blinks, the creeping Opposite-leaved Golden Saxifrage and, at high altitudes, the nationally rare grass Alpine Foxtail and the drooping pink flowers of Alpine Willowherb.

On wet cliffs and ledges is a very distinctive community of mosses and liverworts including the striking golden-green plumes of *Palustriella commutata,* which often forms thick carpets, tumbling over cliff faces and down rills, the reddish *Bryum pseudotriquetrum* and the glossy, pale green shoots of *Brachythecium rivulare*. Characteristic liverworts include *Pellia epiphylla, P. endiviifolia, Conocephalum conicum* and *Aneura pinguis*. Accompanying these bryophytes is a variety of small herbs such as Red Fescue, Alpine Bistort, Cuckooflower and more primitive plants such as Lesser Clubmoss *Selaginella selaginoides*.

Some interesting plants of the Carrifran area *
Crinan Alexander

The area of the Moffat Hills around Carrifran has long been recognised by botanists as being special. It was a target for Victorian botanists and fern collectors, and the late Derek Ratcliffe, one of Britain's outstanding ecologists and conservationists, wrote one of his early papers on the 'The mountain plants of the Moffat Hills'. In *A Nature Conservation Review*, the 1977 work that laid the foundations for the system of designated conservation sites throughout Britain, Ratcliffe reiterated the importance of the area, which is considered the most diverse for upland communities and flora south of the Highlands.

Common Butterwort is one of the striking plants growing in flushes on low ground

One of the pleasures of getting to know an area botanically lies in discovering which rarities or unexpected plants are to be found there, and also which likely candidates have not been found. Useful information on these topics can be gleaned from distribution maps and publications on conservation. In Britain, distributions are mapped systematically by the Botanical Society of the British Isles (BSBI) using a basic recording area of 10×10 km - the 10 km square, so for any species we know which 'squares' it has been found in. Thus, basic information about what grows where is easily come by. Another important factor is the status of each species in the British Red Data List. This is not necessarily related to rarity but is an assessment of the degree of threat that species may be under.

In Britain we are fortunate to have several very active 'amateur' societies devoted to making detailed observations and records in the field. Without such a pool of enthusiastic and unpaid labour it would not be possible to find reliable basic information on plant distributions. It is a pleasure to acknowledge help from members of the Botanical Society of Scotland (BSS) and many other amateurs and professionals in gathering information on the flowering plants, ferns, mosses and liverworts, fungi and lichens found at Carrifran and nearby. Many of the Carrifran records mentioned below result from a BSS field trip led by Douglas McKean in June 1998.

Descriptions of the Border hills as 'over-grazed sheep walk' and 'wet or green desert' belie the fact that, though they are relatively low in diversity, especially among trees and shrubs, they are still home to many interesting plants. Some species found at Carrifran, while not listed as nationally rare or threatened, are locally rare or very scarce in southern Scotland. Several of these, which are plentiful in the Scottish Highlands, have outliers in northern England and the Southern Uplands of Scotland including Carrifran.

Roseroot – one of the special mountain plants of the Moffat Hills

This willow, surviving on an inaccessible ledge, turned out to be a hybrid

Serrated Wintergreen (*Orthilia secunda*) is an attractive dwarf herb with greenish white flowers, mostly found in pine and birch woods and on rock ledges in the Highlands. In the last 20 years it has been recorded in only three squares in southern Scotland, including Carrifran, and in a few more in NW England. It was found in the 1950s near the Grey Mare's Tail waterfall but has not been seen there since. Alpine Willowherb (*Epilobium anagallidifolium*), with small rosy pink flowers and rather yellowish green leaves, has a similar distribution, though at higher altitudes. It is well-represented in the Highlands and has a small stronghold in northern England, but in southern Scotland the records are scattered and mainly old. However, it is present at Carrifran and has also recently been found nearby.

Much rarer than either of these, though not regarded as threatened, is Alpine Foxtail (*Alopecurus borealis*), a grass with compact, egg-shaped flowering heads that are often grazed by herbivores. It grows in high altitude springs and flushes, especially where snow lies late in the year, and we have found it in several flushes in Firth Hope. Since 1987 this species has been seen in only 21 squares in Britain, mostly in the Cairngorms, with five squares in northern England and just two in southern Scotland.

Also quite scarce, and now known to have similar distribution, is Hoary Whitlowgrass (*Draba incana*), not a grass but an erect grey-hairy herb with small, cross-shaped white flowers, favouring limestone, calcareous dunes and poor base-rich soils. Although well scattered in northern Scotland and NW Ireland, with one stronghold in northern England, it was not known at all in southern Scotland until found at Carrifran in 1998.

Much more familiar than either of these is the conspicuous, fleshy Roseroot (*Sedum rosea*), often seen on cliffs by the sea and inland watercourses. Though widely spread in the British Isles, mainly in western Scotland, it is quite scarce in southern Scotland. At Carrifran it flourishes on crags above about 300 m. Pale Forget-me-not (*Myosotis stolonifera*), with very pale blue flowers and bluish-green leaves, has a very different distribution, being mostly confined to base-rich springs and flushes in northern England. Until 1982 its Scottish distribution was confined to a few squares in the south; it has now been found in two squares near Perth and about 20 in southern Scotland. At Carrifran, it occurs in several springs and flushes, having been found there during the 1998 BSS excursion.

Shrubby willows can be quite taxing to those trying to identify them, not least because they hybridise promiscuously, the resulting hybrids often being fully fertile. One that is easy enough to recognise by its small, round, shiny leaves and diminutive stature (often being only 5 cm high) is Dwarf Willow (*Salix herbacea*). It enjoys exposed and demanding sites, rarely growing below 600 m. It is a northern species, but has outliers in the mountains of northern England, Ireland and Wales, and a few stands in southern Scotland. At Carrifran it forms an attractive dense sward in a few windswept areas high on Carrifran Gans, also occuring in rock crevices in other exposed places. The much more robust hybrid willow *Salix x tetrapla*, originally resulting from crosses between Tea-leaved and Dark-leaved Willows, both of which occur in the area, has a diffuse distribution in the Highlands, southern Scotland and northern England, favouring damp, rocky ground and river banks. While its distribution is uncertain, due to confusion with one of its parents (Dark-leaved Willow), it is confirmed in six squares in southern Scotland, including Carrifran, where it was found in 1998 on more or less inaccessible ledges on Raven Craig; it may also be present elsewhere in the valley.

Among the 20 or so species of fern known from Carrifran two are worthy of comment. Holly Fern (*Polystichum lonchitis*) is officially 'vulnerable'; though recorded from well over 100 squares in the British Isles, mostly in the Scottish Highlands, it is regarded as a 'poor competitor' and has problems becoming established. It grows in well-drained base-rich sites such as boulder-screes and limestone pavements. Like many attractive ferns, it suffered at the hands of nineteenth-century fern enthusiasts. Its only site in southern Scotland is at Carrifran, where it was discovered during the 1998 BSS excursion. The nearest other records are just north of Glasgow and in the northern Pennines. The

Victorian fern collectors

In 1857 John Sadler published a pamphlet in Moffat, under the title "Narrative of a ramble among the wild flowers of the Moffat Hills" in which he described a walk by a group of botanists up the Grey Mare's Tail to Loch Skeen and White Coomb and then down the waterfall now christened Firthhope Linn at Carrifran. Sadler wrote: "This was now the longed-for spot where we anticipated finding the tiny fern.....It was not until after more than an hour's patient search in this secluded dell, that a joyous shout was heard from our fern collector, waking every echo of the humid depth. There was he perched upon a dangerous ledge of rock, overhanging a tremendous gap, with the roaring stream far beneath him. He now waved in his hand the long-hid treasure, at which we leaped for joy, as we looked upon his success as our own. It was a small, green, delicate fern, about 2½ inches high, and of a downy appearance. It has been called Woodsia ilvensis, in honour of Woods, a noted English botanist. The plant does not seem to be very plentiful where we visited, five small tufts being all we observed, of which we took four, leaving the other as an "egg in the nest."
As far as we are aware this is this last record of this fern at Carrifran.

Dwarf Willow is flourishing on this exposed ridge now that grazing pressure is reduced

Downy Willow scrub is being established in a few places high up at Carrifran

Right: Firthhope Linn provides a rich habitat for lower plants

very elegant Wilson's Filmy Fern (*Hymenophyllum wilsonii*) is listed as 'near-threatened' in the British Red Data list. It is a delicate, spreading moss-like plant with translucent dark-green leaves, growing in moist shady places. It is widespread in western Britain but appears to have lost ground in southern Scotland since the 1960s. However, it is still established in Rispie Lairs at Carrifran and also grows below the Grey Mare's Tail waterfall.

Having touched on a few of the more interesting plants that have been found at Carrifran, it is amusing to conjecture which 'glamorous' species, known to be nearby, may yet be found there. One candidate is Pyramidal Bugle (*Ajuga pyramidalis*), similar to the common Bugle but with smaller, deeper blue flowers and much hairier leaves and stems. It grows on shallow peat in heathland and grassland and in rock crevices and is listed as 'vulnerable' in the Red Data List. It is almost entirely restricted to the extreme north and west of Scotland and Ireland, with an outlier in Westmoreland and a single record from a few decades ago, very close to Carrifran.

Alpine Cinquefoil (*Potentilla crantzii*) is a more montane species with yellow Silverweed-like flowers and palmate leaves, which favours base-rich habitats. It occurs mainly in the central and northern Highlands and the mountains of northern England and north Wales, but it occurs in one square in Galloway and another in the hills above the Grey Mare's Tail. Alpine Saw-wort (*Saussurea alpina*) is a more widely distributed and more western species, with its main strength in the Scottish Highlands. It is a pale-hairy, knapweed-like plant with purple flower-heads, growing on mountain cliffs and screes. It has been found in several parts of the Southern Uplands, including several places close to the Grey Mare's Tail, but not yet at Carrifran.

Purple Saxifrage (*Saxifraga oppositifolia*) is a very striking, prostrate, mat-forming plant with pinkish-purple flowers appearing in early spring. It enjoys damp conditions on lime-rich screes and rocks, especially by streams. It is widespread in the Highlands and also occurs on mountains in western Ireland, North Wales and northern England. There are three fairly recent records from southern Scotland, one of being a strong colony near the Grey Mare's Tail waterfall, but it has not yet been found at Carrifran.

While the previous four plants are all rare or very uncommon in southern Scotland, there are also surprising gaps in our records for some very common species that are found nearby at the Grey Mare's Tail. These include Mountain Everlasting (*Antennaria dioica*), Mountain Melick (*Melica nutans*), Greater Stitchwort (*Stellaria holostea*), Wood Vetch (*Vicia sylvatica*) and Moonwort (*Botrychium lunaria*). Further searching at Carrifran may well add them to the list.

Fungi at Carrifran

Non-mycologists, who probably think of woodland as the prime habitat for mushrooms and toadstools, may be surprised to know that no fewer than 123 species of fungus have already been recorded from Carrifran. While many of these are inconspicuous microfungi, such as the rare white-crust fungus Atheleopsis lembospora *found on a cold day in May at the base of old rush stems, the whole area is of national importance for its diverse range of waxcaps and pinkgills. One of the latter group is* Entoloma (Leptonia) cruentatum, *a sky blue or mauve agaric which is rare in the British Isles and which has apparently not been recorded in Scotland except at Carrifran. Both it and other macrofungi are of course present throughout the year as underground threads (mycelium) only revealing themselves when the spore-bearing bodies are produced, usually in late summer or autumn. More visits to record fungi at Carrifran are planned, and it is anticipated that the list will soon be considerably longer.*

Roy Watling

Three other interesting species not found at Carrifran but with wild populations nearby are among those that have now been planted, the first two being part of our planned woodland restoration and the third as part of the Scottish Rare Plants Project (see Chapter 12). Dwarf Cornel (*Cornus suecica*) is a northern rather than a western species, occurring commonly on mountains in the Highlands, with outliers mainly in northeast England. There are a few strong colonies in exposed situations in the hills above the Grey Mare's Tail. Downy Willow (*Salix lapponum*), regarded as vulnerable, is a species of the central and northern Highlands, with isolated populations in the Lake District, Galloway and on the Grey Mare's Tail side of White Coomb. Oblong Woodsia (*Woodsia ilvensis*) is one of our rarest and most endangered ferns, with only eight scattered populations known to survive on British mountains, one of them close to Carrifran. The species was formerly much more common but, like Holly Fern (above), was subject to the depredations of Victorian fern collectors.

Lower plants
David Long

Carrifran glen nestles amongst some of the highest hills of the Southern Uplands, immediately south of the Tweed/Solway watershed, where the south-west aspect induces a higher rainfall than in the Moorfoots and Lammermuirs to the east. The high rainfall, together with the large range in altitude and the occurrence of calcareous substrates, enables the valley to support a rich flora of bryophytes (mosses and liverworts) with a blend of montane, oceanic and calcicolous elements. So far, 179 species have been found at Carrifran. Several of the species that are widespread there are much rarer further east and contribute to the more 'western' flavour of the bryoflora. A full list of mosses and liverworts, including the recommended English names, can be found on the Carrifran website www.carrifran.org.uk.

The flush communities are extensive and a wonderful feature of the valley. Most are calcareous to varying degrees, with many characteristic species. Nine of the 16 species of *Sphagnum* recorded were found in these flushes; they include the very rare *Sphagnum platyphyllum*, new to Dumfriesshire. The rocky sections of the Carrifran Burn, where surviving relict trees are hemmed into the ravine, out of reach of sheep and goats, occur intermittently from close to the main road to near the cairn at the foot of Priest Gill and beyond. They contain scraps of woodland with tenacious relict trees of ash, rowan, birch and hazel. Although these trees are few in number, they valiantly support a number of epiphytic bryophytes, and the shaded and often calcareous rocks provide surfaces to which many woodland species cling. The woodland relict bryophytes, although pushed back into tiny refugia, will hopefully have a new dawn under the new regime.

Higher up, the ravines become steeper and more montane in character, with particularly interesting gullies, cliffs and waterfalls in Games Gill and Firth Hope. In the former, the montane elements include calcifugous species and also calcicoles such as the very local *Amphidium lapponicum*. In the latter, the mosses include the very rare oceanic calcicole *Trichostomum hibernicum*, growing on wet rocks. Above Games Gill lies the eroded blanket peat of Rotten Bottom, dotted with cloudberry but yet to be studied for bryophytes, whilst above the rocky sentinel knoll of Games Castle are some bryophyte-rich springs and flushes notable for large populations of the lovely bright pink *Bryum weigelii*, a handsome speciality of the Moffat Hills. The stream where it plunges over the cliffs has very fine colonies of two species of aquatic mosses.

Dwarf Cornel has been planted in small numbers high up at Carrifran

The animal life

When we found Carrifran valley late in the 1990s, it was intensively grazed and had a fauna characteristic of this man-created landscape. It inevitably lacked the native mammals which may have roamed Scotland in the distant past but became extinct centuries ago (see Box in Chapter 5) but also missing were the numerous other animal species (vertebrate and invertebrate) which are still present in some places in Scotland and which would have lived in the valley at a time when the vegetation was more natural. Their absence was mainly due to the limited variety of habitats in the denuded hills, which severely limits the number of ecological niches available. Many species, for instance depend on woodland plants for food or require a habitat more complex and three-dimensional than heavily grazed sheep walk.

Mammals were scarce, apart from the domestic sheep and cattle and the feral goats. Roe deer visited occasionally, but the close-cropped sward offered them little. Brown hares were present at low density, and on the plateau mountain hares could be seen, though they were not abundant. Field voles were always present, though varying in abundance from year to year, and wood mice and common shrews could also be found. Water voles have still not been recorded in the valley and the only bats seen have been pipistrelles.

Rabbits were present in large numbers at some times in the past. Haig Douglas, who farmed at Capplegill during the middle of the 20th century, told Ann Goodburn that during World War II, when meat was

A volunteer's tent provides a new hunting ground for a lizard resident high up at Carrifran
Photo: Mike and Alison Baker

scarce, a trapper worked in the area, and that in 1942 he took 1000 couple off the [Saddle] Yoke hirsel. In the post-war years rabbit control on farmland was legally enforced and a great many rabbits died during the hard winter of 1947. The local population seems to have become extinct under the onslaught of myxomatosis in the 1960s. It is a salutary thought that if it had not been for this disease, establishing trees at Carrifran might have been almost impossible. The only rabbit seen recently at Carrifran was killed by a volunteer's dog near the car park in 2007.

Among predators, foxes were actively persecuted and remained scarce until recently. Badgers had a sett on Todcastles and probably ranged over the whole valley, and otter spraint could be found along the burn and as high up as Rotten Bottom. There were no records of mink. Stoats and weasels were scarce, but moles were present wherever the soil was good enough to support earthworm populations: molehills could be seen along the top of Raven Craig and in Firth Hope, as well as in many places lower down. Wildcat, polecat and pine marten were absent, and we have still not seen hedgehogs in the valley. There have been two sightings of large unidentified predators, one of them in the late 1990s by John Barker, who saw a large, dark, cat-like animal crossing the valley in the early morning, and the other by one of our fencers.

The birdlife of Carrifran was extremely limited. Peregrines probably nested regularly on Raven Craig, although the nest was sometimes robbed. Ravens also nested there, and maintained a presence throughout the year, while carrion crows were to be seen everywhere. Buzzards and kestrels were often seen, but probably nested in the nearby spruce plantation, while herons and goosanders were regular visitors. Black grouse were occasionally seen, but large leks were not recorded. The only abundant songbird was the meadow pipit, ideally suited to the open habitat, but skylarks were present in some parts and wrens were widely distributed. A few pairs of ring ouzels were present in summer, along with wheatears and a few whinchats and stonechats. Along the burn dippers and pied and grey wagtails could be seen. A number of other species visited the valley from time to time, but woodland birds were almost entirely absent. Changes in the birdlife during the past decade are described in Chapter 12.

The common (or viviparous) lizard seems to have been well established in the valley from the start of the project, but it is rarely seen, and two of the high campers in Firth Hope in spring 2007 were startled when they found a lizard inside their tent. Our first evidence of adders was finding a cast skin in 2006, followed by a sighting in 2007, but it is likely that small numbers were always present in the valley. Frogs were abundant at Carrifran in the 1990s and can be found in almost every part of the site. Puddles along the track always have frogspawn in early spring, but the tadpoles probably survive only in exceptionally wet years. We have not found toads in the valley, but smooth newts have been seen and one observer reckoned that he had seen an alpine newt, a European species which has gone wild in some parts of Britain.

We do not have full knowledge of the invertebrate animals of Carrifran at the turn of the millennium, but we have information from several sources. Preliminary pitfall trapping of invertebrates was done by Pam Moncur in Rotten Bottom in the late 1990s, and Philip did a systematic pitfall trap survey of beetles and spiders in 2000/01. Pitfall trapping is one of the most effective ways of assessing the ground invertebrates of a heavily grazed area. Plastic cups containing a little antifreeze as preservative were set out in July 2000, with the help of Wildwood supporter Edward Milner. There were 12 groups of traps, in a variety of habitats from near the mouth of the valley up to Rotten Bottom and Firth Hope. The idea was to collect the catch every couple of months for a full year, but foot and mouth disease kept us off the site between February and June 2001, which meant that the last samples were in very poor condition.

Our late friend Arthur Ewing identified 113 kinds of beetle from the traps, and was somewhat disappointed that they did not include any rare or especially interesting species. The beetle community at the start of the project seems to have been typical of upland sheep walk in the south of Scotland. The spiders from the traps were identified by Edward Milner, who found 96 species (five more species have been collected since). The vast majority (81) belong to the family Linyphiidae (sheetweb weavers and dwarf spiders) as was to be expected in a denuded landscape in northern Britain. However, there were seven species of Lycosidae (wolf spiders) some of them very numerous. Half a dozen of the linyphiids had not previously been found in Dumfriesshire, and these included several noteworthy species typical of mountains. Additional hand-collecting would probably produce some more montane specialists, and we should also remember that pitfall trapping at only a few sites for a short period would not be expected to provide complete information on the species present in the valley.

Foot prints and probing beak marks left in Rotten Bottom after a feeding visit by snipe
Photo: John Savory

This is not a tent but a trap for flying insects

Some investigations entail night visits – catching moths in Hazel Linn

A trap for flying insects was run for several months in summer 2000 by Keith Bland of National Museums Scotland. Not all the groups have yet been studied, but the catch included 37 species of moth. Between late June and mid September 2003 Jeff Waddell ran a light trap at Carrifran on three nights and also made one visit to catch day-flying moths. He found 68 species of the larger moths ('macro moths'), of which 12 had also been found by Keith. Jeff commented that he expects the total fauna of macro moth – even before the woodland is properly established – to be around 200 species.

Jeff analysed the species he caught according to their ecology, finding that 52 were generally common and widespread. The other 16 were habitat specialists but only five of these (all common) were woodland species. This suggests both that the moth fauna of Carrifran at the start of the project was unremarkable, and that in 2003 the planting had not yet had a significant effect. The most notable moth recorded was the northern rustic, which is associated with cliff and scree habitats and in Scotland has usually been found on the coast; its future at Carrifran seems assured since the scree habitats will not be destroyed by planting. Another species of interest is the grey mountain carpet, which is also typical of exposed rocky places such as ravines.

Poplar hawk-moth caterpillars are sometimes easy to find on newly planted aspen and willows

Butterfly records were collected in the early years by John Randall and others. The species seen were green-veined and small whites, orange tip, red admiral, small tortoiseshell, peacock, meadow brown, ringlet and small heath. In recent years butterfly diversity appears to have increased (see Chapter 12).

Adrian Sumner, one of the Wildwood Founders, recorded molluscs and other invertebrates during visits in 2000. There was nothing unexpected, and Adrian was struck by the relative scarcity of slugs. However, an introduced species of slug was present at Carrifran cottage. The only land snail was a minute species that might not be native to the site, found under a delivery pallet. Adrian pointed out that other non-indigenous species would almost certainly reach the valley with our young trees.

Full lists of the animal species recorded at Carrifran are held by the Wildwood volunteer recorder, John Savory, and can also be found on the project website www.carrifran. org.uk

The Carrifran Burn
Neville Morgan

Carrifran Burn is an excellent example of a characteristic upland river system. The whole catchment of the burn and its tributaries, with the exception of a small area at the very head of Priest Gill, lies within the boundaries of Carrifran Wildwood and is thus protected from man induced changes of water quality, caused by run off from agriculture, sewage and industry, or from damming or straightening. The catchment lies on greywacke bedrock, a hard sedimentary rock which yields a low nutrient level to the water.

The altitude range, of over 600 m descent from the principal sources to its discharge in the Moffat Water, and the steep valley sides give rise to a rapidly flowing burn throughout its length which is in places torrential. This combined with a relatively heavy rainfall leads to a heavy scouring of the substrate which subsequently varies from a mixture of gravel, stones and boulders, in varying amounts, to places of bare bedrock. This means that very little organic matter derived from dead terrestrial vegetation is retained in crevices under the stones. These hostile conditions, nutritionally poor and physically severe, limit the species of aquatic plants and animals to those well adapted to them.

The Carrifran Burn flows mainly over bare rock or clean pebbles
Photo: David Geddes

Flowering plants, such as the pond weeds, are virtually eliminated as their roots are not strong enough to resist the drag of the water currents. The vegetation is therefore limited to algae, liverworts and mosses which can fix themselves closely to the surface of the stones. They form a source of food for some of the invertebrates.

The fauna consists predominantly of aquatic invertebrates resistant to the strong water currents. Some, such as flatworms, leeches, shrimps, snails and beetles spend the whole of their life cycle as true aquatics, whereas the caddisflies, stoneflies, mayflies, non-biting midges and blackflies spend their larval stages in the water and emerge from it as free flying adults, later laying their eggs in or at the edge of the burn, to start the new generation. Some species fly upstream to lay their eggs as a strategy to compensate for the displacement of their larvae downstream by the strong current.

Different species within the same family adapt to different life styles to combat the current. Thus some of the mayflies are streamlined and fast swimmers, others are dorsiventrally flattened and able to shelter in narrow spaces under stones, whereas others burrow into the sediments to shelter from the current. Most of the caddis larvae have cases, often of sand particles, and roam searching for food, but the smaller group of caseless caddises spin nets to catch particles, swept in by the current, upon which they feed. Stream invertebrates are usually either herbivores grazing on the algae, or carnivores preying on other animals. Others are omnivores whilst some – such as freshwater shrimps – feed on organic debris, which very much limits their abundance at present. However, as the new forest grows and an increasing quantity of leaves enters the burn their populations will increase, as will those of other detritivores and probably also fish.

Before BFT bought Carrifran the fish populations were investigated by Nick Chisholm of the Annan Fisheries Board. The only species found was brown trout *Salmo trutta*, which is a major predator on the aquatic invertebrates. Sea trout, the migratory form of *Salmo trutta*, may reach the burn, but it is thought that salmon do not penetrate as far as this up the Moffat Water system. Eels and lampreys may be present but have not yet been recorded. However, Stan Tanner found himself in company with a stone loach when snorkelling in the burn one summer day (see Box in Chapter 10). The apparent low diversity of fish is not atypical of upland streams of this character.

Archaeological remains in the Carrifran valley
Fi Martynoga

The Rotten Bottom Bow – some 6000 years old – is the oldest piece of evidence of the human past surviving from the valley. There are no archaeological features that can be directly related to it. All we know is that this yew bow was left in a pool or mire that became the peat bog of Rotten Bottom, at the head of the Carrifran valley. It lay preserved in the peat until it was found there, by chance, by Dr Dan Jones when he was out hillwalking in 1990. His interest in strange bits of wood led him to collect it. A year later, Dan visited an archaeological dig near Melrose and mentioned to the Borders Region archaeologist in charge that he had a curious bit of wood at home. He went to fetch it and when it was examined it was shown to be two-thirds of a longbow or perhaps more correctly a flatbow.

Alison Sheridan of National Museums Scotland wrote:

"The bow was claimed under Scottish Treasure Trove law (which, unlike its counterpart south of the border, applies to all ownerless goods, not just to those of precious metals) and Dr Jones was rewarded. It is only the second prehistoric bow to be found in Scotland, and the sixth from Britain. A fragment was sent to Oxford University for radiocarbon dating, and the result – 4040-3640 BC – makes it the oldest bow in Britain and Ireland, and older than the one recently found with the 'Ice Man' in the Tyrolean Alps."

Dan returned several times to Rotten Bottom, but never managed to find the other part of the bow. The bow is now an exhibit in the National Museums Scotland in Edinburgh. How the bow came to be left in Rotten Bottom is the subject of continuing debate. It may have broken in use, and if the breakage happened during a hunt it might have been discarded. Alternatively, it might have been hidden to be retrieved later, or have been left there because the hunter died.

The next oldest features within the Carrifran area are probably Bronze Age in date. It is fortunate that they occur at places where we have no intention of planting trees. One is a burial cairn on the upper slopes of White Coomb, very near, though actually outside, our boundary. This is on bare hill, above our tentative treeline in Firth Hope. The others are almost at the lowest point, not of the main valley, but at the foot of Peat Hill.

Towards the southern end of the hill's lower slopes, below Todcastles and towards Spoon Burn, there are three monuments known as burnt mounds. Two, like the burial cairn, are on the fence line. The third is slightly to the north of a fine sheepstell that dates from the improvements of the early nineteenth century. Here a horseshoe shaped bank can easily be seen. It is overgrown but excavation would undoubtedly reveal a pile of burnt stones. These would have been heated up on a fire before they were plunged into a tank in order to heat water. If you look carefully within the horseshoe mound, you can make out a change in the vegetation, which reveals the rectangle of the tank, still there after nearly four thousand years. Archaeologists debate whether such tanks were used for cooking or whether they were bath houses, sweat lodges, or even (on Orkney) breweries. The evidence for their culinary use is pretty scanty in Scotland, so maybe we should imagine the tribal people

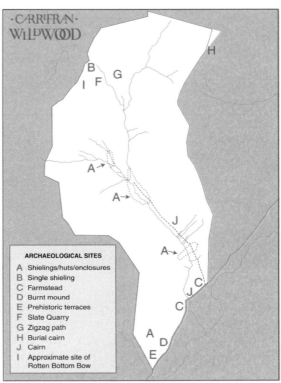

Archaeological sites at Carrifran

For six thousand years the bow lay in the peat in Rotten Bottom, above Raven Craig: perhaps a good place to search for arrowheads!
Photo: Ann Goodburn

of Bronze Age Carrifran enjoying their equivalent of a sauna.

An archaeologist has recently noted a scoop in the slope not far from this burnt mound. It appears on the National Monuments Record of Scotland simply as a 'farmstead' but it could be a dwelling dating from roughly the same time as the burnt mound. Associated with it is a series of agricultural terraces. These run northeast to southwest through the boundary fence above Spoon Burn. They are easy to make out in the winter but become obscured by bracken later in the year. Below them on the floor of Moffatdale, outside the Carrifran boundary, there are field-clearance cairns. They were probably created around the same time, when people were clearing ground in order to till it.

Most of the other archaeological features on the site are from the Medieval period or later. Most notable are the footings of two farmhouses. The first is a little below the boardwalk that leads from the car park to the old track up the main valley. The outlines of its buildings, with associated banks and ditches that denote fields, have recently been reappraised by Historic Scotland and it is now considered of sufficient national importance to become a Scheduled Monument. The second is to the south of Carrifran Burn, on the apron of land that runs above, and parallel to, the road to Moffat. Both seem to have been substantial buildings. The former appears to sit on a former turf dyke that was probably the old 'head dyke' that marked the highest extent of enclosed arable land. The latter has an extensive range of out-buildings, which string along the narrow, flat apron of land for two hundred yards. Whether these are of a single date or represent a succession is impossible to say. They seem to suggest a long period of farming activity.

Associated with these farms, or possibly with others in Moffatdale, are many clusters of shielings further into the valley. These were small huts built to house the folk who came each summer with flocks, mostly of sheep and goats but possibly of cattle, too. For the few warm weeks of each summer they would let their animals graze the high pastures. This made use of the best of the summer grass as well as serving to keep the animals away from sown fields nearer to their usual dwellings.

The shielings appear either as banks of a roughly rectangular shape or else as similar shapes of drystone wall footings. There is a group of the former near Carrifran Burn in the vicinity of the shelter (itself probably a later shieling) not far downstream from the cairn above the confluence of the small burns with the main one (the shelter has been roofed for use by volunteers and for tool storage during the planting period). Another simple, rectangular structure can be seen on Rotten Bottom, just below Games Castle.

If you want to see a larger group of shielings with remaining stone walls, climb the well-marked track to the north of Spoon Burn. Scan each natural terrace on your right as you come to it, and you should see evidence of these simple buildings. Associated with one group there is a small pen. This may well have been a 'bucht' – an enclosure into which sheep were driven when they were to be milked.

The transhumance system of which the shielings are evidence probably went on well into the 18th century. As it finished, a new way of thinking was taking hold and the style of agriculture changed from subsistence to stock farming for profit. Carrifran Cottage belongs to this period. It is hard to say whether it was built as an independent farmhouse or simply as a stockman's house for Capplegill; it was certainly the latter in the 20th century. Either way, evidence for the improved agriculture abounds in the valley. A good example is the circular stell which houses our interpretation boards, to the right of the track at the top of the the glacial deposit that obstructs the mouth of the valley. There is another stell to the west of Carrifran Burn, clearly visible on your left, about halfway up the track into the valley. Two more are close to the Moffat road, on the same apron of flat land which is home to both the Medieval farm and the possible prehistoric dwelling already mentioned. Stells are

Old enclosure on Todcastles which may be a 'bucht' or pen for milking sheep

sheep shelters, designed so that the animals could always find a place to get out of inclement weather. Many of them doubled as handling pens. The walls that radiate out from some of them improved both of these functions. A few larger pens with broken down drystone walls can also be seen, notably above Carrifran Burn on the lower slopes of Peat Hill.

The archaeological survey carried out before we started the planting programme revealed two other features. One was a small slate quarry on Raven Craig. This may be the quarry mentioned in the 1791-99 Statistical Account of Moffat, which states that *"There is a slate quarry lately opened in the parish"*. It was probably short-lived, since the later Statistical Account, written in 1834, says explicitly that no roofing slate was worked in the parish. The quarry would have been started to supply the demand for roofing slate that arose as people aspired to build permanent, stone houses rather than the dry stone and turf dwellings they had formerly used. Once road (and later on rail) links were created to link Moffatdale with a wider area, better slate would have been brought from further afield, and this quarry forgotten.

The other feature is a zig-zag path that leads up the nose of hill at the head Carrifran valley, between Games Gill and Firthhope Burn. It may have been the very path used by packhorses when slate was being extracted from the quarry. It is also possible that it was used by people digging peat from Rotten Bottom. There are plenty of peat exposures or 'hags' up there but it is not clear whether they are all natural or whether there has been peat digging in some places.

In accordance with the Management Plan, all of the sites mentioned in this account (or several representatives where there are many examples) have been respected by our planting. In centuries to come it should be possible to stumble upon mounds, footings or the odd rickle of stones, which will show how the land, over several millennia, was used by people as pasture or, on the lowest slopes, for crops.

7. Planning the restoration

No precedent to guide us—native woodland conference—establishing credibility—advice from experts—communal development of the management plan—natural regeneration versus planting—which areas to plant—maintaining the vision in the context of bureaucracy—which trees and shrubs to plant—aiming at 'original-natural' woodland—woodland types—Ecological Site Classification and National Vegetation Classification—working out the species mix—Woodland Grant Scheme—approaches to silviculture—avoidance of mechanical ground preparation—spot spraying with herbicide—minimal fertiliser use—stock fence, not deer fence—cell grown rather than bare rooted plants—tree protection.

* * * * *

Facing up to the task ahead

In mid 1997 it became clear that we would be able to negotiate a legal option to buy Carrifran. It was therefore time to face up to the extraordinary challenge that we had taken on. One of our well-wishers with much experience of land management confessed after an early visit to the site that he was appalled by the 'enormity' of the task, and one of the staunchest members of the Wildwood Group privately expressed scepticism that we could get trees to grow on the steep rocky sides of the valley. We took these reactions to heart, but realised that the second at least was a reflection of the lack of any folk memory of naturally wooded hills and glens in the Southern Uplands.

Few, if any, ecological restoration projects so radical in their vision and on so large a scale had ever been attempted in Britain. We could share the philosophy of those who were working to restore ancient pinewoods in the Highlands, but both our organisation and our site were very different. We therefore had to find our own way. The uniqueness of our opportunity stemmed partly from the high relief of

The high relief at Carrifran will make it possible to re-create woodland at many levels and of many types, as here in the Lake District

the site that we planned to buy with an altitudinal range from less than 200 m above sea level to more than 800 m, and with steep slopes facing almost all points of the compass. We could try to re-establish the full spectrum of native vegetation – and eventually of fauna – suited to the diverse situations that Carrifran offered. The woodland would be composed of a rich mix of mainly broadleaved deciduous trees, with high forest in the lower part and smaller trees and shrubs on the steep slopes, grading into montane scrub and heathland near the summits.

By late 1997 the option on Carrifran had been signed, but the two years needed to raise the money gave us time to pick some brains. The first move was to organise our second conference, this one under the banners of Borders Forest Trust and the Biodiversity Unit of Edinburgh University. It was organised by members of the Wildwood Group as a one-day event at the Royal Botanic Garden Edinburgh, under the title 'Native woodland restoration in southern Scotland: principles and practice'. About 180 people attended, including many of the best known names in Scottish forestry, ecology and conservation. The title was general, but we did not attempt to hide our primary aim, which was to allow speakers and delegates with wide expertise and experience to help us lay the groundwork for the ecological restoration of Carrifran.

We also stood to gain a less tangible benefit. The development of a large-scale and obviously high-risk enterprise by an inexperienced group was likely to invite sceptical reactions from old hands. As well as asking members of the public for hundreds of thousands of pounds to enable us to buy the land, we would be applying for grant aid on a similar scale to fund the tree planting and management. Furthermore, we were planning to make fundamental changes in the ecology of a designated nature conservation site. It was vital that we should have credibility with the Forestry Commission, Scottish Natural Heritage and all the other public bodies with which we would be interacting; by mounting a high profile and well organised conference, we hoped to demonstrate our professional approach.

Most of the conference day was spent assessing the nature of the broadleaved woodlands that had once clothed the Southern Uplands and considering how some of them might be re-created. Topics included the pollen record and its application to ecological restoration, historical analysis and the composition and structure of native woodlands. We also discussed establishment techniques and the restoration of treeline habitats and heard inspiring accounts of relevant projects from further afield.

One key contribution came from Richard Ennos of Edinburgh University, who studies the genetics of native trees. His underlying thesis was that the aim of woodland restoration efforts should be the creation of a dynamic and expanding woodland resource, ready to meet future challenges. He implied that in choosing the sites from which our planting stock was to be derived, we should be guided by two key criteria. First, to ensure successful establishment, the seedlings should be genetically suited to conditions in the places where we intended to plant them, bearing in mind the great range in altitude at Carrifran. Second, the planted trees of each species should collectively contain enough genetic variability to enable the population to evolve – over future centuries – in the unpredictable ways required to

Seed collection sites needed to be local, and as similar to Carrifran as possible

maintain their adaptation to local environmental conditions, as these became different from those prevailing today. For instance, variability in characteristics such as drought tolerance and the timing of bud-burst within the new Carrifran populations would give them a better chance to evolve in response to changes in climate.

This timely advice led to a determination to collect as many of our own seeds and cuttings as possible, rather than relying on commercially available stock (see Chapter 9). Our collection sites needed to be as local as possible and similar to Carrifran, with particular attention being paid to altitude. At any given site, seed should be collected from many different trees, so as to encompass the full genetic variation within the source population. We also needed to collect seed for each species from a number of different places, to guard against the risk that some small relict source populations might be inbred and thus genetically impoverished. Maximising diversity within our new populations would also ensure that even if some individuals within the planting stock turned out to be unfit for the places where we planted them, others would be better suited. Self-thinning among young competing trees is a normal feature of developing woodland, the best adapted individuals tending to dominate the woodland stands as they mature and thus providing most of the seeds for following generations.

An equally important contribution to the conference was made by Richard Tipping, specialist in Scottish woodland history, whose analysis of pollen from the peat of Rotten Bottom (near the site of discovery of the ancient bow) is described in Chapter 6. The bow dates from about 6000 years ago, some four millennia after the last phase of the Ice Age. There had thus been enough time since the retreat of the ice for all the major species of native trees to spread within Britain sufficiently to reach the Southern Uplands, establishing the richest tree species assemblages ever seen in the region. This was also the time at which local human populations were making a gradual transition from a Mesolithic hunter-gatherer way of life to a Neolithic society based on settled agriculture, a change that led to an increasing impact of humans on the natural environment. We therefore decided to use the deduced vegetation of 6000 years ago as the basis for our attempt at restoration. The implication was that we would aim to establish all – and only – the species of trees and shrubs that had been in the area at that time. The pollen record would provide a basic list, but we would also need to use other lines of evidence if we were to create woodland with the full natural richness of species.

George Peterken, a specialist on native woodland, retained as a consultant by the Forestry Commission, visited Carrifran with us on the eve of the conference and spoke about it on the day. He injected a note of caution, pointing out that although we might aspire to re-creation of the last truly natural woodland that had existed on the site (what he has termed 'original-natural' woodland) in practice we could not simply turn the clock back, since there had been a series of climatic changes since that time, and the soils and fertility of the site had been altered by natural processes as well as by human intervention. These points are clearly valid, but we reckoned that the altitudinal range and variety of conditions at Carrifran would allow us to find appropriate places for nearly all the kinds of trees and shrubs that had been present 6000 years ago.

Communal development of the management plan

Armed with these and many other insights acquired at the conference, we were in a position to develop a plan for the ecological restoration of Carrifran. Our Mission Statement spoke of re-creating *an extensive tract of mainly forested wilderness with most of the rich diversity of native species present in the area before human activities became dominant*. It said nothing about how this was to be achieved.

The matter was fairly urgent since we planned to apply for funding for our planting from the Forestry Commission under the Woodland Grant Scheme (WGS) and wanted to have this funding in place when we acquired the site. However, the grant application itself was not the biggest job. We knew that because of the large scale of the project and because Carrifran lay within a Site of Special Scientific Interest (SSSI) and was soon to be a Special Area of Conservation under the European Habitats Directive, an application for WGS funding would need to be accompanied by an 'Environmental Statement' which would be considered by various statutory consultees, including the local authority and Scottish Natural Heritage.

Environmental Statements are bureaucratic documents with a largely prescribed structure, but based on a management plan. They are typically prepared by consultants, and in April 1997 – when we first realised that one would be needed for Carrifran – we invited a professional forester to make a presentation to the Wildwood Group. The sample statements that he showed us were impressive, clearly involving a lot of work and technical expertise, but as we left the meeting, Adrian Newton commented that he saw no problem in doing the statement ourselves. Adrian was then a forest ecologist at the University of Edinburgh, but also a Peebles resident and member of the group, and he volunteered to co-ordinate the preparation of the management plan and the Environmental Statement derived from it.

Research at Carrifran

Many of the people involved with the Wildwood project have connections with universities, so the idea of having research projects at Carrifran came naturally to mind. From the start, however, we were determined not to forget that the aim of the project was the practical restoration of a wild woodland ecosystem, in which natural processes take over and the influence of people is kept to a minimum. Since Carrifran is so accessible from Edinburgh and Glasgow, we saw some danger that the valley could become almost a research park, with scientific activities reducing the feeling of wildness that is a key objective. We therefore ask those who propose research at Carrifran whether the work could actually be done equally well elsewhere. We also stipulate that projects should offer clear potential benefits to the Wildwood project and should not interfere with the main objective (as research in nature reserves occasionally does). We also try to ensure that any research is as unobtrusive as possible, by avoiding, for instance, the use of conspicuous markers.

Examples of research benefiting the project include the work on soils that helped to guide our planting and a recent study of the glacial geology of the Moffat Hills, which has helped us to understand the forces that have made Carrifran the way it is.

Soils tutorial for Wildwood Group members

Adrian suggested that the work could be done by our Ecological Planning Group, which he chaired. The group had a loose membership of about 25 people with a wide variety of experience and expertise – not necessarily in ecology – and we also consciously fostered continuing input from many other sources. Early in 1998 we started a series of evening meetings of the group in a Peebles pub, at roughly monthly intervals. As a start, members with relevant knowledge produced draft documents relating to the characteristics of the site and the approaches we might use. Each month, using these and additional material, Adrian would develop and distribute a draft of a chapter of the management plan, which would then be discussed in detail at the next meeting. Adrian chaired these meetings brilliantly. When he presented his first carefully worked section to the group, he came up against the fact that our diverse backgrounds resulted in challenges on many points: we all had something to contribute and the discussion was often spirited. Adrian listened to everyone and modified his draft accordingly. Later meetings followed a similar course, so that each part of the plan was the result of a genuinely communal process. Topics considered included public access, archaeology, geology, deer control, fencing, fauna and flora, monitoring, seed collection and propagation, research and the selection of tree species, as well as various aspects of silviculture including ground preparation, tree protection and the pros and cons of using fertiliser and herbicide.

During this work we received a salutary comment from Bill Mutch, one of the most experienced forestry professionals associated with the group, who said that in a lifetime of working on forestry schemes around the world he had never come across a management plan that had not been drastically modified as time passed. This insight cut two ways: on the one hand, it made us more determined to ensure that our plan was based on principles that would stand the test of time; on the other, it showed the need for adaptive management, a preparedness to respond to emerging challenges by making appropriate changes to the way we worked, but without diverging from the principles embodied in the Mission Statement.

Another valuable input at this stage came from results of the first of several research projects by students at Edinburgh University, mainly organised by Adrian. Since successful establishment of the Wildwood depended on a scientific and practical understanding of the task ahead, relevant research was particularly welcome at the start. Muir Sterling, in his MSc project, dug soil pits in various parts of the valley and assessed nutrient and moisture characteristics. Combining this information

Intriguing research results

Shortly after the planting started at Carrifran two projects relating to the genetics of the trees were undertaken. Christopher Kettle studied rowan and his results carried the disconcerting implication that the planting stock we were using at that time – grown from seed collected in two relict woodlands nearby – had lower genetic diversity than the small population of adult trees surviving in the Carrifran valley. This work underlined the need to collect seeds from many different trees in a number of different ancient woodland fragments, so as to maximise diversity – and thus the potential for future evolutionary change – in the newly created woodland.

Cecile Bacles' thesis on rowan and ash was for a PhD at Edinburgh University; like Chris' shorter study it was supervised by Richard Ennos, a colleague of Adrian and Philip who had provided valuable advice when we were planning the project. Bacles used parentage analysis of seedlings based on molecular markers to study dispersal in ash. Her results implied that not only was the pollen of ash trees widely exchanged among scattered woodland fragments, but also that a large proportion of the seeds germinating around the surviving ash stands at Carrifran had been blown in from places outside the valley. This latter counter-intuitive result – if replicated at Carrifran or elsewhere and confirmed as a normal phenomenon – will have significant implications for conservation and restoration of native woodlands.

on soils with existing data on vegetation and climate enabled him to identify the best places for the principal types of tree.

A key decision, which would have a major effect on the way in which the project developed, was on how much of the site should be planted. In principle we could rely entirely on natural regeneration, but the extreme scarcity of old trees at Carrifran meant that even for the species that were present, regeneration would be extremely slow and sparse. It is known that in some tree species, only very small numbers of seedlings become established more than 100 m from established trees, so we would have to wait a long time for the arrival of species not already represented in the valley.

One group member suggested that we should plant relatively small stands of trees, allowing these to mature and provide seed sources, thus promoting gradual development of woodland over the rest of the site. There was no doubt that this would represent a more natural process than large-scale planting and that it would produce woodland with an attractive, irregular structure. However, even this degree of reliance on the uncertain process of regeneration was problematic, since the dense sward that would inevitably develop after sheep and goats were removed would

It was important to get input from staff of Scottish Natural Heritage at an early stage

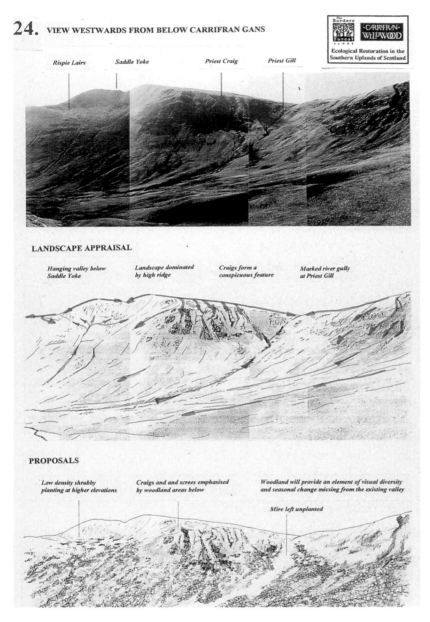

24. VIEW WESTWARDS FROM BELOW CARRIFRAN GANS

Rispie Lairs   Saddle Yoke   Priest Craig   Priest Gill

Ecological Restoration in the Southern Uplands of Scotland

LANDSCAPE APPRAISAL

Hanging valley below Saddle Yoke   Landscape dominated by high ridge   Craigs form a conspicuous feature   Marked river gully at Priest Gill

PROPOSALS

Low density shrubby planting at higher elevations   Craigs and screes emphasised by woodland areas below   Woodland will provide an element of visual diversity and seasonal change missing from the existing valley

Mire left unplanted

Input from landscape architect Jim Knight was needed for the Environmental Statement

be likely to prevent successful germination and establishment of many species, especially those with small seeds like birch and willows. A consensus developed in the group that we could not afford to leave so much to chance. Both we and our supporters were hungry for change in the valley and there was a danger that unless progress was obvious during the first few years, the cohesion and involvement of the group – and also the input of funds – would dwindle. Furthermore, one of our aims was to provide an example of what could be achieved by local initiatives, and we wanted Carrifran to fulfill that function soon.

Having made the decision to use extensive planting – and to seek grant support for this – we had to proceed with detailed planning. We quickly realised that we would not have a completely free hand. First, the Forestry Commission, who would be the likely source of grant aid, would have ideas about what we should plant; these are discussed later in the chapter. Second, there were some recognised archaeological sites in the valley (see Chapter 6) and it would not be acceptable to plant trees over them. Third, because Carrifran lay within a designated conservation site, any 'potentially damaging operations' would require permission from Scottish Natural Heritage (SNH).

Increasing awareness of these constraints brought into focus a key feature of our diverse group, which was a healthy scepticism about externally imposed rules. We were not dominated by professionals accustomed to moulding plans to fit with bureaucratic regulations. We were convinced that our vision for Carrifran was ecologically sound and did not want to water it down by continually looking over our shoulders and worrying about what the authorities might say. We therefore decided to develop our ideal plans, and then to consult SNH and the Forestry Commission so as to ensure that we did not hit unexpected roadblocks when we formally submitted our application for permission and for grant aid.

In practice, both organisations showed considerable flexibility, although certain constraints remained. At our 1997 conference – as well as in private meetings – it had become clear that some people within SNH were excited by what we had in mind, and we gained the impression that to a large extent, common sense would prevail when our plans were assessed. Fortunately, the primary reason for designation of the Moffat Hills SSSI was that it contained an array of special mountain plants (see Chapter 6). Since our planting would naturally be focused mainly on the lower parts of the valley it was not likely to damage the high altitude flora.

SNH did request that we refrain from planting in the flushed and relatively nutrient-rich areas near the valley floor, which harbour some scarce mosses, ferns and flowering plants. This seemed reasonable, although some members of the Ecological Planning Group argued that there were other places on the SSSI and nearby where open habitats of this kind would be preserved, while the natural habitats that would develop on these sites in the absence of grazing stock were non-existent in the area; ecological restoration at Carrifran could thus complement preservation of the *status quo* elsewhere. There was greater unhappiness in the group at one other constraint imposed on us by SNH: that we should avoid planting along the sides of the burns in most parts of the valley. Although they admitted the irony that the best fragments of ancient woodland surviving in Moffatdale were narrow strips of riparian woodland in the most precipitous parts of nearby cleuchs, we were not allowed to plant such places – although there was no constraint on natural regeneration.

At this stage we did not discuss with SNH in any detail the question of planting up near the treeline. We suggested that in general we should establish trees up to about 450 m, but in sympathy with the landform and avoiding a sharp woodland edge. In the zone above this, where there is much scree and heather moorland, we would depend largely on natural regeneration. Nonetheless, we made no secret of the fact that we had longer-term ambitions to establish treeline woodland and montane scrub at high altitude on Carrifran, and later negotiations regarding this are described in Chapter 11.

The text of the Environmental Statement was finalised in the following year. As well as the text we required extensive illustrations,

Only the cold screes slopes below Priest Craig are appropriate for pine, here photographed in the Cairngorms

Aspen stands can occasionally be found within ancient oakwoods in the Southern Uplands

which brought in the skills of other members of the group, including a landscape architect. The result was one volume of text, another of appendices and a portfolio of A3 maps, diagrams and photos. After we submitted it in late 1999 we heard that local Forestry Commission staff considered it one of the best such documents they had seen, and this resulted in unusually rapid approval of our whole scheme.

Species for planting at Carrifran

Appendix B is a summary of the species of trees and shrubs that we considered for planting at Carrifran. We used several approaches in compiling this list. One was to look at the small native woodlands that survived in various parts of the Southern Uplands, including the fragments in the valley itself. The discovery of a considerable range of native species within a tiny and largely coniferised patch of woodland in Gameshope valley had been one of the triggers for the idea of the Wildwood back in 1993. Visits to other cleuchs and remote hillsides showed that many of the same species were often present, countering any suggestion that their occurrence was due to planting. We also had a useful list of species present in ancient woodlands of the Borders, prepared for the 'Restoring Borders Woodland' conference by Chris Badenoch, who had an unrivalled knowledge of the natural history of the area.

Richard Tipping's data on the pollen record (see Chapter 6) gave us an idea of the species present in the pristine woodland at Carrifran and drew our attention to a few trees and shrubs that we might not have taken so seriously if we had depended only on modern distributions. Scots pine was a particularly intriguing example, but aspen, hazel and juniper were also relevant. Scots pine was much more prominent in the first half of the pollen record (before 6000 years ago) than it was subsequently. Tipping felt that even without human intervention it would have survived – if at all – only in relatively dry sites at high altitude, especially on cold, east facing slopes. He suggested that at Carrifran it might be planted on free-draining slopes of this kind, as well as in sites tucked into the foot of the corrie. George Peterken suggested that pine might also be appropriate in heather-dominated ground at the tree line. A later instalment of the pine story is told in Chapter 10.

Hazel is a species of special interest, since Richard Tipping mapped it as being as important as oak in woods in the Moffat Hills 6000 years ago (see map in Chapter 2) although the woodlands in the rest of the south of Scotland were probably dominated by oak. This suggested that hazel should form a major component of restored woodland at

Carrifran. However, here we were faced by a bureaucratic problem, since hazel was classed as a shrub by the Forestry Commission and their rules for native woodland grants at that time prescribed no more than 10% of shrubs. We had to go along with this, but kept in mind the case for supplementing with extra hazel – and some other shrubby species such as hawthorn and willows – at a later stage.

Juniper was one of the earliest colonists of land exposed when the glaciers melted at the end of the last Ice Age. It appears in the earliest part of the pollen record for Carrifran 10,000 years ago, but it was evidently scarce thereafter and none survived in the valley at the end of the 20th century. It may be that it was shaded out by other species except at high altitudes, and that burning and grazing eventually killed it there. However, small numbers of juniper bushes can still be found nearby and we decided that it deserved planting in substantial numbers, mainly at high altitude.

Aspen is a tree with a poorly understood history in southern Scotland. Its pollen is not preserved well and its current distribution gives little clue to its past role in the area. However, aspen is known to have reached Scotland shortly after the end of the last glaciation. Its status as perhaps the world's most widely distributed tree testifies to its ability to survive in extraordinarily diverse conditions. In Scotland it grows at up to more than 600 m a.s.l. on a wide range of mineral soils (as well as on rocky outcrops almost lacking in soil) although it is intolerant of wet peat. However, it is highly palatable to stock and in spite of its suckering habit, the many centuries of intensive grazing in the Southern Uplands have restricted it largely to steep gullies and cliffs. The presence of tiny, widely separated stands (doubtless mainly comprising single-sex clones) in a variety of habitats in the Borders and Dumfriesshire, some of them within ancient oak woodland and some close to Carrifran, convinced us that aspen was appropriate for planting. Accordingly, we decided to try to obtain planting stock from at least two clones each year, to provide genetic diversity and to ensure that both males and females are present.

Planting yew at Carrifran was obviously an interesting idea, since the Rotten Bottom bow was made of yew. However, that piece of yew may well have been traded from elsewhere and although a single grain of yew pollen about 6000 years old was found in the pollen core from Talla Moss, a few miles from Carrifran, pollen archaeologists are extremely wary of drawing conclusions from isolated grains. The question of whether yew is native in Scotland is still a matter of discussion, but George Peterken, in his contribution to our 1997 conference, pointed out that yew is a highly characteristic crag species on limestone in northern England and suggested that it might be worth including with

Reflections on developing the Management Plan

Looking back, the development of the management plan was a fascinating experiment in collective decision making, and a great learning experience. We were helped by the fact that Peebles possessed one of the highest densities of foresters in the country. We were never short of advice, and in fact actively sought it out. But the more different opinions we received, the more difficult it was to reach consensus, which was always the goal. Agreement was sometimes difficult to achieve and some decisions were hard won. Issues such as the management of feral goats, the use of fences and herbicides, and which tree species should be planted, each attracted a great deal of debate. Yet the discussion, though often lively, was always good-humoured. This is a real testament to the positive engagement with the project shared by so many people, even those sceptical about its chances of success. There is no doubt in my mind that the inspired choice of location and a variety of welcoming local pubs were major factors in creating a constructive atmosphere. Perhaps decisions would have been reached more rapidly in less comfortable surroundings, but the process would have been a lot less fun. The successful development of Carrifran Wildwood is a tribute to all those who took part in the experiment. The project would not have happened the way it did without them.

Adrian Newton

other lime-loving species on suitable calcareous outcrops at Carrifran. Since yew is still found wild in Cumbria within 25 km of the Scottish border, we decided with some hesitation to plant small numbers in the valley.

Small-leaved lime is even more controversial and led to lively discussion within the group, which has continued during the subsequent decade. Several grains of lime pollen were found in both the Talla Moss and Rotten Bottom cores, but there is good evidence that under the climatic conditions of the 20th century, summer temperatures in northern Britain were not high enough for this species to set seed. Peterken considered that it had probably never had native populations as far north as Carrifran, but confessed that he would be tempted to plant a few from Lake District populations on south-facing sites at low altitude. Philip tended to agree, citing the fact that there were recent records of planted lime setting seed in southern Scotland and arguing that climate change might be expected to make conditions suitable for lime at Carrifran in the next few decades. Adrian, however, was always firmly opposed, and on one occasion a decade ago, when Philip mentioned at a conference the possibility of planting lime at Carrifran, a stern rebuke arrived instantly by email from Adrian Newton, who had been in the audience, warning of the danger of undermining the ecological credentials of the project!

Adrian emphasised that when formulating the Mission Statement, the Wildwood Group had decided to try to recreate – on any site that they managed to acquire – woodland as similar as possible to the last known natural woodland on the site. He felt that any shift away from the Mission Statement would run the risk of being a 'gardening' approach – in other words, "let's try planting X here, just to see if it grows". In revisiting these discussions during the writing of this book, Adrian — now living in England — cogently reiterated his view, saying:

> *"Yes, I think the principles are established and for me are not negotiable – unless of course the Wildwood group wants to revisit them! For me the goals were set in stone at the beginning; there was almost a romantic notion of restoring an original wildwood (or as near to it as we could get). Personally I wouldn't want to see that compromised, as it is part of what makes Carrifran special. Very few other restoration projects either share that goal or have pursued it so rigorously. There are many other restoration projects that have had a much laxer view of what they should establish; this is what sets Carrifran apart."*

Back in 1998 (and thereafter) Adrian's view was accepted by the group, so there are no plans to plant small-leaved lime at Carrifran.

Matching woodland types to different parts of the valley

A good deal of what is written in this section is summarised in the main map of the valley in Chapter 6, and the information there may be sufficient for many readers. However, in the text we try to show how the various decisions were made. It is fundamental in any forestry planting scheme that the composition of the planned woodland communities should be matched to appropriate site types. Working out this match is a skilled procedure that was undertaken for Carrifran primarily by Adrian Newton. His main tool was the Ecological Site Classification (ESC) system that had just been developed by the Forestry Commission. This is based on assessment of three principal factors that determine site 'quality': climate, soil moisture regime and soil nutrient regime. Dr Graham Pyatt of the Forestry Commission, a local resident and one of the developers of the system, kindly undertook an ESC analysis of the climatic factors in Moffatdale for us. This information was supplemented by information on soils, water chemistry and rainfall obtained by students at Edinburgh University, to provide a basis for deciding what kinds of woodland would be appropriate for different parts of the valley.

An alternative approach was also available. A survey of the open-ground vegetation of the whole of the Moffat Hills SSSI had been carried out previously for SNH using the National Vegetation Classification (NVC) system, which describes British vegetation in terms of a broad spectrum of plant communities. Woodlands and scrub are classified into 25 categories (many of them subdivided) designated

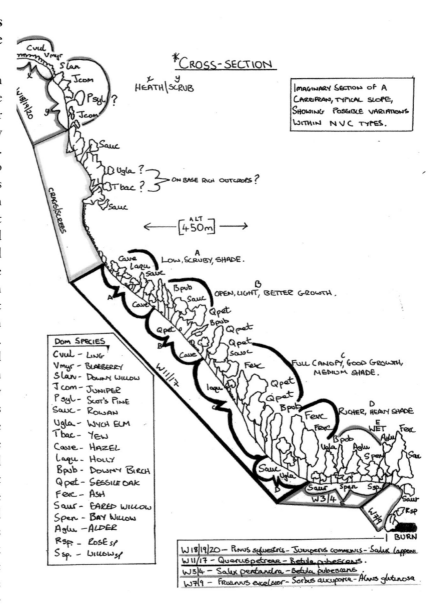

The diagrammatic section of Carrifran by Stuart Adair shows possible variations of the woodland types considered appropriate to the valley

At present there is no example in Scotland of a high level oakwood comparable to this rare example in the Lake District

types W1 to W25. About eight of these were apparently relevant to Carrifran and are discussed below; a summary is given in Appendix C. Both the originators of the NVC scheme and the botanical surveyor Ben Averis had made suggestions as to the woodland types that could be expected to develop in Scotland by a natural process of succession from various open-ground NVC plant communities. Also helpful was the recently published Forestry Commission Bulletin 112 'Creating New Native Woodlands,' by John Rodwell & Gordon Patterson, which is based mainly on NVC analysis and which we had heard about when we asked Gordon to talk to the Wildwood Group at one of our early meetings, in January 1996.

A cautious approach was necessary, however, since the NVC woodland types are descriptive of present day conditions and most of the woodlands on which the categories are based have been managed and modified by humans for many centuries. The woodland types that form the basis of the classification are therefore only semi-natural. We also remembered advice given to us by George Peterken, that in deciding where to plant the various tree species, we should not slavishly follow the fashionable systems for matching species to microsites. He spoke with authority, as the author of an earlier classification of British woodlands, and pointed out that trees are not rigid in their ecological preferences and that colonist trees spread more widely than those in mature woodland. He considered that this was a case for planting some trees on nominally inappropriate sites, allowing the woodland to develop its own characteristics over the long-term rather than attempting over-precise predictions.

It could be argued that there was a more fundamental problem in using either NVC or ESC analyses as the basis for our choice of woodland types, since we were aiming to recreate 'original-natural' woodland, as explained above, while both types of analysis reflect current vegetation, soil and climatic conditions rather than those of 6000 years ago. We were aware of this issue, but felt that the use of NVC and ESC criteria was a pragmatic way of getting as close as possible to the original-natural woodland, while ensuring that the trees were planted in situations in which they would grow. The resulting woodland types would be adapted to the parts of the valley where they were established, and might be similar to the communities at Carrifran 6000 years ago, though not likely to match those in extent or precise location within the valley.

There was no doubt that the ESC and NVC approaches were powerful tools in developing the plan for Carrifran, and there was a fair degree of congruence between them. Crucially, both suggested that on the steep slopes forming the sides of the Carrifran valley, the woodland community that would eventually develop by ecological succession without intervention – provided that herbivore pressure was reduced and fire was not prevalent – would be a form of upland oak-birch woodland. Our aim was to accelerate this process.

Two types of oak-birch woodland are widespread in upland Scotland. NVC type W11 occurs on moist but free-draining, base-poor soils. Sessile oak and downy birch are dominant and other trees include rowan, holly and sometimes aspen and ash; the dominant shrubs are hazel and hawthorn, with juniper in open places, and bluebells are characteristically present. This woodland type develops naturally from heavily grazed grassland, often with great wood-rush and bracken or other ferns. It seemed appropriate for the steep west facing slopes below Carrifran Gans, where the soils are brown earths and there is much scree, and at middle levels on the east-facing bracken-covered slopes near the mouth of the valley.

Oak-birch woodland of NVC type W17 is typical of shallow, strongly leached and acid soils in rugged terrain. It has almost the same composition as W11 in terms of trees and shrubs, although in W17 hazel and hawthorn occur only on the better soils. It is derived by succession from heathland or grassland with blaeberry and heather (although again often with wood-rush and bracken); herbs typically include wood-sorrel

Downy willow – here growing in the Highlands – is the main component of a scrub woodland habitat now rare in Scotland

and tormentil. This woodland type seemed appropriate to the podzols near the head of the valley and the gleyed soils in the west below Raven Craig and Priest Craig. However, experience during the early planting suggested that much of the latter area was wetter than we had originally realised, and well suited to alder and various willows, more typical components of types W4 or W7 (see below), so we modified the plan to some extent.

Both types of analysis suggested that near Carrifran Burn and on lower slopes near the mouth of the glen, woodlands typical of moist mineral soils would be appropriate. The surviving woodland relicts along the burn include much ash, along with downy birch, hazel and hawthorn; in the NVC analysis they are classified as type W7 alder-ash woodland. Although alder was not present at Carrifran at the beginning of the project, it grows well in Moffatdale nearby. W7 woodland is a diverse type, often with patchy composition varying according to the wetness of the slopes. The wettest areas typically have alder, grey willow and sometimes elder, while more stable and drier areas carry hazel, hawthorn and rowan. Other species often found include holly, goat willow, bird cherry, guelder rose, blackthorn and bay willow, with occasional sessile oak.

The ESC analysis also suggested the inclusion in these areas of some W9 upland mixed broadleaved woodland, which typically occupies permanently moist brown soils over a calcareous substrate. It includes most of the same species as W7, although with ash more dominant and alder much less so. The soil data and the NVC open-ground vegetation failed to provide support for type W9. However, many cleuchs in Moffatdale contain wych elm (and dog's mercury in the herb layer) and also show a tendency for dominance of ash, suggesting that some spots at Carrifran might be rich enough in nutrients for a W9 woodland community. It was therefore decided to concentrate W9 species such as wych elm, bird cherry and also aspen in relatively rich microsites within the W7 woodland.

On some high parts of Carrifran there are poorly drained areas with peat or peaty mineral soil and wet heath vegetation, usually with purple moor-grass, deergrass and cross-leaved heath. This is ground suitable for type W4 downy birch woodland, which often includes alder and goat willow; typical shrubs are grey willow, eared willow and bay willow. The obvious areas for this are terraces high up on Peat Hill and the slopes below Dun Knowe at the eastern extremity of the site. As implied above, we also subsequently found that the ground below Priest Craig offered conditions suitable for a mosaic of an alder-rich type W4 woodland with the W17 oak-birch woodland.

The NVC analysis suggested that some restricted areas at Carrifran might be appropriate for type W1 woodland, a willow carr dominated by grey willow, sometimes with downy birch and with occasional pedunculate oak, silver birch, alder and several shrubs. It occurs on wet mineral soils on the margins of standing water and in moist hollows, and it seemed that there might be opportunities to establish it in a few places near the mouth of the valley.

Both of the analyses of potential vegetation, and also the pollen record, suggested that patches of type W19 juniper woodland would once

We decided not to use mechanical ground preparation or to plant in rows like this

have been present on the cold, exposed plateaus surrounding the valley and perhaps in some cold areas within it. This woodland typically includes rowan and downy birch – though these would rarely reach full stature in such exposed conditions – and sometimes also Scots pine (at least in the Highlands). The NVC analysis also suggested that type W20 montane willow scrub was appropriate in the scattered nutrient-rich microsites on the high plateaus, and a form of it survives in a few places on the Grey Mare's Tail property adjacent to Carrifran. In W20 scrub the most frequent shrub species is downy willow, with great wood-rush almost always present, but a number of other shrubby willows sometimes also occur. W19 and W20 would clearly be relevant when we turned our attention to planting at high levels (see Chapter 11).

In 1999, in the last few months before we bought Carrifran, we finalised the Environmental Statement and prepared the Woodland Grant Scheme application for the Forestry Commission.

Avoiding the use of fertiliser and mechanical ground preparation ensures that the developing woodland reflects natural variation in the soils: birches planted in the peaty area (pale) grow more slowly than those on good soil in the surrounding area of bracken

Since all the homework had been done, this was relatively straightforward. However, the decisions we had taken on woodland types for different parts of the site had to be used to generate lists of tree and shrub species and also the proportions of these to be planted in each compartment. The booklet by Rodwell & Patterson mentioned above simply indicated which species of trees and shrubs were considered to be major and minor species in the various woodland types. The original NVC analyses organised by Rodwell included tables on the frequency (consistency of occurrence) and typical extent of dominance of each species in each kind of woodland. When it came down to it, we simply had to use our personal judgement on the percentages for the various species to be used in each part of the valley.

As mentioned above, however, the Forestry Commission rules at that time required that shrubs should not comprise more than 10% of the total. Since several important species including hazel, hawthorn, juniper and most of the willows were classed as shrubs, this was a significant constraint. We felt that the rule was a legacy of the time when the Forestry Commission was focused entirely on timber production and that it didn't make sense in the context of native woodland establishment, but there was nothing we could do about it at the time. On another matter, however, the Forestry Commission later showed helpful flexibility, allowing us to build up the number of oaks gradually as the acorn supply permitted (see Chapter 9).

Techniques for woodland establishment

Apart from deciding on the species to plant and the woodland types that we should aim to establish, some silvicultural decisions were necessary at this stage. As explained above, we had decided not to depend on natural regeneration for woodland establishment. We decided, however, to avoid planting in a few places where mature trees were present, as we hoped to see some natural establishment of seedlings. In the event, rowans – the seeds of which can be distributed over long distances by birds – have been almost the only species regenerating naturally in any numbers, often around craggy places in heathery ground high on the sides of the glen.

Another fundamental decision was whether to use some form of ground preparation when planting. Foresters faced with difficult sites for tree establishment often use techniques such as drainage, ploughing or mounding (using a digger to form small piles of soil on which the trees are planted). These often increase the chance of survival of saplings, but they run counter to principles of ecological restoration. The resulting woodland will not have a natural feel and the drains, furrows or pits make walking unpleasant and even hazardous. We therefore decided to use no mechanical ground preparation at Carrifran.

However, slow growing saplings can be smothered by grasses, so we eventually accepted – after considerable discussion led by the organic gardeners in the group – the need to use some herbicide. The procedure we decided upon was to apply a pre-planting 1 m diameter spot-spray of 'glyphosate' herbicide in all work done by our planting contractors. As a result, at certain seasons during the first eight years of the project one could see hillsides pock-marked with tens of thousands of circles differing slightly in colour from the surrounding vegetation. Looking back after ten years, the more pragmatic members of the group – as well as professional foresters – tend to the view that without herbicide, not only would tree growth have been slower (not necessarily a bad thing) but tree mortality would have been much higher. The arguments against the use of herbicide remain powerful, and mortality could have been avoided by assiduous hand weeding, but on the scale and in the terrain of Carrifan this would have been extremely difficult and expensive.

We also discussed the possible use of fertiliser. On poor soils, fertiliser can speed growth and raise survival rates, but it also has a disadvantage since it can – especially if combined with drainage and deep cultivation – tend to even up the nutrient status of different parts of the site. This is beneficial when establishing a monoculture of conifers, but counterproductive if the aim is to produce diverse native woodland. If ground conditions are patchy, there will be opportunities for different species of trees and shrubs to flourish in different places, and a varied woodland flora is also likely to develop. Furthermore, some types of ground are simply unsuitable for tree planting without major ground preparation and heavy use of fertiliser. At Carrifran there were deep peats associated with the blanket bogs on the higher slopes and plateaux, and some crags and screes. These areas would be better left unplanted – habitats that are more natural in their present state than they would be with trees. Our general decision, therefore, was not to use fertiliser widely at Carrifran, but instead to distribute the various tree species to match the varied conditions. However, in the event, in the treeline planting we used a phosphate and potash fertiliser to give saplings a better start (see Chapter 11).

Another issue was whether to use bare rooted or cell grown saplings for planting. Cell grown trees are raised in arrays of small compost-filled plastic containers rather than in open ground. The use of cell grown stock in woodland establishment projects escalated during the 1990s. When we considered the matter in 1998 some advantages of this approach were already apparent, especially in relation to birch, in which drying out of roots before planting can be a serious problem with bare rooted stock. Since downy birch was intended to be the most abundant species in the valley, with over 230,000 of these trees to be planted, we decided to work mainly with cell grown stock.

During the planning for Carrifran there was much discussion about how to protect the developing trees from herbivores. Roe deer were bound to be a problem and Sika deer were likely to appear eventually (being present in nearby areas), so a perimeter deer fence was something that had to be considered. However, it was eventually rejected, for several reasons. First, since there was no tradition of deer fences on the bare hills of the Southern Uplands, hillwalkers might well be upset if they encountered one, even if stiles were provided. Second, black grouse were known to be present in the area and deer fences pose a risk to low flying grouse, at least in woodland situations. Third, we were aware that some deer always get into large fenced areas, usually through water gates or over drifted snow. We therefore decided to control the deer by culling, and developed a deer management plan to accompany the Environmental Statement, in consultation with the Deer Commission for Scotland.

It was clearly necessary, however, to exclude domestic stock, at least from all areas where woodland was to be established, and we did not want to have internal fences over the long term since they would destroy any sense of wildness. The solution was a perimeter stock fence, and by making it about 1.3 m high we reckoned – correctly, as it turned out – that we could also exclude the feral goats. Some temporary internal fences were needed to exclude stock from planting areas during the period when the previous owner would still be grazing the unplanted parts of the valley, and for this purpose electric fencing was considered appropriate.

A decision on protecting individual trees was deferred until just before we bought the site. All of the main planting was eventually used wrap-around plastic vole guards supported by short canes. The case for vole guards seemed strong, since numbers of short-tailed field voles tend to become especially high when grazing ceases in areas about to be planted, leading to lusher vegetation and so providing extra food

We used herbicide with reluctance and are glad that the pockmarks will soon disappear

Major branching near ground level occurs naturally in exposed places, but not if saplings are grown in tree tubes

and cover. In the winter when fresh food is scarce, the trees are highly vulnerable if they are not protected. It is worth noting, however, that we had no plans to control foxes at Carrifran.

Tree shelters provide an alternative means of protection from herbivores. Their use undoubtedly leads to high survival of saplings and strong vertical growth, with considerable protection against deer browsing and swamping of the trees by the autumn collapse of tall bracken fronds. Their visibility also renders the trees easy to find after planting. However, shelters are also intrusive and are expensive to install and remove. Even 60 cm tubes tend to produce leggy trees lacking low-slung side branches, and it has been shown that sheltered trees invest fewer resources in developing resistance to wind, thus often suffering when the shelters are removed. At Carrifran, we reckoned that we could avoid the general use of tree shelters provided that we could keep the deer under rigorous control. Subsequently, short (60 cm) tree shelters have been used for beating-up in bracken areas and on a small scale in special situations elsewhere. At Carrifran, when short tubes are used, they are normally removed within about three years. Trees that blow over are not pulled upright again; often they survive and regrow in curious shapes that contribute to the feeling of being in natural woodland.

Future trees for Carrifran

We don't worry if some trees are blown over: they may look like this one day

Our careful planning before buying the land enabled us to hit the ground running on Millennium Day, as explained in the next chapter. However, it was inevitable that when the actual work began, some modification of the plans would be necessary, both for practical reasons and as a result of our increasing understanding of the nature of Carrifran. Some of the issues that arose are mentioned by Hugh Chalmers in Chapter 9 and many of them were subject to discussion within the Wildwood Group over the following years.

8. Millennium magic

Volunteer and professional input—Wildwood News—the wider Wildwood Group—Steering Group—Site Operations Team—arrangements with BFT—appointing Project Officer—Millennium Day—Woodland Grant Scheme—approval by Scottish Natural Heritage—funding from David Stevenson for the trees—gift of a quad bike—launch of Stewardships—National Lottery funding after all—access and facilities for the public—interpretation—Founders and Stewards day—facing up to the feral goats—learning from other projects.

* * * * *

During the seven years that elapsed between the initial idea of the Wildwood and the purchase of Carrifran, both the organisation of the Wildwood Group and the actual work was done almost entirely by volunteers, with the group functioning – in the later years – as an autonomous element of Borders Forest Trust. There was no lack of contact and we took care to ensure that the BFT Trustees always included several Wildwood Group members, so consultation was routine, but it was only in the handling of donations that substantial staff time was required.

In mid 1999, when it had become clear that we would be able to buy Carrifran, valuable advice was provided by Alex Smith, a mainstay of Borders Forest Trust at the time. He pointed out that with a complex million-pound restoration project to manage, professional input would be required. We would need someone on the ground to deal with contractors, on-site management and all the paperwork that such a project produces. Some group members were hesitant, but the argument was persuasive, so an approach was soon made to Scottish Natural Heritage (SNH). They agreed to fund a Project Officer, full-time for the first year and half-time for two more years. The half-time support was later extended for a further three years and at lower levels of funding after that.

Joining the Wildwood Steering Group

This is a special experience, the warmth of friendship, organic food, scientific data and passionate debate, transports one to other worlds as good as an exquisite coda in a guitar piece. One element is the mole-grip ownership of the original vision, encountered when I suggested modernising the Carrifran Website. One could hear and feel and struggle with the need to make it more accessible yet not lose the ownership and power of the mission of the project. The outcome of that was very good and a tribute to democracy within the group. Sometimes one has to spectate while two gladiators thrash out an issue, tubes round trees or not tubes round trees was one such debate. Other times one person can take the lead and others follow. Peter Dreghorn

This was a pivotal point in the development of the project, recognising the need to add a highly practical dimension to the somewhat abstract vision of the Wildwood. We knew that we could not afford to keep our heads in the clouds, but several of us were acutely aware of the danger that professional involvement might lessen the commitment of volunteers, thus undermining the grass-roots nature of the project; we took various steps to guard against this.

First, we initiated the publication of *Wildwood News*, a slightly more formal successor to the earlier newsletters, and announced in the first issue (January 2000) that the Wildwood Group would henceforth comprise current members of Borders Forest Trust who were active supporters of the Wildwood project. Since all Founders (and later Stewards) are given introductory membership of BFT, they are automatically members of the Wildwood Group so long as they maintain their BFT membership. However, *Wildwood News* is sent annually even to those whose BFT memberships lapse, since we want to embrace all those who have given major support to the project in the past as well as those now actively working on it. The effect is to maintain a broad group of Wildwood 'stakeholders' – people who feel a real commitment to the project.

Consideration of this group is vital to an understanding of the nature of the enterprise. Carrifran Wildwood is not a 'community woodland' in the usual sense of a woodland in which members of a nearby community play a significant role in management and in which benefit to local people is the primary goal. The majority of Wildwood supporters have never visited the site and will gain no direct benefit from it. They are, however, members of a wide 'community of interest' that stretches across Britain and into many other countries. It unites people who share a conviction that it is worthwhile for individuals to work together in enhancing a small piece of the planet that we share. Of course there are benefits to local people and to visitors from afar, but it is restoration of a 'natural' environment that is the primary goal.

Another way in which the grass-roots could be kept healthy was to create a formal Steering Group, which any member of the original Wildwood Group was invited to join; the only condition was a willingness to attend regular meetings and to play an active role. About 10 volunteers were joined by the Project Officer and the Director of Borders Forest Trust *ex officio*. There were one or two early drop-outs and two key members moved away, but one of these has recently rejoined after an absence in England for some years and several new people have been recruited, including active on-site volunteers.

The Steering Group has met five or six times a year since early 2000 and is never at risk of lacking a realistic quorum. Some might suspect that this is because of the culinary skills of members, since we now usually meet for a shared meal in a member's house. Any supporter of the Wildwood project is always welcome to attend, and we sometimes invite particular supporters or additional members of BFT staff. Our confidence in the long-term survival of the group was raised when Maggie Ashmole, who had been present at meetings since she was a baby, asked at the age of five whether she could become a member in due course.

The idea from the start was that the Steering Group should be the decision making body in the Wildwood project, not merely a consultative one. Although ultimate legal and financial responsibility for Carrifran lies with Borders Forest Trust, the Steering Group is effectively in charge. Membership has been no sinecure, since there have been many difficult decisions and the group was severely tested when the issue of feral goats arose. A feeling of communal input is fostered by members chairing meetings in a rough rotation and by maintenance of the tradition of avoiding formal votes and attempting always to reach a consensus. Various informal subgroups, whose convenors are members of the Steering Group, report to it regularly.

The Steering Group met over supper and drinks in a local Peebles pub

Continuing grass-roots direction for the project was also assured through the establishment of a 'Site Operations Team' comprising the Project Officer, the BFT Director and the Project Co-ordinator, the latter representing the volunteer element in the enterprise. This group meets whenever necessary – often on site – and communicates by email, dealing with day-to-day management of the restoration process. It reports to the Steering Group at each meeting and is sometimes firmly overruled.

Applicants for the job of Project Officer getting a taste of the potential working conditions

In the last months of 1999, when we were closing in on the fundraising target and finalising the Environmental Statement and Woodland Grant Scheme (WGS)

Right: Millenium day — planting the first trees
Photos: Morna Stoakley and Nick Fiddes

Myrtle and Philip plant one of the first trees

application (see Chapter 7), the post of Carrifran Wildwood Project Officer was advertised. More than 50 people applied, so Anna Ashmole, who had wide experience in recruiting staff, spent a day in the BFT office and assembled a 'long list' of promising applicants. This was then narrowed down to seven candidates who were interviewed after six of them came out for a site visit.

The visit was on a dreich November day, with intermittent snow flurries as the applicants trooped up to the high part of the glen, getting a taste of their potential working conditions. During the walk there were plenty of opportunities for accompanying members of the Wildwood Group to get a feel for the candidates. They all survived the day and were then interviewed by a panel made up of BFT Trustees who were also Wildwood people, BFT Director Willie McGhee and also Jonathan Warren of SNH (the funding body) who was to become our main contact within the organisation. The final outcome was that Hugh Chalmers – the one candidate who had been unable to take part in the preliminary open-air interview – was offered the job. His competence on the hills was well known and he had been a member of the Wildwood Group since the beginning. As Philip wrote seven years later, when commenting on the completion of the main planting in the valley:

"The main credit for this achievement is due to our Project Officer Hugh Chalmers, whose dedication to the Wildwood has been extraordinary. His work covers such diverse tasks as working out contracts for fencers and planters, organising visiting groups of volunteers, coping with issues raised by a feisty Steering Group and getting up in the wee hours to stalk roe deer in the most remote parts of the glen. Hugh's unflappability and 'can do' approach to a myriad of problems has made it a pleasure for all of us to work with him".

On 1st January 2000, after seven years of dreaming and planning by the Wildwood Group, we took possession of Carrifran valley and more than 100 people gathered to celebrate and to plant the first trees. Readers in Scotland will be aware that it takes a lot to get 100 people out of bed and into the cold on the morning after Hogmanay, but on this occasion the turnout was high and there was a palpable feeling of excitement and achievement. It was a freezing cold day and the ground was hard, though not too hard to dig the holes. One supporter had composed a special tune for the day and played this on his bagpipes – made by one of the other supporters! Someone else recalls that – *"We all stood around, spades at the ready, and struck the frozen ground as the last notes faded away ... I also very much remember*

Reflections on Carrifran

An eroded forsaken fold in the hills. The dream – to recover it to an image of some original state, shared by enough like-minded folk to make it happen: the vision, singular; the money, multiple; the energy, various. Years of plotting and printing, of approaches and applications. Days on the hills: purposeful, informed, skilled intervention according to the best available knowledge. Slog and excitement. But here comes war!! How could others object to all this niceness?! "The local people ...", said the self appointed one, "Cut through the fences ...", said the righteous one, "Protect our landscape ..." said the defender of the status quo. And there as we stood on the bare hillside, all we had was our dream and our reason and our knowledge and our passion and our innocence. And in this one wee corner of the world these have so far prevailed. So there the seeds are sown and are tended too. And they have grown. This is very good.

John Molleson

the hot wine and mince pies in the cottage afterwards!" At that time we had arranged with John Barker – who had sold us the valley – to use the vacant Carrifran Cottage opposite the mouth of the valley, both for storage of planting materials and for refreshment on volunteer days; this was the first of many days when we used it to brew up and get warm after a cold day planting. The tradition of going to Carrifran on the first day of the New Year persisted for many years – even after we no longer had access to the cottage and had to enjoy mince pies and mulled wine in the car park.

Carrifran Woods

In memory of Doris Stewart 2/7/1910 - 31/10/1999
January 1st 2000

Pete Stewart

The next few weeks were packed with excitement for all of us. First, our Woodland Grant Scheme contract with the Forestry Commission was signed by the middle of January. It related to the first five planting seasons (starting with winter 1999/2000) but the accompanying Environmental Statement also dealt with the subsequent three seasons needed to complete the main planting, which would be the subject of a second contract in due course. The two contracts implied creation of almost 300 hectares of new native woodland, very largely within the lower half of the glen.

A potential stumbling block had arisen at a late stage, since Dumfries and Galloway Council were statutory consultees in relation to the WGS contract and they raised a few issues relating to the Paddock, close to the road at the mouth of the valley. John Barker had originally not been prepared to sell us the major part of this, lying to the left of the track into the valley. He had recently fenced and 'improved' this area, which amounted to about 7 ha. As our purchase of the rest of the site came nearer, we persuaded him to part with it – for an extra £10,000 – and one of our most generous donors agreed to pay for it. The Paddock was thus included in our planting plan. However, the Council planners worried that as our trees grew, they might obscure the view of Raven Craig from the main road, and their archaeologist also pointed out that there were several significant sites within the Paddock. As we talked with them we began to worry that our whole WGS application might be held up because of these complications. The solution was simple: we withdrew the Paddock from the application. This meant that we would not get grant aid for planting there, but we would be able to plant gradually at our leisure with volunteers, without the constraints of timing or density that would have applied under the WGS contract. We did, however, respect the points made by the Council, using shrubs in places where tall trees might block the view and avoiding planting on archaeological remains.

Because Carrifran was part of a Site of Special Scientific Interest, approval of the WGS application required approval of our plans by SNH. We had been talking to them about the project for years, and their consent to the proposed changes soon arrived in the mail. This was an important milestone, since our intentions had been set out in detail in the Environmental Statement that had gone to them as consultees, and their approval of it implied that we did not need further consents for activities that were explained in the plan, including – for instance – the planting of any of the trees and shrubs specified in our lists.

SNH had already offered a grant to cover Hugh Chalmers' salary as Project Officer, and he took up his post in the second week of January, so that the practical work in the valley could gather momentum with full-time professional supervision. With his agricultural training and experience with the Farming and Wildlife Advisory Group (FWAG) he was in his element talking to local farmers and dealing with fencing contractors and planters, and also had the skills needed for the bureaucratic side of the job. However, things were pretty hectic, since we planned to plant 20 hectares of woodland in that first spring. Hugh takes up that story in the next chapter.

Another enormous boost to the project occurred at this time. In mid 1998 a good friend of the Wildwood project had given us an introduction to David Stevenson, son of the founder of the Edinburgh Woollen Mill, who had left the company in 1996 after leading its development into retailing. Two of us went to Langholm to explain the project to Mr Stevenson, who seemed impressed. However, he did not show an interest in contributing in a major way to the land purchase, which was the main focus of our attention at the time, or in funding a building on the site. He did mention the possibility of paying for the trees, but since we couldn't plant trees until we had bought the land, we had to say that we would get back to him when we were sure of our ground.

A year later, armed with confidence that we would be able to buy Carrifran, we made a new approach to David Stevenson and arranged

And then it happened

On the 31st December 1999 I was filled with fear, anticipation and hope. And then it happened. I was staying in Wiston Lodge at Biggar with a group of 60 or so of us who have holidayed together over the New Year for 25 years, with music, dance and celebration. Our final farewell to the old century was the release of a hot air balloon and we watched it drift away over the trees. The next morning I checked the world for changes. It looked OK; fresh, crisp and inviting; birds sang and Biggar still existed despite the largest ever bonfire in the town centre. We drove to Carrifran and planted different varieties of hardwood trees. I drew the Carrifran hill and it emerged from the page as the damp mud blended with stark white. The New Century had broken and we had set out our cards to appreciate the wonder that we lived in; the companionship of friends, the need to preserve and care for our earth and a future that we could look forward to without fear but with anticipation and hope.

Jane Chisholm

Our Millennium Day celebration was featured in the 'New Scientist' — thanks to one of our donors

for him to come and meet some of us one morning at Carrifran. It became clear that he might give us major help with the trees, but there was an unexpected proviso. We had planned to walk up the valley with him, but he was more interested in looking at it from the entrance. He waved his hand across the view and said that he felt we should also acquire the conspicuous slopes of Peat Hill immediately to our left, so that there would never be a hard edge – too much like the edge of a commercial plantation – between our maturing trees and the heavily grazed land beyond. This amounted to a Royal Command, and was accompanied by a hint that he might be able to provide a loan to help with this extra land purchase, if it was needed. We were anyhow in complete agreement about the value of protecting our western flank and took the matter forward at once.

The slopes of Peat Hill, an integral part of the entrance to the valley, were purchased a year later

Negotiating with John Barker was always tough, but we eventually made a deal to buy the whole of the area that we now call Todcastles, which would enable us almost to link the Wildwood with a lovely narrow strip of surviving woodland in the deep gorge of Spoon Burn, which drained the valley behind Peat Hill. By this time our fundraising campaign had been so successful that there was a certain amount of money to spare after paying for Carrifran itself, and we used this to pay for the extra land.

Once this purchase was under way, David Stevenson formalised his amazingly generous offer to arrange for his trust to pay for raising all the young trees to be planted at Carrifran. Philip explained that we hoped to plant about half a million trees and shrubs, and that the present price per tree (propagated in a commercial nursery from our seed) came out at about 30 pence. This implied – in the long run – a contribution to the project of up to £150,000, which would be by far the largest single donation. The Millennium Magic was certainly powerful, since when we reviewed progress with David in early 2008, we were able to show that we had planted 450,000 trees, following almost exactly the programme mapped out in 1999, and that the average price per tree was exactly 30 pence. The remaining fifty thousand trees were scheduled for planting in 2008-2010.

Another important gift was made at this time. The generous owner of a grouse moor in the Borders, who had long shown an

Carbon Offset at Carrifran

The Wildwood project is about ecological restoration, and the idea of carbon offset played no part in the original rationale. Around the turn of the century, however, there was widespread acceptance of the idea that planting trees was an effective way to offset emissions of carbon dioxide, because trees absorb the gas as they grow. After the Kyoto agreement on climate change, many companies decided to offset their emissions in this way. The Wildwood Group was approached by the carbon 'brokers' Future Forests (now renamed The Carbon Neutral Company) with an offer to pay for the carbon that would be sequestered by the trees growing at Carrifran over the coming century. After careful consideration, an agreement was reached by which the project is paid a fixed sum per hectare when the trees are planted and a further sum after they are established. The money comes from the broker's corporate clients, who are given independent verification of the planting and maintenance of the woodland. The Wildwood Group retains a right to veto any company with which they do not wish to be associated. Over the years, the Wildwood project has received about fifty thousand pounds under the scheme. This sum represents about 4% of the total funding for the project to date, and has thus helped us to press on with the restoration of Carrifran glen.

interest in the project and had offered down-to-earth advice on land management, presented us with a brand new quad bike and a road trailer for transporting it. The quad has been indispensable, enabling our Project Officer to take materials to some of the most awkward parts of Carrifran (as well as being useful on other BFT sites) and in spite of one mishap in the early years it is still going strong in 2009.

In spite of this extraordinary support, we were aware that we would depend on donations by ordinary individuals for many years, since it was clear that the work of restoration would cost roughly twice as much as the land. It seemed inappropriate to continue offering Founderships to new donors but we needed to continue fundraising, so we started a scheme in which 'Stewardships' would take the place of Founderships. Using a brochure along the same lines as our original one, we asked people to become Stewards for £250 or £500. This proved highly successful, with many Founders also becoming Stewards or establishing Stewardships for relatives and friends. Some Founders and Stewards take out membership of Borders Forest Trust or become volunteers or visitors to the site, but we keep in touch with the others through the annual newsletter *Wildwood News*. The future seems assured, since by 2009 over 70 of the Stewardships and Founderships had been established for children.

Though much of the Stewardship money is spent as it comes in, we have been careful to keep a substantial proportion of the funds for future use, since fence renewal will be needed within the next couple of decades and there are ongoing management costs, especially for deer control and the care of trees that are not yet established. This work over the past decade has been funded largely by standing order payments made by supporters of the project, many of whom are also Founders or Stewards or both.

An intriguing feature of the start of the year 2000 was that our relationship with the National Lottery came full circle. When the Wildwood Group was formed in autumn 1995, we had high hopes that the Millennium Commission would provide most of the money to buy a site through the Millennium Forest for Scotland Trust (MFST). As explained in Chapter 3, time was against us. By the time we found Carrifran in 1996 all the relevant deadlines had passed and we had abandoned hope of getting money from MFST. In the years that followed we almost forgot about lottery funding and it was something of a surprise when in May 1999 John Hunt, Programme Development Manager for MFST, approached us and explained that as a result of underspending in a few of their projects, some lottery money already allocated to MFST had not been spent and could in principle be applied to other woodland projects.

John advised us that we might be able to get funding for things like fencing, interpretation and work needed to facilitate access to the site. He even helped us with the budget for the business plan that was needed in support of a renewed application to MFST. (John's support did not stop there, since he remained in close touch even after his job with MFST came to an end, and eventually became Chair of Borders Forest Trust.) The application was successful and the resulting funding enabled us to fence the perimeter of the site and to install some temporary internal fences within the first year.

Lottery funding could also be used for improving the accessibility of the site and enhancing the experience of visitors. Our Mission Statement made it clear that in the Wildwood *"Access will be open to all"* and Carrifran valley – especially the ridge over Saddle Yoke, which forms the western boundary – has long been popular with hillwalkers. Early in the planning of the project some of us had envisaged an educational centre on site, with associated facilities. A building would make it easier to accommodate volunteers and might even provide accommodation for a warden. However, we had mentioned this idea when walking up the valley with Andrew Raven of the John Muir Trust, long before we had bought the valley. He queried whether it was wise to think in these terms in relation to a relatively small site where a feeling of wildness was an aim, since this can be lost quickly in places where visitor pressure is high. Andrew suggested building a small and discreet car park and not developing other facilities on site, apart from providing information about the nature of the project. In October 1998 we had a special meeting to discuss issues relating to public access to Carrifran and a clear consensus along these lines emerged.

We all agreed that visitors were welcome and that we wanted interested people to learn about ecological restoration. Casual picnickers, however, would be better served a few miles up the road at the well-known Grey Mare's Tail, owned by the National Trust for Scotland, who were keen to have lots of visitors and who had a large car park. We abandoned the idea of a building providing scope for interpretation and education. This was partly as a result of asking ourselves 'Will it plant more trees?' As time went on, this question became our benchmark for many decisions. A building and its maintenance would be likely to absorb funds and valuable volunteer time, and thus divert energy from the primary business of ecological restoration. We thought, however, that in the long run we might need a base for a warden and left open the possibility of trying to buy Carrifran Cottage.

Shelter for volunteers was still an issue, however, and one of our first educational activities was led by Anna Ashmole, then working as Environmental Co-ordinator at Edinburgh University, who arranged

Interpretation and display boards

The Wildwood group was clear from early on that most man-made things should disappear from the valley. Yet the award of funds from Millennium Forest for Scotland gave us an obligation to communicate with the general public about the project. The obvious way to do so was with interpretation boards. Members of the group worked on the text for these before it went to James Carter, an interpretation specialist. It was fascinating to see paragraphs reduced to a few, potent sentences and brought to life by illustrations. Kate Charlesworth, a New Scientist cartoonist who is also a Wildwood Founder, contributed two of the panel pictures. The other two were watercolours by Zoe Hall, of Studio Z, who worked on the design of the panels. One panel went in the carpark, where it remains. The others had to go in the open to begin with, though strictly within the paddock area. Once we had access to the main sheep stell the boards were moved there, where they were on the walking route but unobtrusive. Apart from some superficial cracking, seven years on they are still legible and colourful.

Fi Martynoga

The growing trees around the car park will soon provide an effective screen

Carefully constructed stepping stones, with a hawser hand rail supported by stanchions in the shape of shepherds' crooks, were washed away in a major flood

Right: Founders and Stewards Day
Photos: by participants

for a party of architecture students to visit the site and – as part of their course – to develop plans for a structure useful to volunteers. Some ingenious designs were submitted for more or less movable structures that could ease the lot of people working in the valley in wild weather. In the end, however, we decided to make do with temporary shelters and a re-roofed drystane shelter part way up the valley.

In the matter of the car park we followed Andrew Raven's advice, aiming to accommodate up to about eight cars. By the road was a place where gravel had been extracted in the past, so we hired a digger and created a high bank to prevent people seeing parked cars when driving past, and arranged a discreet gated entrance. Our feeling was that people who wanted to find the Wildwood would do so, even if the car park were obscure. When we applied for planning permission one neighbouring landowner objected, but the planning officials agreed with our proposals. Overflow parking is rarely needed, but is available near the bridge 100 m away. The car park is still visible from high up near the mouth of the valley, but the hollies and other trees planted around it will soon provide an effective screen.

We wanted to make it easy for a wide variety of people to appreciate the Wildwood without necessarily penetrating right into the valley, so we developed a short trail offering a walk of half an hour or less. This would provide visitors with opportunities to see most of the species of trees and shrubs planted in the valley and also to walk through a variety of habitats. It led – with boardwalks over the wettest parts of the route – up to the sheepstell at the top of the Paddock, which provides a magnificent view of the rest of the valley, then down to the Carrifran burn – crossing it twice – and finally back to the car park.

One of the crossings was a simple oak bridge built by sculptor Jeremy Cunningham, a member of our group. The other was a set of stepping stones designed and constructed by Matthew White, another supporter who farmed further down Moffatdale. He had worked for much of his life with sheep and designed the steel stanchions for the hawser handrail in the form of shepherds' crooks, evoking the sheep farming history of the glen. Sadly, we had to abandon the stepping-stone crossing in 2005 when it was badly damaged by a major flood. The bridge was also washed away, but we found it half a mile downstream and retrieved it with the help of John Barker and his tractor; it is now

Take note!

more secure, with a braided steel cable tether. The lottery funding also allowed us to commission a set of interpretation boards.

On 12th May 2005, five years on from our first planting season, we invited Founders and Stewards of the Wildwood to a daylong celebration. This started off at a local village hall, with a welcome from Willie McGhee, BFT Director. Philip then talked about the first five years and introduced Hugh Chalmers, our Project Officer, who many of the audience had never met. We then collected our packed lunches and moved off to the valley. Three walks were planned, each accompanied by several members of the Wildwood Group. The stalwart group who opted for the 'Montane Scrub Walk' set off ahead, while the 'Holly Gill' and 'Moraine Trail' walkers gathered in the sheepstell for the ceremonial opening of its transformation into a low-key information and viewing point. With minimal modification it now afforded an excellent view up the valley, with space for a stone and wooden seat designed by Jeremy Cunningham. During our picnic lunch it appeared that no one was going to be satisfied with the short 'Moraine Trail' so everyone walked up the valley as far as Holly Gill – a stiff walk, but without the climbing that the Montane Scrub walkers were doing. Later we all returned to the hall where a superb meal was laid on, and Aubrey Manning gave a characteristically lively 'after dinner' speech. The final event was an auction of generously donated local arts and crafts, which raised welcome funds for the project.

We were always aware that the most positive experience at Carrifran would be to gain a sense of being in a wild place. We predicted that only serious walkers and people with a real interest in the project would want to go far into the valley. For this reason the short trail and interpretation boards were placed near the mouth of the glen. We decided to try to minimise the visible influence of people everywhere north of the sheepstell. Old drystane dykes would be left, but all modern fences would be removed, no trails would be maintained and no signs would be erected. The existing track up the valley would be made as inconspicuous as possible, by developing a few wiggles in it and planting trees and shrubs. We hoped that in this way the valley could accommodate a good many people without losing a feeling of tranquillity.

There was one aspect of the time following Millennium Day that was less magical for us. A project bringing fundamental change to a site as large as Carrifran is unlikely to be entirely plain sailing in relation to public opinion. Some local objections are to be expected, and in this case it was the 40 or so feral goats that spent much of their time in Carrifran that caused problems. Although the Carrifran goats represented only a small part (less than a fifth) of the Moffat Hills population, legitimate concern was expressed that this population might have a somewhat less secure future if Carrifran was removed from the total range. We were, however, clear from the start that Carrifran was an ecological restoration project and that goats – as well as sheep – had to be excluded from the valley if it was to succeed. Apart from anything else the money to buy Carrifran was raised on the understanding that we were aiming to restore a natural ecosystem. In the presence of non-native feral goats that would be impossible.

Mention feral goats in any gathering of ecologists and you will elicit reactions ranging from outrage to resigned depression. The word 'feral' refers to descendants of domestic animals that are now living wild, and feral mammals (especially goats, pigs and cats) have caused untold ecological damage to natural communities of plants and animals on islands and continents around the world.

Goats were probably first brought to the Moffat Hills as domestic stock by Neolithic people a long time ago. Although they may have been kept under control at first, eventually some became feral. Since their natural range did not include Britain and they are highly destructive to native vegetation, feral goats are an invasive species, analogous to the coypu in eastern England (now eliminated), the grey squirrel and the American mink, and of course a number of plants like Himalayan balsam and giant hogweed.

In the Middle East and other places where goats are native, plants have evolved all manner of defence mechanisms, although even there the large numbers of goats maintained by people may be largely responsible for the widespread absence of forests. Here in Scotland, the plants have not evolved alongside goats and they mostly lack adequate defences. There is no doubt that goats in the hills of Scotland bear much responsibility for the destruction of the forested landscape, especially on steep areas that would have been inaccessible to sheep and even deer. Much of the damage was doubtless done by tended goats – probably numbering a million or more in Scotland in the 17th and 18th centuries – but it continues wherever feral groups persist, often entirely preventing expansion of native woodland fragments beyond cliffs where they survive.

That is the down-side, but there is no denying that a close encounter on a remote hillside with an ancient-looking, shaggy billy with its great

And some people wonder why there are no trees up here!

After four decades, the oak woodland on Rum is well established but still struggles to maintain a canopy, which is tattered by the strong winds

horns, or a nanny with a new-born kid, is a memorable experience. In the absence of so many of the native wild mammals that were once present on our hills and in the glens, it is not surprising that many people view the feral goats as an asset in the countryside.

When we gave talks in and around Moffat about our vision for Carrifran, some local people, unsurprisingly, objected to our plans to remove the goats. Signatures were collected (on the basis of a complete misunderstanding or misrepresentation of what the project was about) and letters were written to local newspapers. We attended local meetings and had lengthy correspondence, explaining that we understood the objections and realised that people valued the presence of goats in the Moffat Hills, but that natural woodlands were also of value and worthy of restoration in at least one area, and that it would be impossible to restore Carrifran in the presence of feral goats.

We consulted SNH about the possibility of simply fencing out the goats to disperse onto adjacent parts of the Moffat Hills Site of Special Scientific Interest, but they were concerned that higher numbers on that land might do further damage to the vegetation. We therefore decided to round them up and take them to places where they could play their part in heathland restoration projects (see Chapter 9).

Throughout the discussion over the goats at Carrifran we were conscious of a striking irony in the situation. Although it was rarely mentioned, the people most concerned about the feral goats knew that local farmers and the forestry authorities had been routinely shooting them – in some cases by the hundreds – for many decades. Furthermore, goat-stalking opportunities in Dumfriesshire had been featured quite recently in tourist brochures. It was infuriating – but at the same time understandable – that the Wildwood Group of Borders Forest Trust, whose aim was to restore a whole valley to its rich and beautiful former natural state, should be the sole target of protest.

The final version of the Feral Goat Management plan for the Moffat Hills, developed by SNH, emphasised that the best solution was to ensure that feral goats survive in places where they do little damage and can be enjoyed by members of the public, while keeping them firmly away from areas where habitat restoration can eventually provide major enrichment of the environment, benefiting all forms of native wildlife as well as the human population. Feral goats can be observed at close quarters in the Galloway goat park and also at the Grey Mare's Tail near Carrifran, where they sometimes come down to the car park in the hope of handouts from visitors.

During the fundraising period and in the years following purchase of the site, we went on trying to learn about the practicalities of ecological restoration from the experience of others. The conference at the Royal Botanic Garden Edinburgh in late 1997 and the Highland study tour in September 2001 were the most important events, but our Ecological Planning Group also organised several day trips, following on from those that we had during the search for a site. In August 2001 David Mardon of the National Trust for Scotland showed us his fenced exclosures in the National Nature Reserve on Ben Lawers. In his early years at the site, Dave had noted that the tiny number of junipers and downy willows on the site were declining year on year as old, straggly bushes fell off the cliffs where they had found refuge from browsing animals. Recruitment of new plants – and thus the long-term survival of the populations – appeared impossible without effective protection of more accessible land from grazing. This insight inspired him to undertake the first serious attempt in Britain to restore natural montane scrub habitats with sub-arctic willows and juniper, and the work there and on the nearby Tarmachan range provided much insight relevant to our restoration of treeline woodland and scrub at Carrifran (see Chapter 11).

In May 2003 we visited Glen Finglas in the heart of the Trossachs, a flagship project of the Woodland Trust, restoring native woodland and providing recreational opportunities while maintaining a working farm. Our visit came three weeks after a wildfire that had destroyed 350,000 recently planted trees (we had lost only 10,000 trees in our own fire a fortnight earlier – see Chapter 9). Jane Begg, who was in charge of the site and whom we knew from her time in the Borders, was showed extraordinary resilience in the face of this major setback, and took

---

The Highland study tour

In early September 2001 six members of the Wildwood Group (plus one representative of the next generation) went on a week long study tour to the west coast. High above Loch Etive we were shown work by Forest Enterprise aimed at restoring mixed woodland with oak, holly, birch and rowan, which had been largely destroyed by earlier coniferisation. On Rum we were able to walk under the canopy of the small woodlands established by Peter Wormell when working for the Nature Conservancy in the 1960s, which demonstrate that environmental conditions on this exposed island will permit growth of trees and imply that the largely denuded state of Rum results from human management of the land. In a short seminar and site visit to Morvern we learned about ecological restoration on the Ardtornish estate, and met the managers of the Forest Enterprise Sunart Oakwoods project and of the Rahoy Hills Scottish Wildlife Trust reserve. The final visit of the tour was on Mull, where we went on a wet and inspiring walk with David Wathen, who is bravely attempting to establish native woodland on a bleak upland site where vole damage to young trees has been a major problem.

Dave Mardon at Ben Lawers was one of the many people who helped us understand the complexities of the job ahead

the time to show us the ancient wood-pasture on the site, which the Trust plans to maintain.

Other study trips during the past decade by groups of Wildwood members have been to the Wild Ennerdale project in the Lake District, to a community-led woodland project at Dun Coillich near Schiehallion and to the College Valley Estate and a Forestry Commission direct seeding trial in northern Northumberland. Most recently three members on the way to an aspen conference in the Cairngorms spent a fascinating afternoon in Glen Lochay in Highland Perthshire. The estate manager had introduced himself in an email headed 'kindred spirit' and offered to show us round and explain the estate's plans to restore part of the long-lost 'Forest of Mamlorn'. As we were driven far up the winding denuded glen, the wet stumps of some of the long-lost trees, protruding from a peaty hollow, glinted in the afternoon light.

9. Getting down to work

By Members of the Wildwood Group

Collecting seeds for the Wildwood—commitment to stock of local origin—propagation by volunteers—need to involve commercial nurseries—matching seed supply to needs—special efforts for aspen, juniper, oak and pine—organising fencing—planting contractors—getting rid of the feral goats—foot and mouth—the fire—controlling the deer—liaison with the Forestry Commission—planting plan—anti-clockwise round the valley—bracken problems—beating up.

* * * * *

Seed collection and propagation
Michael Matthews

Seed collection and propagation of native trees in the area around Peebles was started by Tweeddale Countryside Volunteers (TCV) several years before the Wildwood project was conceived. As soon as purchase of Carrifran became a real possibility, TCV began to focus on provision of planting stock for the Wildwood.

It was decided that the trees should be grown, as far as possible, from seeds of local provenance and origin (provenance is the place where the seed tree is growing, origin the position of its ancestral wildwood, which is sometimes different). While determining a tree's provenance is only a matter of accurate record keeping, its origin is more problematic, since there are no genuine wildwoods in Britain today. In practice, the best that can be done is to collect seeds in 'Ancient woods' and 'Long Established Woods of Semi-Natural Origin' as defined and listed by Scottish Natural Heritage (SNH), and also in remote patches of native woodland, too small to be listed, where past planting seems unlikely. It was also decided that – as far as possible – we should collect seeds and cuttings from trees growing in similar conditions of soil, climate and altitude to the eventual planting site.

145

Tweeddale Countryside Volunteers

TCV was a group of people based in Peebles doing work of value to conservation or public amenity for Borders Council, the Forestry Commission and private landowners. In 1992 the group established a small tree nursery in the old walled garden at Neidpath Castle (and later at Barns House), by kind permission of Wemyss & March Estates. Members of the group collected seeds from local trees and bushes, and sowed them, after stratification in the nursery. The object at this stage was to provide seedling trees for any conservation plantings in the district in future years. In practice many of them came to Carrifran.

In the early days of the TCV tree nursery, seeds were collected from small woods, roadsides, and hedges close to Peebles and many of these sources didn't meet the more stringent requirements of the Wildwood. Luckily, the hazel source was an ancient nut wood near Peebles, so these hazels were acceptable and provided most of the saplings for the planting ceremony on New Year's Day 2000.

As the search for a Wildwood site continued, we realized that since no commercial nursery was growing stock meeting our criteria, we would have to collect seeds ourselves and build up a stock of saplings so as to be able to start planting as soon as a site was secured. The whole process from seed collection to delivery to the planting site would take from 1-4 years depending on the species and growing conditions. Furthermore, as the plan was to establish hundreds of hectares of new woodland in ten years or less, an initial stock of tens of thousands of saplings would be needed if we were to get off to a good start. This was far beyond the capability of volunteer nurseries, so we would have to get involved with commercial ones.

At this time all funds raised by the group were going towards the purchase of Carrifran. In this dilemma we consulted Alba Trees, a large nursery in East Lothian which was very helpful at the beginning and throughout the project. Rodney Shearer, the Nursery Manager of Alba, visited Peebles to give advice to a group of volunteers, and subsequently Alba agreed to grow plants from our seeds as separate batches without certainty of payment by us; if the project fell through, Alba would add the plants to its own stock. Later another local nursery made a similar agreement with us. However we still planned to grow as many trees as we could for ourselves. To improve our understanding of propagation, Michael attended a training day organised by Flora Locale at Alba Trees and a group of us visited the Argyll nursery of Peter Wormell (who had supervised much of the Nature Conservancy's planting on Rum in the 1960s) and the nearby nursery of Peter McCracken.

In the autumn of 1996, as we started serious negotiations to buy Carrifran, we began to collect seeds for the Wildwood. It turned out to be a very good year. At this stage, there was no definite planting plan but we had a good idea of which species would be needed and that the commoner species such as birch, rowan, sessile oak, alder, hazel, hawthorn and willows would be needed in large numbers. Ash, bird cherry, holly, elm, blackthorn, juniper, burnet rose and dog rose were needed in smaller quantities and would mostly be more difficult to find. Parties of volunteers visited the few semi-natural woods listed by SNH and also the smaller patches of native woodland in cleuchs and steep slopes of the Border hills, collecting whatever seeds we could find. The more uncommon species were tracked down with the help of botanical

The hazel nut mystery

Our chosen collecting sites for hazel nuts are usually very steep and the picking teams have to scramble on the rocky slopes, picking nuts from low branches and raking through the leaf litter for fallen ones. My daughter Maggie became a squirrel on one of these expeditions and the squirrel then started eating the nuts she gathered. Both squirrel and human collectors had to work hard as only about a third of the nuts at this site were viable and it was not easy to distinguish the empty ones without opening them. They were also rather small.

During the early years of the project we were using two main nurseries to grow seed on for us – as well as raising some of the rarer species in our back-garden plots. When, following one autumn harvest, we took delivery of healthy saplings from nursery A, our sharp-eyed Project Officer noticed that some of the nut shells that were still in the peat plugs with the trees seemed larger than the ones we'd collected. Luckily, some of the same batch of nuts had been sent to nursery B, and measurement of shells with trees grown by them confirmed that they were far smaller – there was no overlap between the two batches. It was therefore obvious that nursery A had given us trees grown from seed from somewhere else. We did not plant the stock at Carrifran and realised we needed to be certain that any nursery we used could keep track of the seed that we gathered with such care. The hazels were unwelcome proof that verbal assurances were not enough.

I was working as an auditor of food processing factories, looking at the integrity of organic food production, and decided to apply the same criteria to the nurseries. I made an appointment with nursery A and went round with the manager, following the path which would be taken by seeds from the point they arrived at the nursery to the point where the young trees would be despatched to us. I looked at how the seed and trees were looked after, how they were labelled and what paper or computer records were kept. The nursery was trying to keep track of its stock but it was a tough task because the numbers changed at each stage – for every 100 seeds maybe only 50% would germinate, then another 20% would fail to thrive, 5% later die over the winter etc. Also, the stock was constantly moved around the nursery – the seeds were frozen to imitate winter, planted in trays in

one polytunnel, grown on in cells in another tunnel and then hardened off outside. There were several weaknesses in the system and one point where there was simply no way of matching up two lots of paperwork. When faced with this the manager just threw up his hands in despair and said "well, we just do the best we can". The hazel trees he'd sent us were clearly not from the seed we'd collected and the gap in the record-keeping meant that it could happen again, so we clearly couldn't continue to use the nursery for this project where seed origin was so important .

So, on to nursery B, which also had some of our seed and young trees. Thankfully, this nursery regarded keeping track of the stock as an interesting challenge. They acknowledged that it was a complex business and were handling hundreds of different batches of seed every year but had put in a good deal of thought to making sure that all their customers got trees grown from the seed they'd requested. I found one or two weak points in their system, but the manager welcomed my suggestions and between us we worked out some improvements on the spot. We used this nursery for most of the rest of the Carrifan trees.

Anna Ashmole

Agile volunteers are needed for autumnal seed collecting excursions

inventories supplied by SNH. We sent most of these seeds to Alba, keeping some for growing in the TCV tree nursery and for members of the group and supporters to grow in their own gardens.

We collected little seed in 1997 as it was a poor year but from 1998 onward, with purchase of Carrifran becoming a realistic proposition, collection was stepped up, and as our Ecological Planning Group developed the planting plan, it became more focused. The organisation was informal. As Convenor of the Seed Collecting and Propagation Group, I (Michael) decided how much seed of the different species was needed for each year, on the basis of the planned schedule for planting. I kept a record of volunteers and as the seeds of the desired species ripened, contacted volunteers and assembled collecting parties, generally of 2-6 people. We also extended our collecting area into Dumfriesshire, including Carrifran itself. By the time that planting began at Carrifran in 2000, there were about 31,000 plants available at commercial nurseries and 4400 at volunteer ones.

The collectors mostly enjoyed these seed gathering excursions, which took us into remote parts of the Border hills, off the established tracks. Once into the cleuchs, you are in a different and more colourful world, particularly in early autumn when the leaves and mosses are still green and the rowans are red. Of course there were also days of heavy rain and strong winds, which can be quite scary when you are hanging out on the edge of a rocky cleuch, trying to hook a seed-bearing branch. On one occasion we even came to the attention of the police when a lady, living alone in an isolated house near our collecting site, became alarmed at the sight of six rather scruffily dressed strangers deploying from their cars.

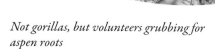

Not gorillas, but volunteers grubbing for aspen roots

Some species had particular requirements. Aspen rarely sets seed in Scotland, but we were given an advisory leaflet describing a method of propagation from root cuttings developed by Forest Research at Roslin. Not having the equipment, we couldn't use mist propagation in a heated greenhouse as recommended, but found that small heated propagators in a cold greenhouse would do instead. Aspen is scattered over the Borders and Dumfriesshire in small stands. We collected it from two rocky cleuchs near the head of Moffatdale, several places in the Forest of Ae, in Dumfriesshire, and others in the Tweed and Yarrow valleys.

Juniper is found in many places in the Borders, mostly in very small stands. We were lucky that BFT had commissioned a survey of juniper sites in 1997. We explored most of these sites in the western Borders but found that Juniper Craigs, just south of Peebles, was so much larger and more promising than the others that we concentrated our efforts there. However we had difficulty in finding ripe berries there though there were always plenty of unripe ones. Eventually

Juniper survived mainly on crags and scree at this site near Peebles, but is now spreading in long heather

in September 2001, four volunteers – working in heavy rain – managed to gather 2.8 kg of berries. This was enough for around 9000 plants, which more than met the immediate need. Juniper Craigs is a dramatic site, with juniper and burnet rose growing in streaks up a steep scree slope and wide views towards the surrounding hills.

Oak was a particular problem. It was required in large numbers to meet the planting plan, but was hard to get. Climate and soil conditions indicate that sessile oak is well suited to Carrifran, but pure stands of this species are scarce in the Southern Uplands, and only produce acorns infrequently (pedunculate or common oak has been widely planted but may not be native in the area). After several unproductive searches in Dumfriesshire, we had to look further afield, and in October 2000, volunteers made several visits to National Trust oak woods around Keswick in the Lake District and collected a considerable quantity of acorns. We also visited the spectacular high-level oakwoods at Keskadale and Birk Rigg, and collected a small number of acorns at the latter site. These didn't germinate, but a collection was made there some years later, with greater success, and we were also able to buy some Keskadale seedlings at a later date, for planting at the higher levels at Carrifran. We were greatly helped in relation to the Lake District collections by Ken Mills, a retired forester living locally, who also collected acorns for us at Acorn Bank, a National Trust park near Penrith.

Meticulous work with seedling trees

In the following year, we started to collect acorns in Buchan Wood by Loch Trool in Galloway, an ancient wood with sessile oaks, which is owned by the Forestry Commission but managed by a voluntary group, Cree Valley Community Woodlands Trust. Their Director, Peter Hopkins, gave us permission to collect, and was very helpful in telling us when the acorns were ready. Though only 80 m above sea level the

Oaks from acorns

The pursuit of the sessile acorn has involved more collecting days than any other species at Carrifran. Amongst the problems were a shortage of suitable sources, the unpredictability of any harvest and, having overcome the first two, the mobilisation of a large body of volunteers at short notice and the completion of quantities of paper work which, ideally, should have been submitted before one even knew if there was a crop to collect. Being someone who sees disaster round every corner, I thought I would enjoy the inevitable risk assessment, but even I drew the line at the suggestion that the focal length of spectacles worn by any participant should be checked for suitability to the task in prospect. The vast majority of Quercus petraea to be planted at Carrifran were collected in 2001, 2004 and 2007 from Glen Trool by kind permission of the Forestry Commission and the Cree Valley Community Woodlands Trust and our thanks go to them for all their help. This is a very beautiful place – visit if you can. Most of the sites where I have collected seed for Carrifran have been precipitous – it was a joy, for once, to be on almost level ground even if it meant I could not include the possibility of landslide as a likely risk.

Jane Buchanan-Dunlop

wood is otherwise well matched to the Carrifran environment; it is also reasonably pure sessile, and so preferable to most of the Lake District woods, many of which are either pedunculate or hybrid. In later years, large numbers of acorns were collected from Glen Trool.

Meanwhile propagation at the tree nursery continued and was supplemented at the Redhall Walled Garden of the Scottish Association for Mental Health, and by people growing trees for Carrifran in their own gardens. These volunteers took on seeds or small seedlings and grew them on to planting size. It was easier to find volunteers to work in this way at their own convenience than to work at the TCV nursery, which was eventually run down and closed. The last task at Barns was lifting the remaining trees, most of which had grown large and deep-rooted. At this stage a group with learning difficulties, who were a great asset, being willing, strong and cheerful, helped us. The back garden nurseries expanded until at one point there were 14 of them in operation in the Borders and Edinburgh. As funding for production at the commercial nurseries became available, this effort diminished, although small batches of special plants are still usually cared for by volunteers.

Philip takes up the story, after Michael moved to Devonshire in autumn 2002

Michael's departure left a gap in our group that was not easy to fill. During the following year Mark Rayment organised a number of successful collecting parties involving lots of children, and John Blyth helped with liaison with the Forestry Commission. After Jane Buchanan-Dunlop joined the Steeering Group in 2003 she took on some of the seed collecting responsibilities, and until Michael's return in spring 2008 she and Philip organised seed collections, with substantial input from Hugh.

Since Michael had fully documented the seed-collecting sites that he had found suitable, the ongoing work was generally straightforward. However, there was one problem, related to our determination to plant only trees of the most appropriate genetic type. As mentioned by Michael above, we had become worried about hybridisation of Lake District oaks, and sparse fruiting by sessile oaks in Dumfries and Galloway left us short of oak saplings in some years. We had made the decisions on the proportions of each tree species to go in different parts of Carrifran, but our Woodland Grant Scheme contract from the Forestry Commission now required us to achieve these numbers.

Luckily, we had anticipated the intermittent fruiting of oaks and had negotiated a special arrangement. If oaks were lacking when we were due to plant a particular compartment, we planted extra birch to make up the numbers to the target density of 1600 trees per hectare, thus enabling us to draw down the grant aid. The only problem was that we had to add the oaks later. This was expensive but was ecologically appropriate since the offset in time would give the birch a head start, reflecting the sequence of natural succession (though on a much compressed timescale).

Finding acorns would probably be easier for wild boar

By 2004 we had built up a substantial deficit of oaks, but in the autumn our contact in Galloway gave us early news of a good acorn crop, so we mobilised volunteers for collecting and eventually collected about 40,000 acorns. Because of a nasty fungus that attacks germinating acorns, only around half of these gave rise to plantable saplings, so we were still left short of about 10,000 oaks to complete the scheduled planting. In autumn 2006, although there were few acorns in Galloway, our friend Ken Mills sent word that there was a crop at Birk Rigg in the Lake District. The oaks here go up to about 400 m and so constitute one of the highest oakwoods in Britain. Although it is impossible to prove that oaks have not been planted there, the remote situation on an extremely rocky slope strongly suggests that the wood has an ancient origin. The high proportion of oaks suggests past weeding out of other species, but survival of the woodland has doubtless depended on the roughness of the ground inhibiting browsing animals, as in Wistmans Wood on Dartmoor and other high level woods elsewhere.

This oak, hardly higher than the surrounding heather, is probably decades old and has an acorn (bottom right)

Philip went to stay with Ken in the Lake District, and although the stunted trees had only relatively few and small acorns, four person-days of work and subsequent good survival led to the eventual production of over 3000 plants, the first of which were planted in autumn 2008. Rodney Shearer at Alba Trees commented that these oak seedlings had noticeably low 'apical dominance', meaning that they tend to produce spreading, well-branched growth. This suggests that they are genetically adapted to the exposed, high-level habitat of Birk Rigg, which makes them suitable for the places where we are planting them, just below the rim of Carrifran valley.

In the following year, the Carrifran acorn story came to a satisfactory conclusion when another mast year in Galloway gave us

Careful siting of a yew to ensure its best chance of survival

These pines at Kielder may be very special

an opportunity for a final collection. Four carloads of of volunteers were organised and about 25,000 acorns collected. Along with the small acorns from Birk Rigg – which mostly needed two or more years to reach plantable size – these produced just enough saplings to achieve our desired overall numbers of oaks in the valley. However, establishing these trees is not a simple matter, since many of the places where oak is most appropriate are now infested by bracken, which has flourished since removal of the sheep and cattle.

Ken Mills is also an authority on the ancient yew trees in the Lake District, and along with the Birk Rigg acorns, Philip brought back nine young yews that Ken had grown for us from cuttings taken from some of these trees. In 2008 these were planted out in carefully selected sites, and although we can never be sure that yews grew naturally in the area 6000 years ago, these trees will provide a token presence of the species in Carrifran valley, where the ancient yew longbow was found.

Another species requiring special attention is juniper, which has become increasingly important in the planting programme at Carrifran as we move uphill. Junipers were probably once abundant on the plateau around the rim of the Carrifran valley, but may have been largely prostrate in form. As any gardener knows, juniper comes in a multitude of different growth forms, testifying to the importance of genetic variation in this group, and we have therefore tried to collect from the highest possible sites, where the plants are likely to have a genetic makeup suited to exposed situations. Apart from Juniper Craigs, which Michael mentions above, a stand on a high and exposed saddle on the Pentland Hills has been a useful source, and we have had one good batch from Ullswater.

In several years we made spring collections of juniper cuttings from more or less prostrate bushes at several sites, but raising juniper from cuttings is a tricky business and we had a frustrating time attempting to get them grown successfully for us. In 2008, therefore, we went back to seed collecting, mainly from Juniper Craigs where there was a good crop, and as a result we should have a good supply of plants for treeline planting in 2011 and 2012.

It was not until 2007 that we began thinking seriously about Scots pine. As explained in Chapter 7, we had been advised during our 1997 conference at the Royal Botanic Garden Edinburgh that at Carrifran, pine might reasonably occupy heather ground at the treeline, or cold east-facing rocky slopes around the crags. Getting seed suitable for Carrifran seemed problematic, but a decade after that conference we heard –

Williams Cleugh Pines

The six old Scots pines growing in Williams Cleugh, at the northern fringe of Kielder Forest, may be very special. In 1961 Herbert Edlin and others published notes in the Journal of the Forestry Commission under the title "The wild pines of Kielder Forest – are they truly native?" Comments by Dr Carlisle (co-author of the classic book on the native pinewoods of Scotland) were cautious, arguing that it was impossible to decide whether this stand was a remnant of a natural pinewood or a result of regeneration from planted pines. Nonetheless, foresters and botanists were still intrigued. In 2004 Russell Anderson of Forest Research pointed out that if they were a naturally surviving group, they could represent the only known ancient pinewood remnant in England, and arranged for coring of the trees. The annual ring counts showed that they could not represent a single planting. There were three distinct age classes: one tree was 153-160 years old, one (separate from the rest) was aged 125-133 years and the remaining four (close to the first) 59-80 years. Angus Lunn, in his New Naturalist book on Northumberland, mentioned botanical evidence that the area of Williams Cleugh was a relatively intact native moorland habitat with vegetation showing similarities to Highland Scotland, and inclined to the view that the pines might represent a relict population. We thought it was reasonable, therefore, to use seed from these trees in establishing a small pine population at Carrifran.

bizarrely, from an academic in the Australian National University in Canberra – of a group of six Scots pines in northern Northumberland, which were suspected of being survivors of an ancient pinewood (see Box). SNH agreed that this stand of trees would represent the most appropriate provenance for a small number of pines to be planted at Carrifran. In 2008, with help from the Forestry Commission, we began trying to obtain planting stock. It proved easier said than done.

The first attempt was in mid March, when a carload of our volunteers met the local forester at Kielder, who kindly opened a locked forestry gate and saved us a long walk in. However, ripe cones still on the trees were out of reach and there were very few cones on the surface. We grubbed up several hundred from within the moss layer, but suspected that most of them were years old. When heated gently the scales opened and we got masses of seeds, but only a couple germinated. Fresher cones were clearly needed. In August we went back and found a good many small cones on the ground. Our propagation attempts still gave germination of only around 10%, and the seedlings proved frighteningly susceptible to damping off. However, in spring 2009 we laid out tarpaulins under the trees and left them so that cones and loose seeds would accumulate. At the time of writing, one batch of seeds has been collected, so we shall soon see if Alba Trees can obtain a better rate of germination than we did.

The quad bike and trailer have been indispensable for our Project Officer

Establishing woodland at Carrifran
Hugh Chalmers

On the 21st of January 2000, the Forestry Commission Woodland Grant Scheme (WGS) contract for the first five years of tree planting at Carrifran was approved. Our way was now clear to start the practical aspects of the restoration and to get trees in the ground. The plan was to plant roughly 40 ha (64,000 trees) each year for seven years, advancing round the valley in an anticlockwise direction. During the negotiations to purchase Carrifran, John Barker agreed to remove sheep from the valley in stages. We divided the valley into four major compartments and constructed internal fences as needed. The compartments excluded substantial parts of the valley where Scottish Natural Heritage or the archaeological authorities had asked us not to plant trees.

We subdivided these four main compartments into convenient-sized areas and specified the year of planting for each. The WGS contract specified a tree density of 1600 stems per hectare, giving an average distance between trees of 2.5 m, but we planned to make this distance very variable, attempting to mimic a natural distribution with a mixture of dense clumps, sparse areas and irregular gaps. Furthermore, although the grant was paid for the whole planting area in each compartment, Forestry Commission rules allowed us to designate up to 20% of this area as open ground, to create open glades and to protect particular features, scree and places with interesting wetland plants. Since we made full use of the 20% allowance, so as to increase the habitat diversity of the valley and avoid creating unbroken woodland cover, the total number of trees planted initially was only about four fifths of the number obtained by multiplying the overall area of the compartments by 1600. However, extra trees were later added to many compartments to offset losses – a process called 'beating up' by foresters.

As we were on a tight deadline to get some trees planted before the end of the season in late April 2000, we quickly arranged for construction of the first of our internal (infernal) fences, to keep sheep out of the first 25 hectares. The fences consisted of four plain live wires with an earth wire running at the base and posts five metres apart, as a compromise between effectiveness and cost. The first fence was powered by a battery but for a later, longer one we tapped into the mains at John Barker's farm, a mile and a half down the valley: it was a long route with plenty of potential for shorting out!

Planting tenders were sent out to local woodland management companies, specifying the use of short (at first 30 cm, later 20 cm) plastic wrap-around guards – supported by single 45 cm canes – to provide protection from voles. We felt that this minimal protection was essential, as short-tailed field voles can have a devastating effect on

Planting trees on contract

If there was a job description for tree planting contracts at Carrifran, I'm sure the words 'Mountain Mule' would be in there somewhere. A truly wild wood on wild terrain, planting each compartment has provided many physical challenges but with an equal number of rewards. The views have unfolded year after year, revealing different angles from which to assess what lay ahead, or to look back on what had gone before. Working on a single part of the hill for weeks at a time, has increased my awareness of how the sun moves across this deep valley, and has led to an intimate knowledge of landmark boulders, crags and burns. In early morning fog, I have exchanged looks with an owl at close quarters. On hot summer days I have been re-born in pools beneath waterfalls. And in blizzards retreated off the hill altogether, possibility of landslide as a likely risk.

The randomness of the Carrifran ground plan is not the only thing that has made working there different from other tree planting contracts. Hugh and his enthusiastic volunteers have created a feel where more people are brought along. Friends and family have come along to have a look and plant a tree for themselves. My parents, Lawrence and Rosemary, joked in 2002, while planting some holly near the track, that they won't be around to see the trees mature, but in 2009 are now talking about coming back to see the growth. A first ever camping trip with my nieces, Rebecca and Tara, showed that the very young, as well as the very old, are capable of negotiating Carrifran's wild terrain, as Tara, aged two at the time, walked from the bothy to the waterfall without being carried. Maybe there is another mountain child in the family. I had spent many nights camping in the higher reaches of the valley, seeking out six foot of flat ground on which to pitch a tent, but it was that night around the campfire with family that I will remember the most.

The transformation that has taken place since the spring of 2000, when I planted my first trees on a bare hillside, has been astounding. Not every tree came from Alba Nurseries. I remember unwrapping a bundle of hazel saplings carefully tied up in newspaper, after their successful propagation in a back garden nursery; another testament to the human interest in getting the wildwood started. The numbers of trees planted have gone from thousands to tens of thousands, and the increase in bird numbers was an early indicator of the changes being made. No longer are sheep seen dotted around the upper slopes, and the trees have been slowly taking advantage of the limited direct sunlight that reaches the valley floor. The resident fox still trots away from the frequent visits of outsiders tramping up the track, but now is surrounded by a growing forest that will seed itself into the next generation, putting trees in places that all the anonymous tree planters could not reach.

Tim Holden

Vole guards protect the trees. Herbicide, though used reluctantly, reduces competition from surrounding vegetation while the trees get established

newly planted trees. One potential contractor was unhappy with the specification, fearing that in such an exposed site the trees would be damaged by abrasion against the sharp upper rim of the vole guard. In the event this was not a significant problem, since any trees that lost their leading shoot typically regrew in a robust bushy form.

The systematic seed collection described earlier in the chapter had ensured that plenty of saplings were available. Some were bare rooted and had been grown – and were now planted – by volunteers, but those needed by our contractor planters had been cell grown in local nurseries. Most of them were in non-peat compost in 200 ml cells and stood around 20-40 cm tall. The trees are removed from the cells in the nursery and wrapped in bundles of 15, and if kept moist they can survive like this from November to April if necessary. The decision made at the planning stage to use mainly cell-grown stock soon proved to have been a wise one, since it enabled our individual contractors to work steadily through the planting season whenever weather permitted, without too much worry about deterioration of the stock.

By mid May 2000, less than six months after site acquisition, the first 20,000 trees were in the ground behind a 2 km sheep fence. This was a considerable achievement, due in large part to the careful planning by volunteers during the previous two years. However, as the summer wore on the practical challenges of successful tree establishment started to become apparent. First, there was a worrying dry period as the last saplings were being planted, although rain arrived just as they began to suffer. However, in our rush to get trees planted I had taken on some casual help from a team of hard working path makers who were living in Carrifran Cottage. We later found that some trees had been planted in bundles of 10 or 15 to save time and effort; although I had subsequently re-planted some of them and fresh leaves had appeared, our diligent Forestry Commission Woodland Officer was not too impressed when carrying out the inspection of the planting that was needed before the grant could be paid.

As the soft and delicate pale-green leaves of the new birch, rowan and ash trees emerged at Carrifran that first spring, with roots firmly wedged between rocks, some very strong gusty winds got up and blew them off! I have now become accustomed to these freakish winds, especially in the valley bottom, where mini-tornados will advance with a roar, and throw you to the ground if you are not prepared by dropping to your knees.

The Cheviot ewes of Carrifran were not too pleased at being fenced out of their choice grazing, and it was a struggle to keep all sheep

Courtesy Neil Bennett

away from the new trees. This meant regular patrolling and occasionally disentangling them from the live wires of the fence. The feral goats seemed more wary of the pulsing wires and generally kept well away. By mid July, it was obvious that hand clearing around the plants which had been planted among bracken was going to be a big job – it had not seemed so strong at first, but with no trampling by sheep, the robust fern grew tall and strong, shading out our delicate trees. Bracken can be killed when at full frond with a chemical which though specific to ferns will suppress broadleaved trees too, so the decision was made not to spray, and generally to use as few chemicals as possible. By August, teams of volunteers armed with sickles and sticks were wading through head-high bracken, trying to save suppressed trees that were deprived of light. This battle continued for some years, with the use of some slightly larger tubes helping to solve the problem in the most difficult areas.

Surveying the upper boundary of planting under Raven Craig

At the same time, we had to face up to the construction of the perimeter fence around the whole of Carrifran, a distance of more than 11 km, most of which would be above 500 m altitude and over some very steep ground. We had decided early on that a deer fence could not be kept proof against roe deer, as the high winds, snow and ice would soon tear it down, as well as such a tall fence being ugly and a barrier to hillwalkers. The jumping ability of feral goats was considered at length. These goats seemed to be able to climb most rock faces at Carrifran and to get over the traditional 5-wire sheep fence. We took an educated guess that a 7-wire fence about 1.3 m high would keep sheep and goats out on a permanent basis. The line wires were made from heavily galvanised 5 mm diameter mild steel, with posts of treated Scots pine every 1.8 m. This was to be a fence built to last. Even the staples holding the wire were specially long and barbed for extra hold.

Twelve gates and stiles were incorporated, with short spurs of fence close to the gates to help in driving out any marauding sheep or goats. Short lengths of wood were also threaded on the wire on the steep sections of the fence up to 500 m altitude, with the aim of making the fence more visible to black grouse and so preventing collisions.

Eleven kilometres of perimeter fence to keep out sheep and goats

There were two obvious contenders for the contract, and we accepted a reasonable quote from Charlie McCrerie from Denholm, who had already built some fine fences in Ettrick for Borders Forest Trust. Charlie set to work getting materials in place, and with the use of a helicopter, placed over 6000 fence posts and tonnes of wire around the perimeter. Over the next nine weeks, based in Carrifran cottage, Charlie, with Jock and Bob his foremen, worked 12 hour days through July and August to complete the job on time, using quad bikes where possible. Knowing they were up for a big day on the hill, the men would

Erecting the perimeter fence

Erecting the new Carrifran boundary fence was a wonderful challenging experience – ten weeks holiday with pay. Working in an area of rolling lowland hills with a climate to match the more rugged Highlands. We stayed in the cottage opposite the Carrifran car park. Self-catering, working for two weeks at a time then the luxury of home for a weekend. Carrifran has more than its fair share of low cloud and rain, a population of midges to match anywhere in Scotland, and more often than not the first area in the south of Scotland to see winter snow.

Memorable moments: starting fencing after all the preparation – marking out fence line and helicopter drop sites – preparing material bundles for aerial drops – getting material laid out with helicopter – first day across Rotten Bottom on quad bikes – looking across valley from Peat Hill and thinking there was no chance of being across the other side in nine weeks – sighting eagle on two separate occasions – goats got quite unfazed by our presence – getting lost in mist one Saturday night coming off Whitecombe on quad bikes – arriving back at cottage on night of my wedding anniversary to find my wife and Helen Middlemass had motored up and surprised us with a three-course meal – and of course fence finally reaching the bottom of Carrifran Gans.

Still walk the boundary as often as possible just to keep an eye on it and to enjoy the scenery. And when working in the Borders gaze over to Whitecombe and reminisce.

Charlie McCrerie

Photos: Charlie McCrerie

pack up to 18 'pieces' for the day, and despite this, they all lost weight.

Nine years on, the boundary fence is holding up well. It has been checked on a monthly basis since mid 2001 by a hardy group of Boundary Wardens (see next chapter) and incipient problems have been nipped in the bud. Some staples have come loose, gaps have developed below the bottom wire and needed plugging with rocks, and lightning has damaged a few posts. More seriously,

Checking the boundary is essential. Wires crossing a dip in the ground contracted in a cold spell and pulled stobs out of the ground, letting sheep through
Photo: Crinan Alexander

increased tension in the wires caused by contraction in a very cold spell pulled some posts out of the ground where the fence crossed a hollow on Carrifran Gans, allowing sheep to get through. The fault was noted by a Boundary Warden and the marauding sheep were quickly evicted and emergency repairs made, pending attention from the professional fencer. One section near Rotten Bottom where we raised the height of an old fence rather than building a new one may need replacement fairly soon, but the new fence should last at least another decade.

Two special internal fences were built at the same time as the perimeter fence. Another local contractor, Derek Murray from Beattock whose father had been a shepherd at Carrifran in the 1940s, did this work. These were deer fences two metres tall, constructed around areas with small remnants of native trees, one around Hazel Linn – a shallow gorge along the burn a kilometre into the valley – and the other around the steep ravine of Holly Gill. This would allow us to see how trees would grow without any deer browsing, and also allow tree seed to fall from the nearby remnants and perhaps regenerate trees naturally. We had planned a third deer-fenced 'exclosure' close to the road on the eastern boundary of the site, in an effort to inhibit incursions by deer from the nearby conifer plantations. However, we abandoned this idea shortly before the purchase when the owner mentioned that he had seen a blackcock displaying nearby.

At this time, after discussion with the Deer Commission for Scotland, we took on a professional deer controller. We were well aware that our new trees in pasture clear of sheep would become very attractive to roe deer. In the long run, roe deer will become an integral part of the Wildwood, but in the early stages, without predators, they would

159

prevent new tree growth. Our policy was to control them to the point where the damage they inflicted was 'acceptable'.

From watching the grazing and movements of the feral goats that first summer, it was obvious that some were resident in the valley whilst other groups spent time wandering the land to the east and west of Carrifran, which was, up until August 2000, unfenced. By the time the fence was completed, around 40 goats were still within the fence. Due to the rare plants on neighbouring cliffs SNH did not want us simply to relocate 'our' goats next door to Black Hope or elsewhere. We were obliged to move them to a place where their influence would be more positive.

By October, we had found two lowland heath restoration projects that were keen to have our goats to prevent trees from colonising; this seemed an ideal though somewhat ironic solution. The challenge was to get our goats to Windsor Great Park in Surrey! In preparation, the upper deer fence at Holly Gill was modified to create a funnel into which goats would be driven, with the last 50 m of fence shielded by a 2 m high hessian 'scrim', which would keep the goats calm.

On a rather inauspicious day in late October 2000, a team of volunteers walked high into the valley before dawn to rendezvous with a neighbouring shepherd, who failed to turn up. Strong winds, rain and patchy clouds made spotting goats difficult, but soon a talented farmer neighbour and his sheepdogs were quietly driving a group of 21 goats down through steep crags towards the funnel. Once in the penned area, they were firmly placed in a sheep trailer and taken down by quad bike to a larger stock trailer beside the road. Unfortunately, the second attempted gathering proved a complete failure when the rest of the goats decided to run towards the refuge of Raven Craig. By this time the weather and steep exertions had taken their toll on the dogs and volunteers, and we left with the job half done, but knowing it was possible. The 21 goats were whisked away to spend the night on a Pennine farm, and the next day down to Windsor and to the appropriately named 'Wildwood Park' in Kent. We would have to wait until we had weathered some more pressing difficulties before we could say goodbye to the rest of the Carrifran goats.

Planting in the late autumn of 2000 had proved quite straightforward, with around 15,000 new trees behind a new temporary internal fence, and at the turn of the year we had the next 30,000 trees delivered and about to be planted. The scheduled planting site, on the east-facing slopes of Peat Hill, was particularly steep, rocky and with large patches of bracken. The site rises steeply from the road at 180 m above sea level, to just under 500 m – quite a challenge, and with limited potential to use any machinery for transport.

Then, with the sudden arrival of Foot and Mouth Disease, all movements on farms were off limits. A strange kind of hysteria pervaded the south of Scotland, with farms near to Carrifran being culled out – all sheep and cattle killed and burned on site in what may now be thought of as drastic policy compared with the alternative option of vaccination. Carrifran was at first only in a high-risk area, but then, because of a 'Dangerous Contact' – a farm vehicle commuting between Carrifran and Moffat – it was decided by 'The Ministry' that livestock should be culled at Carrifran. The Cheviot flock, which had been resident for hundreds of years at Carrifran, was summarily herded up and slaughtered, then burnt at Capplegill. Marksmen were despatched to shoot any animals that had escaped the initial gathering of sheep, and over 30 stragglers were left dead on the hill. Luckily for the remaining Carrifran goats, they were not shot. However, goats on some of our neighbouring land were shot. Restrictions were lifted in June, too late for planting.

Our deer culling was also put on hold by government ruling, and soon it was common to see – from a distance – groups of deer happily ensconced among our small trees, with no way of preventing them browsing fresh foliage. We watered the trees stored at Carrifran cottage until the spring which supplies the water ran out, and then had to move them elsewhere to water them whilst still in their bundles. This proved to be not a good idea, as the bundles of trees tended to shade each other and they all became weakened, so storing up problems for the future.

Planting the delayed areas on the steep hillside under Peat Hill started in October 2001, followed by the next scheduled area of 35 ha (56,000 trees) on the slopes beneath Carrifran Gans, the east side of the valley. This took its toll on our contractors, and we eventually had to agree to a compromise settlement and find other contractors to finish that job. In later years, a small number of independent tree planters emerged, and from then on showed their grit and determination to get the job done well. Gradually too, volunteers became accustomed to the challenge of the steep slopes; as well as planting 10% of the trees, they were involved with wildlife monitoring, bridge repairs, bracken control and removing redundant fencing (See chapter 10).

From then on, we settled into a well thought out routine to get trees planted efficiently. In July, we would use canes to mark out individual tree planting sites in a random distribution to mimic natural patterns, but always following Forestry Commission criteria for overall tree density. A one-metre diameter spot spray of the herbicide glyphosate (usually sold as 'Roundup') – which is considered to be a relatively harmless chemical – was then used to suppress weeds. By October, it was possible to arrive with tree and vole guard and plant into

Unplanted saplings were not as healthy as this by the end of the summer

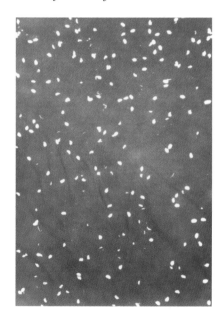

No straight lines please, and no evenly spaced trees. Petals fallen from a cherry tree were used as a guide to planters of what we meant by random spacing

A warning

After the fire

the herbicided spot. Spreading the work out like this, over the summer and then into winter, made the job easier, though it did have serious cash-flow implications, as the first instalment of FC grant money is paid only once the trees are planted.

With volunteers, however, we have generally avoided the use of herbicide and instead used 'screefing', clearing the ground vegetation from where the tree is to be planted with a mattock or spade. The trees are then usually planted with a 'spear' – a robust, narrow and pointed spade that can be used to lever a small space between rocks – or some kind of mattock. Planters are encouraged to think of the 'microsite' when deciding where to put a tree. For example, a sheltered spot behind a rock may give some extra shelter from winds and thus help the tree become established.

As the planting programme took us further into the valley, with much of the work being done high up on steep slopes, we tried to help the contractors by getting the planting materials as close to them as possible. Hiring a crawler tractor and driver each year from Murray the fencers in Beattock turned out to be very worthwhile (and more effective than an overloaded quad bike which did overturn on one memorable and expensive occasion, luckily with no injury!). One day in July each year got the canes and vole guards in place and a day in November dealt with the trees. The tractor could tackle impressively steep slopes and the driver seemed unfazed on one occasion when it slid sideways a hundred feet or so down the hill. Some scarring of the ground was caused, but it has healed pretty well. We were also able to ease the contractors' problems in late 2006, when we had hired a helicopter to take materials up to Firth Hope (see Chapter 11) and arranged for it to make several drops of bundles of tree tubes and stakes high up on Peat Hill, where we were doing some replacement planting in a difficult area. A couple of the bundles broke apart as they were deposited, so for a week or so there were conspicuous 'cascades' of tree tubes down the side of the hill.

On the last day of March 2002, following a sustained dry period, our neighbour decided to rejuvenate his heather and grass on the land next to Peat Hill by setting fire to it. Unfortunately, or perhaps inevitably, strong winds got up and the fire raged across his land, burning his quad bike, leaping through our new fence, creeping downhill and consuming 10,000 newly planted trees. The fire burned for much of the night despite the best efforts of the local Fire Brigade. No helicopters were available as they were busy fighting bigger forest fires in Ardnamurchan and on the Pennines, and at the Woodland Trust's new plantings at Glen Finglas. Luckily a brief shower of rain overnight stopped the advance of the fire at Carrifran, but we were left with 10,000 melted plastic vole guards and a mile of burnt fence where some of the posts had been completely consumed by the fire. The galvanising of the wire was checked and found to be unaffected, and posts were quickly replaced. The final bill (paid by the farmer's insurance) for clearing plastic, fence repair and replanting came to over £17,000, a substantial disincentive to further irresponsible muirburn! That autumn, our contractor Davy Cairns, who had planted most of the original trees, planted another 10,000 to replace them.

We always had our eye firmly fixed on the Woodland Grant Scheme contract conditions. This money was essential to help to pay for tree planting, herbicide use and vole guards, with the propagation of the trees themselves all paid for by the David Stevenson Trust. The total planting grant was £1050 per hectare, of which 70% was paid immediately after planting, with the remaining 30% (£315/ha) five years later when the trees became 'established'. Our main concern was to make sure the trees became established in sufficient numbers. 'Established'

Fire damages protected and unprotected trees alike, but even a devastating fire can leave some saplings alive
Photos: Hugh Chalmers

in this case meant that the trees should be at least 60 cm high and able to grow with only basic protection from deer and domestic herbivores. Failure to establish trees would require the repayment, with interest, of all Forestry Commission grant, and by May 2004, with over 150 ha planted, we had over 240,000 vulnerable trees. Grant repayment of over £110,000 was impossible, so failure was not an option.

The tree survival monitoring technique that we use, developed by the Forestry Commission, involves using a 5.6 m length of cord as a radius to describe a circle (of area 0.01 hectares) at each of a series of evenly spaced points along several transects across the compartment. The average number of trees within the circles multiplied by 100 gives an estimate of tree density per hectare. At least 30 of these circles are

Unprotected saplings are vulnerable to nibbling by voles and fraying by deer. However, protection tubes with sharp edges can also cause damage

measured in any compartment and the condition of the trees within them is also recorded. We make these measurements in the third season of tree growth in each area, giving an opportunity for remedial action where necessary, before the official inspection after five years.

At this time it became obvious even from casual observation that some areas were in need of further weed control, with trees being smothered by grasses and bracken, whilst other had been browsed. A little bit of browsing damage on broadleaved trees does no harm, but severe browsing will kill a tree. In addition, too many of our larger trees had been bark-stripped by the fraying of roebucks as they established territories. In the worst areas, severe browsing was suppressing 70% of the trees. In the summer of 2004, sheep and feral goats were still in part of the valley, and we had to decide whether it was just deer which were causing the browsing damage, or whether sheep or goat incursions into the planted areas were part of the problem. Sheep did get in occasionally, but they were always evicted – sometimes with considerable difficulty – and we became convinced that deer were the key agents.

From the beginning we had been culling roe deer, but the extent of damage that we were now seeing and a visit from a Deer Commission for Scotland adviser convinced us that we needed to do a lot more deer control. Night shooting and out of season shooting under licence would be required, as well as participation in deer control by a professional, the Project Officer and a team of well qualified amateur stalkers. By summer 2005, recovery of most of the trees was under way, with strong shoots growing tall from previously suppressed trees. This task is ongoing. The deer-fenced areas within the valley showed the clear benefit of adequate deer control.

Late in 2004 we realised that we could no longer delay removal of the remaining feral goats. John Barker was due to remove the last of his sheep and we needed to start planting the western side of Carrifran. During the development of the feral goat management plan for the Moffat Hills, SNH had arranged a census which had shown that at least 230 goats were still present in areas other than Carrifran. By this time we had attended several meetings with SNH, local landowners and a group calling themselves 'Friends of Moffat Water' (who were concerned about the future of the Carrifran goats). It was agreed that as some goats had been shot during the Foot and Mouth crisis on neighbouring land, there would now be room there for the remainder of our goats without causing undue harm to the vegetation.

Accordingly, we obtained the necessary permissions and recruited groups of fit volunteers on three separate days to herd the remaining goats (and a few stray sheep) through gates in our perimeter fence into adjacent areas. It was an exhausting and frustrating business and more than once they disappeared into the low cloud above Raven Craig. On the third day a tiny group repeatedly evaded us by taking refuge on the steepest parts of the cliffs; with regret, we shot one initially, and two more a little later. It was an upsetting end to the most difficult part of the whole Carrifran project.

With the removal of the goats and the last of the domestic sheep from the valley in autumn 2004, the re-wilding of Carrifran could take big steps forward. Volunteers dismantled over 6 km of internal fences and the traces left by humans started to heal. The deer-fenced exclosure in Hazel Linn was also removed in 2008 by volunteers, since we reckoned that the trees were big enough to avoid serious damage by deer. Its removal has made a striking difference to the feel of the lower part of the valley, where the only conspicuous modern artefacts remaining are some tree tubes that can soon be removed. The deer fence around Holly Gill will be kept for a few more years, since this is a tougher place for tree establishment.

Hugh emerging from his own version of a hunting lodge

One of the marauding roe deer escaped the rifle but not the camera
Photo: John Savory

Stalking experience

I really enjoy stalking at Carrifran. Sometimes it is easy to see the deer – if they move – but then the challenge is to get close to them, with the lack of deep cover on the open hill. Carrifran is very rough underfoot and that too makes moving hard work. Sometimes traversing high on the hill can be good, as deer often hide up in the high gullies. I have spent hours stalking around a deer only for it to disappear into the gullies or mist. It is great to see all the other wildlife like black grouse and peregrines and to watch foxes hunting voles. The trees are doing well now, and maybe there will soon become a time when less stalking will be needed. The only time I don't enjoy stalking at Carrifran is when the midgies are bad!

Scott Speed

Its upkeep costs have already been significant, since the water gate on Broomy Gutter was badly damaged during snow melt floods one spring, and the main water gate on its southern end was washed away – with an adjacent stretch of fence – during a severe flood a few years later.

The seven year tree planting programme is now complete, and we have received second instalments of the Woodland Grant Scheme (payable after five years) from the Forestry Commission on almost all areas where it is due, implying that they consider the trees to be established. The exception is the lower compartment on the steep side of Peat Hill, planted in the aftermath of foot and mouth disease, for which the establishment grant was deferred. Here, drying out of unplanted trees held over the summer, bracken smothering and deer browsing all took their toll, and we have planted around 10,000 extra trees protected by 60 cm guards. This will stop the trees being smothered and give more protection from deer. The last compartments planted under the original plan (in autumn 2006) will be due for their five-year inspection in 2012, and are currently looking good.

The area known as Todcastles, at the southern limit of Carrifran on the long stony slope above the road towards Moffat, was purchased separately from the main valley (see Chapter 8) and was not included in the Woodland Grant Scheme funding from the Forestry Commission. In 2007, with funding from LloydsTSB bank, we planted 10,000 trees on this land, using 60 cm tubes and spraying the bracken by helicopter. This approach was chosen because of the dense bracken and the challenge of deer control. The planting was at lower densities than on the FC-funded areas and included a larger proportion of hazel than would have been allowed by them. This seemed a good opportunity to create an area of hazel-dominated woodland similar to a few native hazel woods on south facing slopes in the area.

We continue to plant oaks from acorns which were initially in short supply, and also extra aspen from isolated clones in steep ravines in the Southern Uplands. We have started to remove vole guards and in summer we can now sit in the dappled shade of trees, listening to woodland birds that have recently appeared. The focus of the hard work has shifted to the highest parts of the site, where we are attempting to establish treeline woodland and scrub. This part of the project is described in Chapter 11.

At Carrifran, we took a risk in planting trees without deer fences and with only very small individual tree protectors. We initially suffered a lot of browsing from deer and some from brown hare, and in the years when trees shared the valley with sheep (behind a temporary fence) escapees did browse some trees. Weed control was an issue until we began spot spraying in summer where the trees would be planted the following autumn. With more rigorous deer control effort (between 10 and 20 deer culled per year) tree growth has been good. We will be able to relax a bit more in a few years time, when all the planting compartments at Carrifran have received their second stage (establishment) payments. In the meantime, volunteer Boundary Wardens check that the fence is in good order, volunteers plant extra trees where needed and do various tasks to assist tree growth (including bracken control and deer culling) and to make the valley look more like a Wildwood – especially tree tube and vole guard removal.

He climbed every mountain!

10. Volunteers in the valley

*Grass-roots nature of the Wildwood initiative—back-room volunteers—website—
dirty-hands volunteers—monthly volunteer Sundays—visits by organised
groups—advice and recording by visiting experts—Tuesday volunteers working
with the Project Officer—weekend high planting camps—boundary wardens—
volunteer deer culling—sponsored walk—long-term volunteers.*

* * * * *

The Wildwood project, from its inception, was a grass-roots volunteer
initiative. Its development depended almost entirely on all the dreamers,
planners, searchers and fundraisers who generously contributed their
time and expertise. Volunteers come in many guises and their vast range
of background and attitudes ensures that we rarely have a dull occasion.
Most of these people got together very early on, as described in previous
chapters, and their combined efforts have carried forward the Carrifran
project.

When we bought Carrifran, our website www.carrifran.org.uk
was redesigned and set up by Pete Stewart, who then kindly serviced
it for several years. We felt that it was attractive and gave a wonderfully
clear impression of the nature of the project. However, technology had
moved on by 2008 and there were concerns about 'accessibility' of the
site and the need for it to conform to international norms, in an era
when these things loom large. It was with regret that we decided that a
complete reorganisation was needed. In the event, the process was both
interesting and rewarding. It was masterminded by volunteer and IT
specialist Simon Poots, who was convinced – to our surprise – that he
could find website designers prepared to construct the site for nothing,
given the prestige of a leading environmental project. His hunch proved
correct and two firms responded to the careful brief provided by Simon
after extensive discussion with members of the Steering Group. The
outlines they produced were both of high quality, but one seemed more

Left: Volunteers in the valley
Photos: contributed

169

Sunday volunteering

Getting up in the dark in winter, driving out of town as the light increases. Down through the Borders, wondering about the weather the other side of the watershed. Arriving at Carrifran to friendly faces, some old friends, others new to meet. Hearing of our tasks for the day – will it be up, down, along or what? Collecting tools, and perhaps trees, heavily laden, one foot in front of another until the theatre of operations is reached. Chatter en route to catch up on news with friends, or hear about the lives of others, or discuss what's happening at Carrifran, in Scotland or the world. Then comes the work: prepare the place of planting among the stones – it looks hopeless – then put in the little tree, replace the earth around it – and hope! Work and emotion rolled into one: this tiny little whip of a thing is carrying with it your hope for life, for growth to tree-dom, and for the whole future of this little part of an ecosystem which you are helping to re-create. Then on to the next one. And at the end of the day, tea and Fi's cake and a warm glow.

Liz Rogers

orientated towards commercial needs and we were unanimous that the other, by Zach Anthony of Cazinc, showed more understanding of the nature of our project. We decided to work with Zach, and were particularly pleased when he took the trouble to come down to Peebles with Simon to meet the relevant members of the Steering Group. Simon put in an enormous amount of time explaining our priorities and likes and dislikes to Zach, gathering images and distilling over-long text elements provided by Philip. The new Carrifran website duly went live in July 2008 and has had a very favourable reception.

Around the same time Peter Dreghorn drew us further into the IT age and set up the Wildwood Google Group (http://groups.google.co.uk/group/WWood), as a tool to co-ordinate the boundary wardens, post reports about activities in the valley and communicate with volunteers in general. Lots of photos and anecdotes have been posted on it over the years.

The purchase of the site brought an increasing level of professional input, mainly by the Project Officer and his line manager (the Director of BFT) but the volunteer members of the Steering Group and various informal subgroups have continued working in the background all the time. Complementing this, the actual dirty-hands work in the valley has involved hundreds of additional volunteers. Their contribution has been essential for the success of the project, even though the bulk of the planting has been done on contract. In this chapter we try to give the flavour of the volunteer effort, mainly through first-hand accounts by the people involved.

Our initial plans for volunteer work on site were focused on Sunday volunteer days. These were comparable to the event on 1st

Fear not, till Birnam wood do come to Dunsinane

January 2000, when members of the group, along with their friends, children and other supporters of the project, came to plant the first trees (see Chapter 8). From the start of 2000, volunteers have been turning up on the third Sunday of every month except July, August and December, mainly to plant trees, but also to bash bracken, repair paths, remove unneeded fences and generally clear up. The days are led either by the Project Officer or a volunteer, and although they can be quite tough, there is always an attempt to provide a range of tasks, suitable for people with different levels of energy and fortitude. Sometimes people spend half the day working and then go for a walk to see other parts of the valley. Numbers range from a handful up to 20 or 30, many people coming only once but others turning up occasionally or regularly over several years.

Organised groups sometimes turn up on volunteer Sundays and swell the numbers, but such groups often arrange with the Project Officer to come on a different day or for a whole weekend. These groups of volunteers, often from Edinburgh or Glasgow but sometimes travelling from as far afield as the Lake District or Newcastle, come under many different auspices. Student groups include the Forestry Society of Cumbria University at Newton Rigg and the Dirty Weekenders from Edinburgh University, but also groups from further afield, including students from the Czech Republic who spent two weeks planting trees and experiencing the worst of Scottish spring weather. The Lothian Conservation Volunteers, like-minded people getting together to do environmental work at the weekends, have come repeatedly and made major contributions to the planting. Professionals from NGOs such as RSPB, the John Muir Trust and the National Trust for Scotland have sometimes come on a weekday as a staff outing, and Hugh Chalmers has always been ready with suitable tasks for them. Commercial firms,

Leading volunteers

The third Sunday in the month is the time for the general public to volunteer. It tends to be wildly enthusiastic, large groups of environmental students like the Edinburgh University Dirty Weekenders or retired folks with walking backgrounds. They arrive with energy and expectation of leap-frogging Philip Ashmole up the hill (not even keeping up with him!) armed with tubes, saplings, canes, spears and mattocks. As the day progresses they are inspired and in awe of the project, at the same time wondering if they can be the first to depart and will it look bad if they do. Many come only once, but a core of hardy perennials does return, some of whom have planted several thousand trees.

At times I have attempted to involve colleagues from the NHS and found that both the notion and the work were very far from their expectations. For me the experience is about renewal, making a difference and as my own life declines, encouraging growth for the long term. One learns so much too, how holly trees need other trees around else they can keel over in the wind, the difference between cowberries, crowberries and cloudberries and how fieldfares can fly in flocks into gale force wind.

Peter Dreghorn

Volunteering in retirement

The great thing about retirement is that it allows you to do all those things you wanted to do when you were working, but didn't have time for. In my case, during all the years I worked in agricultural research I was a frustrated ecologist at heart, having trained originally in that line. I had inherited my father's love of nature and his special interest in birds, and I enjoy hillwalking. So I was greatly inspired by the vision of Carrifran Wildwood when I learned of it at the fund-raising stage, and my wife and I duly became Founders. I looked forward to helping plant native trees there in spectacular Borders scenery over many years. I was initially unaware that the great majority of trees were being planted by contract planters, but there was clearly plenty for volunteers to do. At first, I helped Hugh prepare things for the intensive tree planting by contractors at the end of 2003, and also with various tasks at other BFT project sites. Then, gradually, other regular volunteers started joining us – Jane in 2004, Stan (a retired forester) in 2005, Les (a retired civil servant) in 2006, Robin (a retired dentist) in 2007, and more, until in 2008 we often had nearer 10 folk at a time.

John Savory

All hands and ages to pull out the water gate, no longer needed
Photo: Hugh Chalmers

There are always jobs to do on Tuesdays

such as Lloyds TSB, Scandic Crown Hotels and Berghaus have also had volunteer work days at Carrifran for their staff. Schools have found it difficult to fit in a long drive and outdoor visit to the valley, but both Hawick High School and St. Joseph's College in Dumfries have contributed a lot of energy and enthusiasm (often involving getting wet in the burn at some point during the day).

A group from the Woodcraft Folk, a countrywide educational movement for children and young people, worked in the valley and camped nearby at Tibbie Shiels, while other groups have taken over one of the village halls in the area for the weekend. Some of the people who come with groups find themselves working in wild country for the first time in their lives, and many are startled by the scale of the project and the steepness of the slopes on which they have to plant trees. Explorer Scouts from Glasgow even camped during a high planting weekend (see Chapter 11).

Over the years, many other groups have come to see what is in the valley or what is going on there, but not to do hands-on work. Though not part of the ordinary volunteering effort, these groups contribute to the project since they tend to include specialists of one kind or another. We often learn a lot from them during the walks, and some contribute wildlife records afterwards. For example, in June 1998, before we bought the valley, the Botanical Society of Scotland held their alpine field meeting at Carrifran. They provided a list of the vascular plants recorded and David Long listed 179 species of mosses and liverworts. Other visits include those made by members of the Royal Scottish Forestry Society, Scottish Natural Heritage Upland Policy Group, Montane Scrub Action Group, delegates from the Society for Ecological Restoration conference in Liverpool, the Borders Farming and Wildlife Advisory Group, Inverness Forestry College students and the woodland group concerned with the Dumfries and Galloway Local Biodiversity Action Plan.

Another major and ongoing element in the Wildwood project is the Tuesday volunteer group. This is an informal group of individuals who come out to join the Project Officer in the valley on Tuesdays. Most people turn up nearly every week, in all weathers, and show an amazing commitment to Carrifran. For instance, Carl Moses, a mature student studying conservation management at Manchester University, but living in the Borders at Yetholm, spent every Tuesday during 2005 at Carrifran, bringing a lot of energy, humour and business experience to the group. Planting young trees has formed the core of the work of the Tuesday volunteers and its scale has been impressive. In winter 2008-09, for instance, the Tuesday volunteers planted more than 7000 trees high up in the valley. However, over the years they have also undertaken a wide

Choosing a planting spot which affords some protection to the sapling

Working with Hugh Chalmers

When the regular Tuesday volunteers gathered as usual at Carrifran at the end of November 2008, it was with some sadness because it was to be our last Tuesday with Project Officer Hugh Chalmers, who had led us so capably for the past five years, and who was moving to a new job. However, we were happy in the knowledge that his participation with Carrifran will continue, and the weather gave us one of those magic winter days with clear blue sky, no wind and fresh snow along the tops. From my first day with Hugh Chalmers, when we constructed an outdoor loo (now invisible in a thicket of willows) in a single visit, I never ceased to be impressed with his commitment and his organisational, practical and interpersonal skills. It was these skills that were vital in the establishment of Wildwood, and it was his stimulating and unobtrusive leadership that was responsible for the establishment of the regular Tuesday volunteer team. He took me to many nice places that I would never otherwise have gone to, and often in weather conditions when I would otherwise have stayed at home! Occasionally he even provided a welcome cooked addition to our packed lunches, and he initiated an 'annual treat' for us in the form of a nice meal in some local hostelry!

John Savory

Tuesday volunteering through a forester's eyes

To create a woodland that would have been on the site if people had never influenced the valley was something that even in my job as a Conservation Officer in the Forestry Commission I would never have been able to establish. My first experience of Carrifran was with Freya, my mountain rescue dog, in horizontal growling rain, compass useless on slate quarry, Firth Linn a white serpent in its black chasm, spewing out at Holly Gill. Another sunny day, so calm we could hear our dogs breathing, such were the differences. Since then we volunteers have come to know the glen in all its moods, day or night, more than just doing a job, discovering some of its secrets that had never been eliminated by man or have come back in since the fouling grazing ceased. Flowers and grasses tell us what range of species of trees should be suited to each piece of ground or left as open space and are hosting a growing list of insect types which in turn suits the birds and their predators. Building a snow igloo or in a tent at 450m and 700m beside black grouse lekking; a bivvy bag at the first planting of Firth Hope seeing four layers of stars at $-4^{\circ}C$; a summer snorkel swim with a stone loach on your palm, roe calf just so close, what is that bird or butterfly doing here, and the experiences go on!

Stan Tanner

variety of other tasks, including bashing bracken, removing old fencing, lugging materials uphill for our contract planters, improving paths in the Paddock, collecting seeds and aspen roots in relict woodlands near Carrifran, and anything else that Hugh (or his successor George Moffat) asked of them. Over the planting seasons, from late autumn through to early spring, the efforts of all volunteers (including those coming out on Sundays) have accounted for some 10% of all trees planted in the valley. Sometimes visiting groups or individuals come on Tuesdays to be shown the valley or to help with planting. John Savory comments that:

> *"One of the joys of being a regular volunteer is to see just how impressed such visitors always are with what they see. Above all, however, it is the gradual familiarisation with one of the most beautiful parts of southern Scotland, which can be stunning at any season, and the ability to see the woodland and fauna and flora there develop year by year, which brings its greatest rewards for the regular Carrifran volunteers. That and the fact that, despite our different backgrounds, we share a common vision, work well together and enjoy good crack."*

Every bit as challenging is the work done by volunteers (including some of the Tuesday group) who have taken part in the weekend planting camps at 650 m in Firth Hope, or have walked up on one or more of these weekend days, during the treeline planting described in the next chapter. More than one of these treeline planters travel up from England to brave the Scottish mountain weather. Dr Barbara Sumner, Editor of the Botanical Society of Scotland News, recently commented:

There are always jobs to do up high

"I'm lost in admiration for the heroic tree-planters who camped high up the glen in February. With that kind of dedication the long-term success of the project should be secure!"

Soon after the perimeter fence and some temporary internal fences were erected in 2000 to keep the grazing stock out of our planting areas, we realised that the fences would need to be regularly checked. Enter quite a different source of volunteers – hillwalkers. A few friends who were not especially interested in planting trees expressed interest in the idea of hillwalking with a purpose, so Myrtle set up the boundary warden scheme in mid 2001. In recent years it has been co-ordinated by Peter Dreghorn, who has made good use of the Google Group to recruit volunteers for the scheme and feed back the reports. The idea is that the whole boundary fence (and also some internal fences during the early years of the scheme) should be checked every month. This involves a walk of 13 kilometres (8 miles) on steep and rugged ground, almost all of it at over 450 m (1500 ft).

One of the initial motives for setting up the scheme arose from concern that our perimeter fence might pose a risk to birds. No data were available on collision rates with stock fences on open moorland, but there was worrying evidence that deer fences (mainly in conifer plantations) in the Highlands cause serious mortality of capercaillie, red grouse and black grouse. The latter two species are relevant to Carrifran and we were especially concerned about black grouse. We expected them to benefit from the ecological restoration that we were undertaking and it would be ironic if they then perished by hitting our fence. However, it seems that our fence does not kill significant numbers of grouse. During the 90 or so boundary inspections that have been done since the start of the project, no definite case of a fence strike by black or red grouse has come to light. Remains of one black grouse found near the fence had apparently been eaten by a fox, but this was near the lek and it is likely that the bird had been ambushed while displaying.

Altogether around 30 people have taken part in the boundary warden scheme, some of them doing a walk each year over several years. Their reports have been invaluable, alerting us to signs of sheep pushing under the wire and any other fencing problems, gathering sightings of deer or deer damage and providing a string of interesting wildlife observations. The boundary walk is easy enough on a summer day in good weather, but in winter – and sometimes at other seasons and with little warning – it can become quite an undertaking, and reports from wardens often record memorable walking conditions. A quick search through them comes up with the following:

Walking the boundary

I have been travelling from East Yorkshire to Moffat for a few years to complete the Carrifran boundary walk once or twice a year. This used to take me two days because of the internal fences which originally divided the area into four. Now there is just the perimeter fence, plus the two small deer exclosures. I usually do the walk anti-clockwise, partly because of the tall bracken on Dun Knowe. I carry a sickle and slash as much as my stamina allows, it being easier to cut when climbing. The walk takes me around six hours, depending on the conditions. GPS technology has made it much easier to identify any problem areas very precisely. The only bit I dislike is Rotten Bottom (well named); it can be tricky finding secure ground in very wet conditions. I rarely see anyone other than a distant contractor, and I have not seen a lot of wildlife. I surprised a fox once (I was surprised too!), and wild goats are fairly common (outside the fence). There are always buzzards, eating the voles, we hope. It is a good day out in an exciting place – all that growth going on.

Terry Holmes

Carrifran by a regular Volunteer

Though there have been tree planting projects nearer to home (Manchester), I've found none have the same scale or depth of vision as Carrifran. The idea of returning a rich variety of life to an entire denuded valley fired my imagination and a desire to be a small part of it, so I was attracted to the work parties, and have made regular trips north for a number of years. What's new there this time, or what has been seen? Conditions not always the ideal but still there's an odd pleasure to be had. Planting in the snow at Carrifran, a group of us struggling up the slopes above Holly Gill, bearing bags of trees, strong winds hurling spindrift and snowflakes through the sunshine into our watering eyes. Probing for soil in which to plant, and hurriedly distributing the contents of our tree bags before sliding down to the shelter of the lower valley. Mad but exhilarating. Alone at Firth Hope, staying on after a high planting weekend for a day of planting juniper, after days of grey, a day of warm sunshine – the first shirt sleeve day of the year and a day of contentment. A figure crosses the valley, pauses to check a map and continues for White Coomb. Did he notice the thickets of tree guards on the slopes and wonder what was going on? Would he return in future years to see what the valley had become?

Dave Bone

"It is good to know that the fence between Carrifran Gangs and White Coomb is capable of stopping an 11 stone man rucksack being blown to Selkirk!"

Raymond Handyside

"Great views of the Solway from Saddle Yoke. At the top the breeze had gone completely and every midge in the south of Scotland decided that we were lunch. As long as we kept moving it wasn't too bad. Rotten Bottom was a challenge – walk softly and think light thoughts."

Mike and Alison Baker

"I climbed over Dun Knowe to the top of Carrifran Gangs, by which time I could barely stand in the gale force wind. I decided conditions would be impossible once I turned the corner at White Coomb, when I would be walking straight into the wind and rain, so I returned the way I had come, thinking that perhaps it would have been more feasible if I had taken the clockwise route."

Terry Holmes

"This was a very 'interesting' descent as there was just enough snow to start you sliding nicely on the grass underneath. No problems with the fence but we were too busy trying to stay upright to be confident we would have noticed anything on the ground."

Mary

"By the time I was on Peat Hill snow was being blasted across the hill which was turning white by the time I'd got to the top of Saddle Yoke ..... By the time I'd finished lunch in the lee of the Saddle Yoke ridge I had turned white too. ... And so up to Firthhope Rig and White Coomb as another heavy snow shower arrived, every wire and every post up there laden with ice. The wires as thick as your thumb."

John Thomas

However, on the whole, the walk is enjoyed. Why else would they do it?

"What a great walk – and a lovely fence! We had a fantastic day, despite low cloud and mist (it stayed dry). We didn't even see into the valley. It took us six hours – we found the climb up hard going, but loved the easy walking on short grass all the way round."

Angus Miller

A less obvious group of volunteers are the people who go out with a rifle to help us cull the roe deer that endanger our young trees. Although a professional deer stalker is now employed to spend several days each month on the site (substituting for the missing lynx and wolves) several qualified voluntary stalkers also visit the site on pre-arranged dates to help search out intruding deer.

At their own pace, all the walkers reached the top of Saddle Yoke – some with a little help from the fence

Welcome refreshments at the end of the walk – while David Cairns (right), who has planted more trees at Carrifran than anyone else, looks on

Sponsored Walk

This was a challenging walk around the boundary of the property, ascending Peat Hill and Saddle Yoke to a high point of 821m at White Coomb, then turning back along Carrifran Gans to descend Dun Knowe: a good six hours, although Davy Cairns raced around in a personal best of just four and a half hours! We were lucky to get a wonderfully dry and bright October day, with tremendous views all around. Our target was £1000, and in fact, the twenty or so walkers raised more than double that. Some of the walkers were regular boundary walkers, while for others, it was their first time around the boundary. In fact, two walkers had thought that it was only a walk up the valley and back, and nearly backed out when they heard how high we were planning to go. Whether it was our persuasiveness or their foolhardiness, I don't know, but anyway, they made it halfway round and then back down the valley, which was quite an achievement for them.

Rosalind Grant-Robertson

In 2007, a group of hardy Wildwood supporters took part in a sponsored boundary walk. This was another occasion to introduce a variety of people to the valley and participants either did the complete circuit, or walked half way and then came back down the centre. It provided good opportunities to discuss the project with others and also proved to be a good fundraiser.

Yet another element in our volunteer effort is provided by several long-term volunteers, both from Britain and abroad, who have come for several weeks or months and worked alongside the Project Officer at Carrifran and at other Borders Forest Trust sites. The first was Anders Skoglund, a forestry student from the Agricultural University of Norway, who stayed for several months and in 2003 wrote a post-graduate thesis about the Carrifran project. Tim Allen, a petroleum geologist, spent several weeks with us between contracts over the years. As a keen walker with a large 4WD, he was particularly useful. Both Tim and Anders now work in Norway north of the Arctic Circle – perhaps Carrifran was a suitable training ground! In spring 2008 Simon Dunster came up from southern England to gain experience of hands-

Long term volunteering

I got to know about the project through its website. Immediately I had the feeling that this is exactly what I was looking for in order to do the internship as part of my course (International Forest Ecosystem Management, Fh Eberswalde, Germany).

No doubt, I was right. When I began as regular Tuesday volunteer, I was introduced to this great bunch of people led by Hugh Chalmers, my supervisor. It felt a bit funny in the beginning, as I was the only female and the youngest. Still had to get used to their speed and endurance. The first task, was taking down the deer fence. Followed by preparing the old fence line for spreading seeds (birch, rowan, hazel) collected at Carrifran. To get an overview of the tree establishment, we spread out to survey growth and general survival. Every day at Carrifran felt somehow special. Harmonic interaction of different people sharing this common sense of 'creation' while spending their time for overall benefit.

A very positive effect of being a long term volunteer is that you see the changes. Of course, the weather can be quite a challenge. Sometimes raining all day and sometimes sunbeams and blue sky. When the weather got too wild, the hovel gave shelter. There was never the feeling of pressure, probably as well due to Hugh's talent of dealing with people. It was a wonderful experience. Looking forward to visit the Carrifran valley and see those great people involved, again.

Nora Jauernig

Committed to Carrifran from Arctic Norway

I first became aware of Carrifran in 1999 and immediately became a Founder. By 2003 I was a committed volunteer, spending many days working in the valley, planting trees and sharing any of the other wide assortment of interesting (and often exhausting) tasks planned by Hugh Chalmers. Fortunately, my work offshore in the oil business allowed me plenty of free time during my weeks onshore away from the rigs. In early 2005, my work took me permanently to the Lofoten Islands in Arctic Norway – a place set in an area of amazing natural beauty. The extensive forests to be found here are mainly birch, with rowan, juniper and occasional aspen and willow, giving way to montane scrub. Not too dissimilar from what the upland Carrifran Wildwood will one day resemble. In several areas the forest is naturally regenerating as the pressure of sheep grazing has been reduced over what were once bare grass slopes. The forests on these mountainous islands are home to moose, reindeer and fox; even the occasional bear has been spotted. Over on the mainland, lynx and wolverine still roam. Sea eagles are a common sight. Living and working here in Lofoten, amongst this vibrant arctic forest, only served to enthuse me further in my support for Carrifran and determination to contribute in some small way, to the success of re-establishing a small part in my home country, of what I now see all around me everyday.

Tim Allen

on environmental work. He proved to be a tower of strength, helping Hugh with a multitude of jobs, including an emergency weekend repair of the boundary fence on Carrifran Gans after a small flock of sheep were found inside it. More recently, Nora Jauernig from Germany arranged a formal internship with BFT so that she could gain academic credit with her home institution for the work she did over here. She came with her partner and two-year old son, and Fi was able to arrange inexpensive accommodation for them in Innerleithen.

End of a wintry work day at Carrifran

11. Going up high

Loss of mountain woodland—raising awareness of treeline habitats—opportunities at Carrifran—the high level trial exclosure—completing the planting up to the valley rim—vegetation survey—preserving the flushes—paucity of knowledge—matching species to planting sites—advice from Forestry Commission—marginal conditions for trees in Firth Hope—fertiliser and tree protection—logistic challenges and solutions—volunteers and high planting camps—new site for treeline planting in Rispie Lairs—Forestry Commission support obtained.

* * * * *

From the early days of the Wildwood idea we were clear that our future site must include high land. In many parts of Britain lowland woods dominated by native species are relatively common – though not fully natural – but high altitude native woods are extremely rare. A few fragments survive on open hillsides, including the woods of dwarfed oaks in the Lake District that reach the 450 m contour and birchwoods that extend above 500 m in several parts of the Scottish Highlands. The latter are often heavily grazed and senile but sometimes include montane goat willow and rowan, as at Creag Meagaidh. More common are cliff faces adorned by precariously clinging trees which cause us to stop suddenly and grab a camera when driving around the Highlands, and the smaller remnants that can often be found in remote glens. These show the potential for many of our native trees to grow in high and exposed situations, and strongly imply the destructive role of browsing deer, sheep and goats.

Hardly anywhere, however, can one see a fully developed 'montane scrub' zone, the natural transition between the 'timberline' (above which trees are not upright in form and with good quality timber) and the prostrate heath of dwarfed heather and other shrubs found on some of the most exposed summits. Ecologists have long been conscious of

Left top photo: The first day of planting in Firth Hope
Photo: Hugh Chalmers

Left bottom photo: View from the high planting site
Photo: Hugh Chalmers

Next page photos:

Top: Sheep ensure that no regeneration occurs in this ancient birch wood high up near Ben Nevis

Bottom: Woodlands with a rich mix of species can sometimes survive in special places, even in denuded Scottish glens: this cliff in Glen Mama held oak, rowan, birch, hazel, holly and ivy.

this missing piece in our jigsaw of natural habitats, which we here refer to informally as the treeline zone. In 1996 – stimulated by a conference held as part of a Millennium Forest for Scotland project – professionals from a number of relevant organisations formed the Montane Scrub Action Group to promote awareness of this special habitat.

Carrifran, with its great range of altitude, offered us an exciting chance to recreate the full spectrum of natural habitats that would once have clothed the hills of southern Scotland, from wet woodland in the floodplain beside a meandering river (still an ambition at Carrifran) to dwarf woodland and montane scrub forming a natural treeline just below the summits of the hills. Official advice on the restoration of the treeline zone has generally been to encourage natural upward expansion of native woodlands already present lower down on the hills, or at the most to plant small clumps of trees and shrubs at high altitudes as future seed sources. This strategy is an attractive ideal since natural processes would play a major role, but the process is chancy and painfully slow. We decided that at Carrifran we must try to help it along by planting substantial numbers of trees and shrubs in a few areas high up around the valley. We wanted to show people – as soon as possible – that this missing habitat could be restored to the hills of southern Scotland

Accordingly, as soon as the main planting in the valley was well under way, we began thinking about establishing treeline woodland. In July 2001, after the end of the foot and mouth epidemic, the Ecological Planning Group spent a day in the hanging valley above the waterfall, an area we later called Firth Hope, which we had always thought was the ideal place. We marked out several sites for possible 'exclosures' – small fenced plots to protect young trees from mountain hares, deer and the sheep and goats that still had access to the area. We knew that establishing trees and shrubs at this sort of height would be difficult, and reckoned that a trial early on in the project, using a variety of species, would enable us to benefit from experience when planting a bigger area in due course.

In May 2002 we heard that a helicopter was going to be used by BFT contractors to lay out fence materials at Broadgairhill in the upper Ettrick valley only a mile or so distant, and arranged for a single inexpensive drop of materials beside the Little Firthhope Burn at 690 m, just below the summit of White Coomb. With strainer posts, stobs and netting in place, and young downy willows and other trees brought up on the quad bike, we were able to construct a 40 metre square exclosure that would keep out anything but a determined roe deer. It was made to straddle the burn (which runs southeast to northwest) and thus provide different degrees of exposure to sun, wind and drifting snow, as well as some variety of soils. About ten kinds of trees and shrubs were planted

The Montane Scrub Action Group

MSAG is an informal partnership of professionals supported by organisations concerned with woodland and scrub at high altitudes, especially Forestry Commission Scotland, Highland Birchwoods, Macaulay Institute, National Trust for Scotland, Plantlife, Scottish Agricultural College, Scottish Natural Heritage and Trees for Life; Borders Forest Trust has been represented in recent years by Hugh Chalmers or Philip Ashmole. The aim of the group is to help raise awareness of the rare tall shrub habitats around the climatic 'treeline' and to stimulate action for their restoration. The group has run meetings and published various reports and pamphlets, and also advises land managers. An informal journal, Scrubbers' Bulletin, is used to disseminate ideas and report on progress. In 2008 MSAG launched a Heritage Lottery-funded project 'Action for Mountain Woodlands' to expand the awareness-raising and also to co-ordinate restoration of montane scrub habitats in several parts of Scotland. This will advise and inform future projects, the most ambitious of which is the proposed conversion of 2000 hectares of high altitude conifer plantation to montane scrub in the moorland fringe of Galloway Forest Park.

and we gained confidence from the fact that many of them survived at this extreme height, though their growth was naturally slow.

Constructing an exclosure at 690 m to see which trees would grow up there

Firth Hope (left) and Carrrifran Gans separated by the Little Firthhope Burn; the exclosure is below the peat haggs at top left

Over the next few years the priority was on planting lower down, but when work on treeline woodland got back on the agenda we realised that there was a fill-in job to be done. In about 2001, at a time when a good many of our planted trees seemed to be in trouble as a result of foot and mouth delays and deer browsing, we had got cold feet about the highest grant-aided planting that we had planned within the valley rim. This was to extend above the 600 m contour on the steep grassy slopes below Carrifran Gans between Gupe Craig and Broomy Gutter, and also right at the head of the valley west of Firthhope Linn. The worry was that if several hectares of planting at this altitude failed, we would have to pay back the grant, with interest. We therefore arranged an amendment to our Woodland Grant Scheme contract, pulling back the upper edge of the planting to a more prudent height. Five years on, however, with renewed confidence that our trees lower down were becoming established, some

fast footwork by Hugh Chalmers secured funding in season 2007/08 from a special one-year interim scheme introduced by the Forestry Commission after the sudden closure of their main grant scheme. This enabled us to plant the most promising parts of the deferred area.

The planting on the rim of the valley west of Firthhope Linn was especially important, since it provided a link between the native woodland developing lower down the glen and the treeline woodland and montane scrub that we hoped to establish in Firth Hope. This hanging valley is invisible from most of the rest of the site but offers up to 30 hectares of ground between the 600 m and 750 m contours. The latter height is roughly that at which one can see a transition from a non-natural and mainly grassy sward to a true montane, wind-clipped moss-heath of mat-forming plants such as woolly-fringe moss (*Racomitrium*), blaeberry and stiff sedge.

We had to consult SNH about planting in Firth Hope. After a site visit, they concluded that the 'anthropogenic' grassland produced by centuries of grazing offered little conservation value in its present state; they were therefore relaxed at the idea of our establishing treeline woodland on it. Within the grassy area, however, there were a number of enriched springs or 'flushes' with some of the special montane plants that were a prime reason for designating this part of the Moffat Hills as a Site of Special Scientific Interest. We suggested surveying the vegetation and mapping the special flushes, so that we could mark them and arrange for our planters to avoid putting trees nearby. SNH agreed to fund the survey, which was carried out by Stuart Adair, a Wildwood Group member and professional vegetation surveyor.

Scottish Natural Heritage asked us not to plant trees near calcareous flushes where some special plants occur

The difficulty in trying to re-establish treeline woodland and scrub on Scottish mountains is that so little is known about what these habitats were originally like. However, it was fairly obvious that we should not aim at continuous cover in an exposed site like Firth Hope with many patches of wet peat, and there would obviously be places where no woody shrubs could be expected to grow. The choice of species was based on the idea that natural treeline habitats would have been diverse, each species occurring at the highest elevations at which it could

Ecological Planning Group in Firth Hope

Dwarf birch

Dwarf birch, a spreading shrub up to one metre tall, is an attractive and rare species much in need of conservation, which we would like to see at Carrifran. However, we failed to convince Scottish Natural Heritage that it was appropriate. We did not include it in our initial plans, since it has not been found in the Southern Uplands recently, but it still grows near Glasgow and in north Northumberland and Cumbria. It was once present in Lanarkshire and an old record for Peeblesshire was confirmed when Crinan Alexander found an 1855 specimen from near Innerleithen in the herbarium of the Royal Botanic Garden Edinburgh.

Dwarf birch occurs on wetland heaths and blanket bogs up to high altitudes, but has been severely affected by grazing and burning so its natural distribution is unknown. Our request to plant it in Firth Hope fell foul of the fact that Carrifran is not only a Site of Special Scientific Interest but also a Special Area of Conservation under the European Habitats Directive. We were informed that since dwarf birch was not mentioned in these designations as a feature of the area: "this proposed introduction of Betula nana *spp[sic] nana could be damaging to the interests of the SSSI and could compromise the integrity of the SAC." Sadly, that seems to be the end of the matter.*

Checking soils above the cloud sea

cope with the low temperatures and exposure and also avoid being outcompeted by other plants.

About 30 species of trees and shrubs have been recorded growing naturally at or above 600 m in Britain, but some of these (especially certain willows) are confined to calcareous sites and would not be suitable for Carrifran. Obvious candidate trees for Firth Hope were downy birch, rowan, aspen, montane goat willow, bird cherry, hazel, hawthorn and holly (marginal). Scots pine was also a candidate, but was vetoed for Firth Hope by SNH, although they agreed that it could be planted elsewhere in the valley. Shrubs that we thought would be suitable included juniper, several willows (eared, grey, downy, dark-leaved, tea-leaved and creeping), dwarf birch (but this was also given a thumbs down by SNH – see Box), burnet rose, honeysuckle, ivy, raspberry, stone bramble, broom, whin and perhaps petty whin.

We soon decided that the drier parts of Firth Hope, including the steep rocky slopes below Firthhope Rig, should have juniper-dominated scrub, with smaller numbers of downy birch and rowan. The growth form of junipers is largely inherited, so we made an effort to collect some of our seed from low-growing plants in the highest stands we could find reasonably close to Carrifran, including one near Peebles and one on a windswept saddle in the Pentland Hills. As a result, we had some seedlings with more or less prostrate growth form, well suited to the most exposed parts of the site. These could eventually form a more or less continuous canopy just above ground level.

The central hollow in Firth Hope, which is damp and peaty, seemed appropriate for eared willow, which is tolerant of moderately acid conditions and which may emerge as the dominant species in much of the lower part of this high valley. This eared willow habitat is likely to develop a rich field layer of tall herbs; it should extend up damp

peaty gullies and also occur in scattered patches in peaty hollows among the junipers higher up. Permanently wet areas at low levels are suitable for clumps of grey willow, and drier spots have montane goat willow, downy birch and aspen.

The steep slopes, both around the lowest part of Firth Hope and higher up along the channels of the Firthhope Burn and Little Firthhope Burn, are generally better drained and offer a variety of aspect as well as some shelter. Here a more diverse mix is appropriate, including larger numbers of downy birch and rowan along with the juniper, and limited numbers of hazel, holly, hawthorn and even a few sessile oak are being tried in relatively sheltered places with a partly southern aspect. Montane goat willow and aspen are associated with rocky outcrops and small numbers of bird cherry are being planted in wetter places. Some of the smaller shrubs listed above will also be tried on these slopes eventually.

Dwarf birch, here growing in Glen Muick, was vetoed for planting at Carrifran

On the steep slopes on the southeast side near the bottom of Firth Hope there are some damp rocky sites where the vegetation shows signs of enrichment. These offer a chance to establish the more demanding montane willows, especially downy willow, but with some tea-leaved willow and dark-leaved willow. In these places there are many small landslips and eroded patches, offering the bare soil and gravel suitable for germination of willow seeds, so that once a few bushes are established, natural regeneration may enable the willow clumps to spread.

We initially hoped to get support for this high level planting from the Forestry Commission, but it was always clear that we would be lucky to succeed, since establishing scattered shrubs and dwarf trees at unusually high altitudes could never be considered as 'real forestry'. However, our application was taken seriously and senior staff climbed up to Firth Hope with us on a site visit, so we didn't lose hope.

However, more significant in the long run was an offer from the Commission to pay for a visit by their soils specialist, Bill Rayner, who spent a day with us in November 2005. He dug test holes with his rabbiting spade, carefully dug up and examined a couple of our birches at lower levels that didn't seem to be thriving, patiently answered penetrating questions from members of our group and gave trenchant advice on the silvicultural approach that we should use in Firth Hope. In his report he provided detailed and helpful notes on the different parts

A long distance volunteer

One of the most remarkable contributions to this planting has been by faithful Wildwood supporter Chris Curry, who came repeatedly from Plymouth to take part in the high planting weekends in 2007 and 2008, walking up on both the Saturday and Sunday each time until the weekend in May 2008, when he joined the overnight camp – his first wild camping experience for many years. We don't ask Chris to work out whether the carbon footprint associated with the drives from Plymouth is fully offset by the trees he plants – we just appreciate his extraordinary commitment to the project.

Trees – and volunteers – would be exposed to tough conditions in the high exclosure and elsewhere in Firth Hope
Photo: Hugh Chalmers

of Firth Hope and the opportunities and problems that they presented. However, there was a sting in the tail, since his final comment was:

> *"I have no doubts to the commitment and resolve of members of the Carrifran Wildwood Project to establish this wood. But, I am not sure if the fiscal critera required by the Scottish Forestry Grant Scheme (SFGS), as I understand them, allow sufficient time and flexibility for the establishment of these high elevation plantings."*

Bill also suggested that we would be wise to ensure that our lower planting was fully established before attempting anything too ambitious at higher levels. It was no surprise, therefore, when our application for SFGS support stalled. In the end, although we did not get funding for the high planting from the Forestry Commission, we determined to push ahead, having confidence in the eventual success of our planting lower down, even though trees in some areas were growing slowly. Furthermore, as we faced up to the logistics of planting in Firth Hope we quickly realised that the failure to get grant support might be a blessing in disguise. Although we now had to raise money to do the job, we would be free to plant the various kinds of trees gradually as suitable stock became available, and to plant at densities and in patterns that suited us, rather than having to adhere to the rules that Bill Rayner had realised would cause problems for us.

In discussing our proposed planting in Firth Hope, Bill had been adamant that we should give the saplings a good start. He recommended screefing around each planting site and then digging down deep enough to reach mineral soil, breaking up any hard pan and mixing in a dose (about 100 grams) of P-K fertiliser. Phosphate and potash would promote the development of the root system, crucial to survival in this tough environment, but nitrogen was not advisable since it encourages tender leafy growth. We eventually followed this advice, using a granular fertiliser based on rock phosphate from North Africa and muriate of potash mined about eight miles down off the Yorkshire coast! We had hesitated over the fertiliser decision because of our general reluctance to do anything to the ground at Carrifran that might even out the conditions in different parts of the site and so reduce the diversity of the forest that we were aiming to create. In Firth Hope, however, we would be planting nursery-grown saplings of several species higher up than they currently grow anywhere in Scotland. If we enabled them to get through the first year or so, we could find out whether they were capable of growing and surviving in this challenging environment. This experience could then be used to guide other attempts to establish semi-natural treeline woodland.

The Forestry Commission also provided us with the climatic data used in 'Ecological Site Classification' (discussed in Chapter 7) which enables foresters to know what tree species – if any – are appropriate for planting in any given place. The 'DAMS' scores, indicated by the colours in the diagram, are an index of exposure (windiness) and the 'ATT' scores (not shown) are a measure of accumulated temperature. As we had hoped, the scores for both measures in different parts of Firth Hope

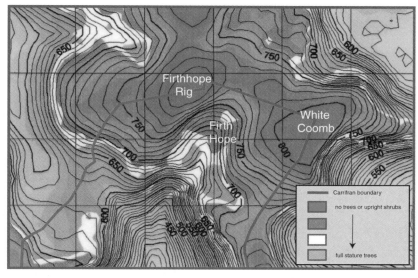

Will Firth Hope one day become the highest wood in southern Scotland? (Information on potential tree growth courtesy of the Forestry Commission)

bracketed the range where growth of trees and shrubs just might – or might not – be possible. This meant that our planting should result in the creation of a genuine climatic treeline, with small trees of several species in the most favorable areas, low-growing shrubs in more exposed areas and the latter giving way to the unplanted mat-like heath in places where no upright woody plant can survive. The situation could be fluid, however, since over a long timescale, mutual shelter provided by the hardiest plants might result in a gradual spread of slightly less hardy species into higher and more exposed places.

Protection of the young trees in Firth Hope from browsing by mountain hares or deer has been an ongoing concern, with no simple solution. In the first year we organised the on-site construction of half height rabbit-wire shelters supported by canes. These were effective for junipers, but the process was laborious. Vole guards are hard to fit on such spreading plants and since juniper is not very attractive to herbivores we eventually decided that we could probably get away with planting this species without protection. For other trees and shrubs we experimented with open-mesh short tree tubes, but the extreme exposure often blew them over and we came to doubt whether they were worthwhile. However, voles are often abundant in Firth Hope, so all species apart from juniper have been given vole guards as a minimum. Tree protection materials were paid for by a special grant from the Konrad Zweig Trust, who had helped us from the beginning of the Wildwood project.

We always realised that planting thousands of trees between 600 and 750 m in Firth Hope would present major logistic challenges. In the event, it has become a triumph, since the challenges were of just the kind that our then Project Officer, Hugh Chalmers, was best at dealing

Even in our high exclosure, fenced against hares, roe deer could occasionally get in and fray the downy willows

189

Heavy loads going up soon after dawn
Photo: Hugh Chalmers

Making the best use of the hire of a crawler tractor

with. It takes most people a full hour and a half to walk up to Firth Hope from the car park and almost as long to walk down, taking a big chunk out of a short Scottish winter day. Hugh's solution was to organise weekend planting camps at 650 m (>2100 feet) in Firth Hope, so that volunteers could walk up on a Saturday morning and work through into the evening and during most of Sunday, going down just before dark.

We could expect campers to carry up their own kit, but it wasn't realistic to expect them also to take up trees, tools, fertiliser and tree guards. Quad bike access to Firth Hope is just possible (though not through Carrifran glen) but ferrying so much material up there on a quad was not a practical option, so a helicopter seemed the obvious solution. In the first season we obtained a grant from the Scottish Mountaineering Trust to pay for a helicopter flight, but finding a day with both favourable weather and an available helicopter proved frustratingly difficult. After many cancellations the helicopter finally arrived a few days after Christmas 2006 and started by making some useful drops high up on Peat Hill where access was difficult. However, Philip then had the infuriating experience of being given a ride in the helicopter to point out the drop site in Firth Hope, only to find that the mission was foiled by cloud that came down to exactly the level that made it unsafe for the helicopter to get to the site, although this was in full view. It was a month later, with the first weekend camp imminent, before we were able to get the helicopter back, and the bill for the two visits was nearly £3000.

A generous private donation covered the extra cost for that spring, but in the following season, when faced with even higher bills for helicopter hire, we remembered that there was a track through the forestry plantation just to the east of Carrifran that gave potential access to an overland route to Firth Hope. Hugh arranged with the relevant forestry company for us to repair a washout on this track, making it passable for a crawler tractor that we had occasionally hired to take materials up steep slopes within Carrifran valley. When it arrived, the driver soon realised that three trips would be needed, and the final return down frighteningly steep slopes on the east of Carrifran Gans was in darkness. It was quite a day, but the total cost was well under £1000 and the track was still passable for use in spring 2009.

The camps themselves ran in three years, starting with mid February, mid April and mid May 2007; in 2008 there was also a March weekend and in 2009 there was camping in March and April. Before the first camps, special appeals for volunteers were made by leaflet, on the website and in person, and over the three years over 30 person-nights by hardy people have been clocked up in Firth Hope. Many other people have walked up on one or more of the weekend days to join the planting effort, but it is always a bit embarrassing to arrive around midday on a Sunday and realise that the campers have already been at work for many hours.

The weather has not yet forced us to cancel any of these high camps, but conditions have often been severe. In 2007 extra shelter was provided by a small geodesic dome, coincidentally designed by one of the campers, Paul Henry. However, the dome eventually suffered under the stress of the high winds and in 2008 we bought a mountain tent to serve as a base where planters could relax and Hugh could dispense hot drinks. The high camp weekends enabled volunteers to plant around 9000 trees in Firth Hope over three years, a remarkable achievement under difficult conditions. The total has been brought up to about 11,000 trees and shrubs by planting left-overs at the end of each season by a couple of our regular contractor planters; for them also, it must represent an extreme planting site.

The second site for establishment of treeline woodland and scrub is Rispie Lairs, a shallow but impressive east-facing corrie scooped out below the summit of Saddle Yoke. It lies mainly between the 500 and 650 metre contours, and together with the scree slopes below Priest Craig to the north provides potential for a maximum of perhaps 14 ha of treeline woodland. This seemed an ideal site to establish juniper-dominated

High camp diary

Tree planting at 700 metres in some of the wildest hills of the Scottish Borderlands was an opportunity not to be missed as a keen mountaineer and tree-lover. Some may say these hills are not mountains, as they have no sgurrs and stobs. Yet the area between Hart Fell and White Coomb has enough Craigs to give a real mountain flavour.

A band of hardy planters set up the first high camp in the lovely coire of Firth Hope, between Firthhope Rig and White Coomb, on a bitterly cold morning in February 2007. It remained subzero for most of the weekend, 'tho the wind was light and the sun shone as we planted juniper. The rhythm seemed easy to find and there is a certain special, hard to define quality in planting in such a wild location. The views from the summit of White Coomb at sunset were astonishing; westwards the Solway shone and Criffel was plainly visible. The second high camp in April was a different affair. Again we were blessed with cloudless skies, but this time about twenty degrees warmer. How different from February, when we tried to dig a snow hole! At night as I lay in my sleeping bag looking at the stars, I imagined my son walking these hills enjoying the juniper and willow that will colonise these crags and boggy hollows and feel glad that I had a tiny part to play.

Paul Henry

Explorer scouts

Explorer Scouts Dylan, Harry, William and Colin, of 30th Inverleith Explorer Scouts, Edinburgh, had hiked in along the Carrifran Burn to a steepening ascent towards Firthhope Linn, the magnificent waterfall beyond Gupe Craig. Reaching the angled high ground, every unnecessary ounce of kit becomes a burden to be noted with muttered curses for future expedition planning! Beyond, the head of the waterfall gives way to flatter ground at last. The tents go up by the crystal waters of Firthhope Burn. We quickly join in the planting: cutting into frosty bog-rush to expose soft peat over mineral soil;

a handful of gritty fertiliser; and a seedling firmed into the barren hillside. Work settles into a routine, to the banter of Explorer Scouts forever seeing the funny side of life under arduous conditions, and the camaraderie of volunteer workmates. The hillside flares in the glow of a late afternoon sunset and with dusk it's time to down tools.

Stars pierce the inky black sky with a clarity unimaginable in town. Later on, a full moon illuminates the mountain for a surrealistic midnight walk onto White Coomb summit. By departure time the following afternoon, the hillside is transformed. With eyes now open to all the planting that can be seen on the way down, we visualise the future wildwood. We long to see it and feel great to be part of it!

Ed Mackey, Leader

woodland similar to NVC woodland type W19, which typically also includes downy birch and rowan, and sometimes also Scots pine.

One of Hugh Chalmers' last achievements, shortly before moving to a new job in late 2008, was to organise a planting grant for Rispie Lairs under the new Scotland Rural Development Programme (SRDP). The scheme has had some teething problems and application is an arduous online process, but Hugh was guided through it by one of our local Forestry Commission Woodland Officers and approval came through just in time for planting in the 2008/09 season. Since the area is so marginal in forestry terms we felt it was sensible to start by using only the best ground, planting 7,200 trees in 4.5 hectares. Given the funding, we were able to get the work done by another of our contractors, who was able to get materials up with a quad bike but was then held up by frozen trees and frozen ground for many weeks around midwinter. In future years, and probably without grant aid, we shall soften the edges of the planting area by adding extra trees at low density in patches round about.

CHAPTER 11. GOING UP HIGH

*Delivery was by helicopter but now
it is up to the volunteers*
Photo: Peter
Dreghorn

From this distance, Rispie Lairs does not look plantable

Seat of Ravens

Who comes unseen to Caer-y-fran?
No-one, the ravens say
For they began their daily scan
When glaciers barred the way.

Did crags reflect ancestral croaks?
Twelve thousand years ago
As summits shed their icy cloaks
Only the ravens know.

Did reindeer on the lichens graze?
Nine thousand years ago
When birk and hazel clothed the braes
Only the ravens know.

Did yew bow break as they flew by?
Six thousand years ago
Did hunter die 'neath wintry sky?
Only the ravens know.

Did trees decay and seedlings fail?
One thousand years ago
As sheep and goats patrolled the dale
Surely, the ravens know.

Did shepherds by the shielings sit?
Five hundred years ago
As cows were milked and midges bit
Only the ravens know.

Millennium Day! Did they watch then?
A short ten years ago
When trees reclaimed Carrifran glen
Of course, the ravens know.

Will they stand by on rock strewn hill?
Some fifty years from now
To take their fill from lynx's kill
We shall, the ravens vow.

Will they yet hear, for some to fear?
A century from today
Howl of the wolf from hillside near
Perhaps, the ravens say.

Will eagles soar o'er ancient oaks?
In time still far away
As crags reflect protesting croaks
They may, the ravens say.

None come unseen to Carrifran glen
Now, or on future day
For Wildwood is in ravens' ken
And ravens still hold sway.

PA

12. Watching changes

Ten years of change—woodland development—fixed point photography—recording biological changes—a series of bird surveys—continuing the work of restoration—enrichment planting—extending the planting at treeline—woodland plants—coping with climate change—allowing nature to take over—the wider vision—another walk into the valley.

* * * * *

After Millennium Day, change came quickly to Carrifran. The little clump of trees planted on January 1st – christened the Millennium Grove – was soon joined by groups of hazels and willows along the route across the Paddock, from the site for our discreet car park up to the sheepstell. All these trees had been growing in volunteers' gardens for several years and were already rather big for planting out.

The major changes, however, came when we started our contract planting and erection of the first of the internal fences needed to protect the trees. By the end of April, more than 30,000 trees had been planted, an extraordinary achievement by Project Officer Hugh Chalmers, newly in post. Fencing the whole perimeter of the valley followed in the summer, along with construction of the car park and the two temporary deer exclosures, one of which was next to the track up the valley.

In the absence of deer, sheep and goats from the fenced areas, we soon began to discover a few regenerating rowans emerging from the dense herb layer, and some of the surviving old trees within them put out dense clumps of suckers. Even more exciting was the first time we noticed our willows producing seed, only two years after being planted. Then came the first rowan berries, and as the years have passed, more and more of the planted trees have become mature enough to produce seeds. Ten years on, we are still waiting to see the first acorns and the first seeds on planted ash and elm, but have already found berries or seeds on planted rowan, bird cherry, hazel, dog rose, blackthorn, downy birch,

> *"Into the woods,*
> *Each time you go,*
> *There's more to learn*
> *Of what you know."*
>
> Stephen Sondheim and James Lapine (1987)

195

One of only three surviving ivy clumps at Carrifran, in 1999 and ten years later

alder, holly, juniper, eared willow, bay-leaved willow, downy willow, grey willow, tea-leaved willow, broom and guelder rose. Aspen has not yet produced seeds (this tree flowers rarely in Scotland) but some of our planted aspens now have suckers coming up around them and so will soon be the centres of little clumps of trees.

We are not the only people watching changes at Carrifran. It was pleasing to see, on the cover of the 2006 edition of the Ordnance Survey Explorer Map of the Moffat area, a photograph of two walkers in the snow high up at Carrifran. Looking inside, however, we were startled to find the whole of our main planting area in the valley coloured green and indicated as deciduous woodland. Planting of the last part of this area was completed only in December 2006, so we can only assume that the Ordnance Survey have access to Forestry Commission grant records. We're happy at their optimism, but sympathise with those walkers seeking woodland walks, who may arrive and find that many of our trees are barely knee-high!

A more realistic official measure of progress is provided by the second-stage payments under the Woodland Grant Scheme, made after five years if the trees are considered established. As explained in Chapter 9, we did not want to be caught by surprise at the time of the inspection by the Forestry Commission Woodland Officer, so we monitored the condition of the trees as we went along and did extra planting when needed. At the time of writing we have received establishment payments on 140 hectares of new native woodland – about half of the total area planted under the scheme – and should be able to claim the rest over the next four years, although trees in some areas are slow growing.

Photographs can give a more immediate indication of progress. Soon after the purchase we therefore set up a series of photographic monitoring points, located by GPS, to record the growth of the Wildwood over the coming decades. David Geddes, the most expert photographer in the group, suggested sticking to 35 mm slide film rather than using digital cameras. He and Philip made a preliminary trip in June 2000, taking several wide-angle shots. Later in the year Philip set up about 30 sites around the valley. The first few photographs were taken at a focal length of 28 mm but subsequently 50 mm was normally used. A planned expansion of the scheme during 2001 was disrupted by foot and mouth disease, but another dozen sites were added. Many of the points are high up, in places that will not show significant change for a long time, and many were taken in late autumn, but repeat shots taken from some of the lower points in early 2009 speak for themselves.

We realised that while these photos would be a good way of showing the progress of woodland development, they would not tell us much about changes in the fauna and non-tree flora of the valley.

View from the sheepstell on fundraising launch day in 1998 and ten years later

Hazel Linn in 1999, with a few surviving trees, and in 2009 (the large birch in the left foreground had fallen over)

The boardwalk in 2000 and in 2009 (the birches in the background will eventually conceal the conifer plantation)

Black grouse

Black grouse numbers have declined in southern Scotland, but at Carrifran they seem to be increasing. In this species, the larger males (blackcocks) compete with each other for the attention of females (greyhens) at display grounds or 'leks'. Before BFT bought Carrifran, a few blackcocks had displayed near the road, but we now know of two leks much higher up, on grassy ridges overlooking each side of the valley. We found one in March 2006, from footprints and wing feather marks in snow, and the other in April 2008, from accumulated droppings and feathers. In May 2008 and in April 2009, two of us camped on the same night, one at each lek. The numbers of blackcocks attending the leks the next morning were seven and two, respectively, in 2008, and eight and three in 2009. These two leks are of particular interest, partly because they are among the very highest in Britain, and partly because they are situated on the boundary fence and cocks actually spar with each other through the fence. However, despite the known risk of collision mortality that fences can pose to flying grouse, no evidence of such mortality has been found. Correspondence with other ornithologists suggests that blackcocks' apparent use of fences at leks is not uncommon.

John Savory

These were likely to be substantial after removal of grazing and browsing stock from the whole of the site and the planting of trees and shrubs in half of it. The results of systematic monitoring of changes in flora and fauna are of great interest to ecologists, and we also knew that everyone involved with the Wildwood project would want to know what effects it was having. Clearly, if we were to detect change, we needed to know what the situation was at the start, so we planned various types of base-line assessment. For this work, we relied mainly on the considerable experience within the group and the expertise of visitors who contributed data. Numerous volunteers supplied natural history records, and we paid for some professional vegetation surveys. Ground-living and flying invertebrates were recorded and some moth trapping was done, as explained in Chapter 6.

We have not yet attempted repeat surveys of the vegetation or most of the animals, but we do have some information on butterflies and birds. Stan Tanner has made systematic observations on butterflies from 2005 onwards. The species list now stands at 16, the most notable records being of small pearl-bordered and dark-green fritillaries and Scotch argus, with small copper and common blue apparently also new for the 10 km map square containing Carrifran. Other additions to the list in Chapter 6 are large white and painted lady. Stan has the impression that many of the species are increasing in abundance, perhaps in response to the more luxuriant ground vegetation that has developed since grazing animals were removed.

Birds are a special case, as systematic surveys undertaken in most summers since Carrifran was selected as the Wildwood site provide numerical information already spanning 12 years. This work is one of the key contributions made by volunteers at Carrifran. The procedure is based on the Breeding Bird Survey of the British Trust for Ornithology, modified to take account of the large altitudinal range within Carrifran. It involves two observers walking three transects of about 2 km in May and again in June, identifying and counting birds seen or heard. The surveys were initiated by Peter Gordon, who as RSPB representative in the Borders was involved with the Wildwood idea from the beginning, and in recent years they have been conducted by John Savory and Joanna Thomson. A special feature of the work is that in 2000, 2007 and 2009 'control' surveys were done in the adjacent valley of Black Hope, which resembles Carrifran in landform but is still grazed and unplanted. The survey data are given in Appendix A, while the black grouse population of Carrifran is discussed in the Box.

Changes in the bird populations of Carrifran as a result of tree planting can be judged by comparing the results of the early surveys (1998, 2000 and 2002) when sheep were present and there were few trees, with those of the most recent surveys (2007, 2008 and 2009) when many trees had been planted and there were no sheep (see Appendix A). Data of this kind always show high variability, but trends in some species are now becoming clear and contrast with the situation in Black Hope. John Savory emphasises the striking change in the wheatear, which shows a marked decline at Carrifran while numbers at Black Hope have been maintained or even increased. Wheatears typically live in open grassland with a short sward, and their feeding areas and nest sites (usually among rocks) have doubtless been reduced by the growth of ground vegetation following removal of herbivores from Carrifran. In contrast, the scrubland species stonechat and whinchat have both become relatively common in Carrifran, while remaining respectively scarce and absent at Black Hope. There are apparent declines in skylark and ring ouzel, but in the latter this may reflect a wider national trend.

Woodland birds are now flooding back into Carrifran as their habitat develops. There are marked increases in willow warbler and chaffinch and a hint of an increase in wren, while other woodland species – dunnock, blackcap, garden warbler, lesser redpoll and siskin – have been recorded during the surveys in the last year or two. Reed bunting and grasshopper warbler have also established themselves in scrub near the mouth of the valley (though this does not show up in the surveys) woodpigeons are commonly seen and there have been recent observations of sedge warbler and several species of tits. In general, the observed changes in the bird species are consistent with predictions made by Peter Gordon in the 1999 Carrifran Wildwood Environmental Statement. A full list of birds recorded from Carrifran is on the project website **www.carrifran.org.uk.**

The tenth anniversary is a good time to assess achievements at Carrifran, but not a good time to call a halt to restoration work. During the years since the main scheduled planting was completed in winter 2006/07, volunteer planters have been working hard enriching the planted areas. Groves of hawthorn and especially of hazel, a species probably present in large numbers in the pristine wildwood, have been added in various parts of the valley, along with more scrub willows and a number

A blackcock taking a rest from displaying at a rival through the fence
Photo: John Savory

Wing tips of displaying Blackcock (Thorburn painting) *leave traces when there is snow*
Photo: John Savory

Wood anemones survived in many parts of Carrifran, but at 700 m in Firth Hope they are often pink

Oblong woodsia, one of the rarest ferns in Britain, has been reinstated at Carrifran

of other species that we felt needed better representation in the developing woodland. In carrying out this planting we are trying to avoid simply filling in gaps with the extra trees, but instead are using the opportunity to ensure that the spacing of trees is as close as possible to natural irregular patterns. This work will be carried on in the future, though probably on a gradually diminishing scale, since natural regeneration can be expected to increase and we want to allow natural processes gradually to take over the work of restoration.

In Chapter 11 we described the efforts to establish treeline woodland in Firth Hope and Rispie Lairs, but we do not feel that this should be the end of our high level planting. As mentioned in that chapter, we have recently concluded that before domestic stock and goats had cleared the trees from the hills of the Southern Uplands, the woodland dominated by oak and ash at low and medium levels may have been complemented by a band of treeline woodland composed mainly of downy birch, aspen, montane goat willow and rowan. Woodland of this kind can be found in many places in the Highlands, a good example being at 450 m on the steep north slopes of Creag Dhubh on Speyside. Our current planting should lead to development of a community rather like this around the top of Firthhope Linn, but we would like to see it extended to other parts of the rim of the valley. Apart from the species mentioned, hazel, holly and hawthorn would be included in places, with bird cherry and shrub willows in damp gullies. Open spaces in the woodland would have clumps of juniper and along the upper edge there would be a transition to juniper-dominated scrub, with willows taking over in the wetter parts.

As the effort to plant trees and shrubs diminishes, we shall be able to pay more attention to smaller plants of the woodland floor. Some have survived against the odds. Wood anemone may once have been mainly a woodland plant, but can flourish in open ground under an extraordinary range of conditions. The bluebell (wild hyacinth) which is a plant typical of upland oakwoods (especially NVC type W11) hung on at Carrifran in small numbers, mainly under bracken, while wood-sorrel survived in many shady places in rock clefts and under relict trees; these plants will doubtless become more widespread as the canopy closes in areas where trees have been planted most densely.

However, many plants characteristic of mature woodlands and adapted to deep shade must have been lost from the valley along with the trees. Some of these may re-colonise naturally, but many have poor dispersal mechanisms and rarely become established in restored or newly created woods that are not adjacent to ancient woodland. It may therefore be appropriate to give some of them a helping hand, when shady habitats

High level woodland at Carrifran could one day look like this wood at 450 m on Speyside

become available. The botanists in the Ecological Planning Group have already made up a list of possible species. One obvious candidate is dog's mercury, which is abundant in some local woodland fragments, including the edges of the burn enveloped in the Polmoody conifer plantations just to the east of Carrifran.

As mentioned in Chapter 6, two small plants have already been brought in to Carrifran: dwarf cornel and the fern *Woodsia ilvensis* (oblong woodsia). The latter is a special case, since it used to occur at Carrifran but was lost from the site, probably through the activities of Victorian fern collectors. One small clump, however, survived in a nearby valley. Spores were collected from this and propagated by staff from the Royal Botanic Garden Edinburgh. Under the Scottish Rare Plants Project, about 250 individuals have now been planted, at Carrifran and above the Grey Mare's Tail; of 60 individuals planted by the waterfall at Carrifran in 2003-2004, 46 still survived in 2007.

We are often asked how the woodland at Carrifran will respond to future changes in climate. Fifteen years ago, when we first formulated ideas for the Wildwood, rapid climate change was not on our minds. In fact, we wrote the Mission Statement and developed the management plan with hardly a reference to the possible future climate. We are not sure how different our approach would have been if we had known then what we know today. As more and more evidence of change induced by human activity has accumulated in recent years, it has become apparent that our dream of reinstating the woodland of 6000 years ago will remain a dream. By the time our Wildwood matures, conditions near the mouth of the valley will probably be more welcoming to animal and plant species from further south, whilst those species unable to

We don't have plans to move animals or plants in anticipation of climate change
Cartoon: Neil Bennett

flourish in a warmer climate may gradually shift their ranges uphill, and eventually die out if conditions even at high levels become unsuitable for them.

However, as implied in Chapter 7, we were always aware that we could not really put the clock back, since quite apart from natural climate changes between 6000 years ago and the present, the soils in the valley have undergone progressive change. In a certain sense the Wildwood Group can be accused of living in a state of denial, since we have stubbornly resisted being derailed from our initial objectives. On the other hand, perhaps that is exactly what makes the project unique. We have remained committed to restoring, as best as we can, what we are certain has been lost. Planning for the future is quite a different matter: in spite of all the modelling and predictions, there are no certainties in climate forecasting. Furthermore, there is a strand of realism in our thinking. A primary aim has always been to recreate a functioning and dynamic ecosystem, gradually losing its dependence on management. To this end, we have tried to ensure that all the founding populations of the species we plant include ample genetic diversity, so as to enable them to adapt quickly to new selective pressures created by changing conditions. If spring comes earlier, for instance, individual trees within a population that come into leaf earlier and thus have a longer growing season, may grow faster and produce more seeds than those that flush later, and so come to predominate in the population. This is evolution in action, and we would love to be here to watch it.

We are well aware that at Carrifran, a sense of being in a truly wild place will come only with time. We also know that some oversight will be needed indefinitely, and are well prepared to ensure this. The Steering Group, after 10 years and 55 meetings, is full of vitality, although an infusion of younger blood will soon be necessary. Difficult decisions are still sometimes needed, but good company and the odd bottle of wine make things easier. The most valuable meetings are the now annual ones on site, where we are joined by some members of our informal Ecological Planning group and can discuss issues while looking at the situation on the ground. Day to day operations, however, are organised by our Project Officer, George Moffat (who took over from Hugh in 2008), backed up by the occasional meetings of the Site Operations Team, in which George is joined by Philip and Willie McGhee. Monthly patrols by the volunteer boundary wardens ensure that fence problems are noticed and can be dealt with, and everyone is on the lookout for deer and for damage to trees caused by them, so that the stalking effort can be well directed.

Members of the Steering Group pause on the way up to Firth Hope

Working with the Wildwood Group

The dynamics of managing this ambitious woodland creation project as a partnership effort between the grass-roots Wildwood Steering Group and staff of Borders Forest Trust is both absorbing and challenging. As an umbrella organization for community groups BFT is used to working at arms length with groups of woodland enthusiasts. The Wildwood is radically different from this in many ways, not least because the volunteer group raised the funds to buy the site but the Trust is the landowner and bears the ultimate legal responsibility. The concept of managing an area of ground by volunteers is not familiar to many foresters or land managers and the interplay between a steering group and executive action can be subject to stresses and strains. And to be fair, over the years there have been moments. However, the sum of the efforts of the Wildwood Group and BFT, visible in the growth of woodland within Carrifran glen and the number of enthusiastic volunteers who continue to be engaged with the project justifies and validates this very special ecological restoration by committee. I have learned that patience is vital to establishing an understanding within a sea of disparate voices and that clear and considered communication underpins a successful working relationship. I have also learned that the democratic process involved in formulating management principles for an ideologically inspired project can be deeply rewarding (if somewhat long winded) and this democratization gives credence to Wildwood's community and social engagement credentials.

Willie McGhee, Director of BFT

Over the longer term the most obvious requirement is to maintain the perimeter fence so as to prevent incursions by domestic stock and goats. Deer culling will also be required for a good many years, since recently planted trees are still vulnerable, while those at high altitudes, where growth is inevitably slow, can be set back badly by browsing or fraying. Apart from this vigilance and routine care, we can expect the woodland to look after itself. Perhaps the greatest risk is of a major fire, which could cause devastating damage. However, we must accept that fire is to some extent a natural phenomenon even in our wet climate, and anyhow complete destruction of the woodland is improbable once trees are established at all levels at Carrifran. Fire would indeed be a major shock, but the process of recovery over the ensuing decades would be fascinating.

We are already trying to reduce the visible influence of humans in the valley. Many artefacts have been cleared away and much of the work of our volunteers in the next few years will be focused on removal of vole guards and tree tubes, odd bits of fencing and other clutter. The track up the valley will be made less conspicuous and contractors' vehicles will no longer use it. The stalkers' hut will eventually be removed, as well as the Holly Gill deer fence just below it. These things we can do, but the rest must be left to nature and to time.

In 1993, at the first 'Restoring Borders Woodland' conference, Chris Badenoch tried to deduce the character of the ancient wildwood of the Scottish Borderlands:

Our new Project Officer in contemplative mood

Commissioned surveys

In the Wildwood project individual donations have normally been used for buying land or planting and caring for trees, and we have avoided paying for any work that could be done by volunteers. Occasionally, however, funding organisations prefer a broader focus. The wildlife charity WWF did not help us with land purchase but funded vegetation surveys by Ben and Alison Averis. Their work gives us a snapshot of the vegetation of Carrifran at the start of the project, while a parallel survey of the neighbouring valley of Black Hope – which remains as sheep walk – provides a 'control', allowing comparison with Carrifran as restoration progresses.

In 1997, a grant from Scottish Natural Heritage funded a team of botanist-climbers to undertake a survey of Raven Craig, where special plants survive on ledges inaccessible to sheep and goats. SNH also helped when we needed their permission for the treeline woodland planting in Firth Hope, by funding a detailed vegetation survey that enabled us to avoid botanically sensitive places when planning the distribution of different tree and shrub species in this high valley (see Chapter 11).

"Much of the forest would have been tangled and irregular due to the natural wastage, disease and physical forces of wind (especially at higher altitudes on waterlogged sites), fire (since small-scale lightning fires are known to occur in this country) and floodwater. From what we know of northern Canada, Russia and Poland, at any time up to 60% of the forest trees would have been dead or dying, providing a habitat for thousands of different kinds of fungi, ferns and flowering plants, insects and other invertebrates, mammals and birds. This dead and dying timber may now be our rarest habitat in Britain."

Another graphic evocation of wildwood – though describing lands of the Duke of Argyll rather than the Duke or Buccleuch or other landowner in the Southern Uplands – comes from a 1751 report from the Clerk of Bralecken (quoted by Chris Smout) pointing out that in the local woods, the oaks made only the smallest share in most places, with many other species such as:

"ash, elm, birch, hazel, alder, rowan, gean, quaking ash, sallies, haw and sloethorn trees ...... so intermixed and grow so thick and close together in the form of a hedge or one continued thicket, galling, rubbing upon and smoothing one another for want of due weeding and pruneing ..."

Carrifran will not reach a state like this for several centuries, but we can help it on its way. For a start, we can avoid the 'tidying up' of the developing woodland that is instinctive (or learned?) in many land managers. Tidy woodlands are common enough, but rare is the forest in Britain that feels wild and natural. So we shall leave fallen trees and branches lying where they fall, we shall walk around tangles rather than cutting our way through, and we shall avoid pruning except where it is essential along the short marked trail in the Paddock.

It would be good to have beavers felling trees near the watercourses and thus ensuring more tangles and a supply of dead wood, as well as creating a variety of watery habitats. Carrifran may be too steep for them, but natural death of trees will eventually provide the dead wood habitats, and blockages of the burns will promote development of wet places. There is a case for bringing in dead wood from ancient woods in the area, along with a cargo of characteristic invertebrates, as has been done in at least one ecological restoration project in Australia. However, there will be little point in this until our planted trees are old enough to ensure a continuous supply of dead wood.

We write this final chapter at a time when BFT is embarking on a new adventure. At the end of May 2009 the Trust reached the £700,000 target of an eighteen-month fundraising campaign, enabling it to buy

the land of Corehead, 7 km north of Moffat at the head of Annandale. The land extends along the main ridge of the Moffat Hills from the iconic landmark of the Devil's Beef Tub in the west to the summit of Hart Fell (808 m) in the east.

At a BFT conference in 2003 – a decade after our first one – we revisited the topic of 'Restoring Borders Woodland'. A major theme in the second meeting was that it was time for Borders Forest Trust to develop a vision for extensive ecological restoration in the 500 or so square kilometres of the ancient Ettrick Forest, a largely unpopulated upland area bordered in the west, north and east by the towns of Moffat, Biggar, Peebles, Innerleithen, Selkirk and Hawick, and merging in the south with the remote expanse of Eskdalemuir, which extends towards Langholm. In his contribution, Philip pointed out that the Ettrick Forest had almost disappeared as a natural ecosystem, and he emphasised the accompanying loss of biodiversity, comparable to that which we mourn when tropical rainforests are felled. The work of BFT in the Ettrick and Yarrow valleys and at Carrifran were the first steps on the way to repairing some of the ecological damage inflicted over past centuries, and the plan for the future of Corehead is another part of the wider vision.

The land of Corehead links the catchment of the River Tweed (off the left) to that of the River Annan (right), while the Clyde rises just behind the viewer. Carrifran is just over the far horizon.

205

There is no expectation that the entire area of the lost Ettrick Forest will ever become wildwood. Instead, the hope is for diversification of the land, bringing both environmental and economic benefits over the long term. The most remote areas could be gradually changed to semi-natural wildwood of the kind we are trying to create at Carrifran. These core areas would be surrounded by a rich variety of woodland, grassland and wetland habitats with low key human management, enhancing the sense of a wild and relatively natural countryside. Much of the area, especially at lower levels, would continue to be managed as farmland.

The purchase of Corehead brings special opportunities. The River Annan rises on the farm, the sources of the Tweed are a stone's throw across the watershed and headwaters of the Clyde are hardly more distant. Corehead might therefore provide a key element in a network of natural habitats linking three great river catchments of southern Scotland. Furthermore, Corehead extends to within 3 km from Carrifran, offering the possibility of making a connection. If sensitive management could be extended into some of the neighbouring land, sufficient suitable habitat might – one day – develop for the lost mammals and birds, including some of the predators whose cause was so strongly espoused by Roy Dennis at the 2003 conference, such as eagles, kite, wildcat, pine marten and lynx, or even eventually wild boar and wolf. The Moffat Hills could then play a key role in promoting the survival and free movement both of these species and the host of other animals and plants whose vanguard is already to be seen in the developing Wildwood at Carrifran.

As populations of more and more kinds of wild plants and animals become established in the Moffat Hills we shall gradually come closer to achieving a basic aim of the Wildwood Group, which is to ensure that in one part of the Southern Uplands, nature takes priority: the needs of wild animals and plants take precedence and natural processes largely supersede human management. Humans will always be welcome in the Wildwood, but we hope they will tread lightly, striving to avoid any reduction in the wildness of the recreated natural habitats. Carrifran and the surrounding hills may then become a beautiful oasis in a stressed and crowded world.

Another walk into the valley

It is summer 2009 and thirteen years have passed since our first walk into Carrifran valley (see Chapter 6). Today, in early June, we take another walk. First we pause at the secluded car park. There are other cars here today, working cars. We wonder whose they are? Leaving the car park we follow the winding path – partly along board walks over wet patches – through clumps of young hazel, blackthorn and rowan, along with alder, bird cherry and guelder rose. There is a glint of water through a screen of young willows, where a developing wetland provides habitat for species lost to past agricultural drainage and heavy grazing. A cock reed bunting stands proudly on the tallest willow branch and we hear the churring song of a grasshopper warbler somewhere in the undergrowth.

Further along the path the woodland is more dense. Willow warblers, great tits and blue tits have found this newly created habitat, and across the dip to our right, among a grove of even taller trees, an infuriatingly secretive warbler is singing strongly. It may be a blackcap, a species that recolonised the valley last year, but doesn't sound quite right. We fail to see it, and continue to the sheepstell at the top of the rise.

Here is the place to pause – to sit on the bench and absorb the changes in the valley. First we look down to the left, where the trees planted in 2000 are now several times our own height. Then we look northwards. There are obvious patches of developing woodland on the slopes of Carrifran Gans on the right, and a few trees break the

Autumn view, 2008

horizon high on Peat Hill, but it is still barely possible to pick out the more recently planted trees in the distant parts of the valley and high up on the steep slopes. We know we have planted nearly half a million, but most are still barely knee-high.

Now we drop down to the old track, still used by the Project Officer on his quad bike, but gradually fading and getting lost in the woodland. We are entering the valley proper. Here we shall see no markers, find

Millennium Grove, ten years on

View out of Carrifran in 1997: today the dots on the hillside are volunteers, not sheep

no maintained paths and see few artefacts, apart from some drystane dykes and remains of older structures built by herdsmen through the centuries. Carrifran is embarking on its slow drift in time, towards a landscape resembling the one surveyed by the bowman as he set off on his hunt, six thousand years ago.

The hillsides are strongly patterned at this time of year, not only with clumps of trees and expanses of bracken and dark heather, but also with sedges and grasses showing up the flushes – patches of green and buff, with occasional darker brown streaks of rushes. Tracks are still visible on the hillside left by the crawler tractor when placing saplings and guards for the planters, but they will disappear in a few years. Close by, some trees are ten feet tall and it is easy to imagine a game of hide-and-seek – impossible on the bare hillsides of the past. What a difference these trees would have made to the Covenanters seeking refuge in these hills three and a half centuries ago!

Above us, bright objects are moving on the slopes – five on one side of the valley and three on the other. Surely not sheep! A decade ago, these hillsides were white-dotted with sheep, along with the occasional goats and many cows further up the valley, but they are gone now. Today the dots on the hillsides are people, whose cars we noted earlier. The job today for these committed Tuesday volunteers is to clear away old tree guards, collecting them in the bright-coloured sacks that caught our eyes.

It is the season for cuckooflower, marsh-marigold, violets, purple vetch, milkwort and parsley fern. Orange tip and green-veined white butterflies are feeding and mating. Some of the puddles along the track still have live tadpoles; most puddles dry up too soon, but some are fed by trickles from the flushes and froglets may emerge from them in time. A hiker walks towards us and passes silently; perhaps we should have stopped him to find out what he feels about the changes in the valley.

Soon we come to a large unplanted area, the domain of the meadow pipits. They, along with the wheatears, may not welcome the developing forest elsewhere in the valley, since they depend on open ground. In the young woodland, however, stonechats are flourishing, since saplings a metre or so high make ideal perches. We wonder about ring ouzels, always scarce in this area and normally associated with bare hillsides, though slopes with patchy scrub of juniper and willow may be closer to their natural habitat. An influx of short-eared owls was expected when we fenced out the stock, since their vole prey flourish in the resulting dense sward, but we have only seen ones and twos occasionally over the years. As we wander along the burn, we find clumps of young rowans, not planted by us; it is evident that self-sown trees, which survived here and around high crags but have long been suppressed by grazing, have at last had the chance to come away. The valley is reviving, even where we have not planted.

Now that we have passed the end of the old farm track, there are only faint paths. Most of the well-worn tracks made by the sheep and goats have grassed over, and although routes followed by planters and

The hillsides are strongly patterned at this time of year

Woodland is creeping up the valley

One has to walk a long way up the valley to view Firthhope Linn

visitors can be made out in some places, they are hardly more conspicuous than those used by the wild animals. Fox droppings are easy to find, but we are becoming aware that badgers – with their low-slung bodies – may be responsible for some of the more obvious tracks. On an earlier walk, Philip stumbled on a badger lavatory at the surprising height of 747 m near the summit of Carrifran Gans, suggesting that the badger patrols at Carrifran are not only within the valley but extend over the plateau above it.

And so we walk on up the glen, encountering more cogent reminders of the transformation that is under way at Carrifran. Although trees are visible in every direction there is never a feeling of being in a plantation because they vary in height, shape, colour and spacing, emphasising the varied character of the land. They are not everywhere – there are glades and wide open spaces – but they pervade the valley; mostly small, but some twice as tall as us and forming visible patches of woodland. There are straight trees, crooked trees, fallen trees and a few dead trees; trees in clumps, drifts and scattered groups, spreading across level ground, clustered in hollows and silhouetted on ridges. As we climb, they are smaller: not struggling – though a few have lost their tips – but most of them proudly thrusting upwards with fresh leaves above the remaining winter-dead grass and. They are less developed the higher we get: summer comes late near the hilltops!

Beside us is the stepped cascade of Firthhope Linn that brings the burn down more than 150 m in a series of ropes of foam into the rocky ravine below. Far above, Firth Hope opens out. This hanging valley, a scoop in the plateau that surrounds Carrifran, still has a relatively uninteresting grassy sward created by grazing domestic stock, but it is now dotted with small tree guards protecting some of the 11,000 shrubs and trees planted up here in the last three springs. We hope that in due course it will be the jewel in the crown of Carrifran, a patchy expanse of re-created treeline woodland unlike anything now existing in Britain. The little trees battling to survive in the extreme conditions high in the hills are just one piece of the ecological jigsaw reassembling itself at Carrifran as we watch, year by year. The efforts of all those who have dreamed, planned and planted are now coming to fruition: Carrifran is becoming a Wildwood once again.

Wildwood December dawn

APPENDIX A. Bird surveys

Species	Carrifran 1998	Carrifran 2000	Blackhope 2000	Carrifran 2002	Carrifran 2004 (15 May / 18 June)	Carrifran 2005 (16 May / 29 June)	Carrifran 2006 (25 May / 19 June)	Carrifran 2007 (10 May / 14 June)	Blackhope 2007 (17 May / 18 June)	Carrifran 2008 (14-5 May / 26 June)	Carrifran 2009 (14 May / 25 June)	Blackhope 2009 (21 May / 18 June)	Carrifran 1998-2002 TOTAL	Carrifran 2007-2009 TOTAL
Goosander	1												1	0
Kestrel		1		1		1	1		1	5			2	5
Peregrine	3		2	1	3	2	2	2	3	2			4	4
Buzzard	1	1		1	2	1		2	4	2	1	4	2	5
Black grouse				1			5			4	4		2	8
Oystercatcher							2		1					0
Common sandpiper			4						2					0
Lesser bb gull	1												1	0
Woodpigeon								1	1	2	6			9
Cuckoo							1							0
Skylark	6	1	4	2			1						9	0
Swallow	6	1	1				1		1	1		1	7	1
House martin									2					0
Meadow pipit	278	267	409	371	282	251	214	282	294	368	331	444	916	981
Pied wagtail	3	1	4		1				1			2	4	0
Grey wagtail	2	4	5	5	4	2	3	3	4	8	8	1	11	19
Dipper	1		5			1		1	1	1	1		1	3
Wren	19	17	43	10	20	19	27	18	14	43	22	17	46	83
Dunnock											2			2
Robin									3			1		0
Whinchat				4	11	11	13			14	7		4	21
Stonechat				1	8	9	22	21	4	15	11	2	1	47
Wheatear	31	28	60	9	13	23	21	8	62	8	11	91	68	27
Ring ousel	5	3	1		1								8	0
Garden warbler											2			2
Blackcap							2			2	3			5
Grasshopper warbler								1						1
Willow warbler	1							4		9	22	2	1	35
Great tit														0
Raven	2	1	3	1	6	1	1	5	3	4	1		4	10
Carrion crow	3	5	1	1	22	9	7	10	11	14	9	1	9	33
Rook	1		29		3				156			41	1	0
Chaffinch	1	1	1	4			1		1	9	12	5	6	21
Lesser redpoll										2	1	4		3
Siskin											1			1
Total	365	331	572	412	376	330	324	358	569	513	455	616	1108	1326
Number of species	18	13	15	14	13	12	17	13	20	19	19	14	22	23

APPENDIX B. Trees and shrubs for Carrifran

Scientific name	English name	Status in 1999	Action
Alnus glutinosa	Alder	Not at Carrifran but in Moffatdale	Many planted
Arctostaphylos uva-ursi	Bearberry	Not at Carrifran but on Grey Mare's Tail	Perhaps plant some
Betula nana	Dwarf birch	Not at Carrifran but in southern Scotland	Planting vetoed by SNH
Betula pendula	Silver birch	One tree recorded	A few needed
Betula pubescens	Downy birch	Some present	Many planted
Calluna vulgaris	Heather, ling	Abundant	No action
Cornus suecica	Dwarf cornel	Not at Carrifran but on Grey Mare's Tail	A few planted, more needed
Corylus avellana	Hazel	A few present	Many planted, more needed
Crataegus monogyna	Hawthorn	A few present	Many planted, more needed
Cytisus scoparius	Broom	Not at Carrifran but in the area	A few planted, more needed
Fraxinus excelsior	Ash	Some present	Many planted
Genista anglica	Petty whin	Not at Carrifran but past records in area	Perhaps should be planted
Hedera helix	Ivy	A few present	Some planted, more needed
Ilex aquifolium	Holly	Two present	Many planted
Juniperus communis	Juniper	Not at Carrifran but near St Mary's Loch	Many planted, more needed
Lonicera periclymenum	Honeysuckle	A few present	Some planted, more needed
Malus sylvestris	Crab apple	Perhaps native to the area	Provisionally no action
Myrica gale	Bog-myrtle	Not at Carrifran but within 10 km	Perhaps should be planted
Pinus sylvestris	Scots pine	Not at Carrifran but present in the past	A few to be planted soon
Populus tremula	Aspen	Not at Carrifran but in Moffatdale	Many planted, more needed
Prunus avium	Gean, wild cherry	Not at Carrifran but in Moffatdale	Some planted, more needed
Prunus padus	Bird cherry	Two present	Many planted, more needed
Prunus spinosa	Blackthorn	Not at Carrifran but in Moffatdale	Some planted, more needed
Quercus petraea	Sessile oak	Not at Carrifran but in Moffatdale	Many planted, more needed
Quercus robur	Pedunculate oak	Not at Carrifran but near St Mary's Loch	Perhaps a few needed
Rosa canina (agg.)	Dog rose	Some present	Some planted, more needed
Rosa mollis	Soft downy-rose	A few probably present on crags	Some needed
Rosa pimpinellifolia	Burnet rose	A few clumps present	Some planted, more needed
Rubus chamaemorus	Cloudberry	Many present	No action
Rubus fruticosus (agg.)	Bramble	Some present at mouth of valley	No action
Rubus idaeus	Raspberry	Some present	No action
Rubus saxatilis	Stone bramble	A few present	None planted, perhaps needed
Salix aurita	Eared willow	Some present	Many planted, more needed
Salix caprea	Goat willow	A few present	Some planted, more needed
Salix cinerea	Grey willow	A few present	Some planted, more needed
Salix herbacea	Dwarf willow	A few patches present	No action
Salix lapponum	Downy willow	Not at Carrifran but on Grey Mare's Tail	Some planted, more needed
Salix myrsinifolia	Dark-leaved willow	Not at Carrifran but on Grey Mare's Tail	Some planted, more needed
Salix pentandra	Bay willow	Not at Carrifran but near St Mary's Loch	Some planted, more needed
Salix phylicifolia	Tea-leaved willow	Not at Carrifran but near St Mary's Loch	Some planted, more needed
Salix purpurea	Purple willow	Not at Carrifran but recorded in area	Probably should be planted
Salix repens	Creeping willow	One clump recorded	More needed
Sambucus nigra	Elder	Not at Carrifran but in Moffatdale	Some to be planted soon
Sorbus aucuparia	Rowan	Some present	Many planted
Taxus baccata	Yew	Not at Carrifran but may be native to area	A few planted
Tilia cordata	Small-leaved lime	Not at Carrifran and not native to area	No action
Ulex species	Whin (gorse)	Not at Carrifran but in the area	A few to be planted soon
Ulmus glabra	Wych elm	Not at Carrifran but in Moffatdale	Some planted, more needed
Viburnum opulus	Guelder rose	Not at Carrifran but in Moffatdale	Some planted, more needed

APPENDIX C. Woodland types considered appropriate for Carrifran

NVC Woodland Type	Informal woodland name	Appropriate trees (major species in bold type)	Appropriate shrubs (major species in bold type)
W1	Grey willow with marsh bedstraw	Downy birch	**Grey willow**
W4	Downy birch with purple moor-grass	**Downy birch** (65%), alder (15%), goat willow (10%)	**Grey willow**, eared willow, bay willow
W7	Alder-ash with yellow pimpernel	**Ash** (20%), **alder** (5%), downy birch (42%), rowan (14%), holly (3%), sessile oak (3%), bird cherry, goat willow	**Hawthorn, hazel, grey willow**, bay willow, blackthorn, elder, guelder rose
W9	Upland mixed broadleaved with dog's mercury	**Downy birch, ash, rowan**, alder, sessile oak, aspen, wych elm, bird cherry, holly	**Hazel**, elder, hawthorn, grey willow
W11	Upland oak-birch with bluebell	**Downy birch** (50%), **sessile oak** (15%), rowan (19%), holly (5%), aspen (1%)	Hawthorn, hazel, juniper
W17	Upland oak-birch with blaeberry	**Downy birch** (50%), **sessile oak** (15%), rowan (20%), holly (5%)	Hawthorn, hazel, juniper
W19	Juniper with wood-sorrel	Downy birch, rowan, Scots pine	**Juniper**, stone bramble
W20	Downy willow scrub with great wood-rush		**Downy willow**, tea-leaved willow, eared willow

Notes: Tree and shrub species appropriate for Carrifran and designations of major and minor species were based mainly on information in Rodwell (1991), Rodwell & Patterson (1994) and Preston et al. (2002). The percentages for tree species are those chosen by us, but are approximate since different mixes were used in different compartments. Shrubs were limited by Forestry Commission rules to a total of 10%. A few extra species were planted in small quantities. Only a little alder was planted initially in W7, but more was added later when the ground proved wetter than we had realised, both there and especially in some areas originally planned as W17. W9 woodland was considered to form small pockets within W7.

Index

Bold type indicates main discussion. Plant species are indexed under their English names, with spelling following Stace (1997). Scientific names for plants are indexed only if these are used in the text, but are included in the index for reference under the relevant English name. Butterfly species are indexed under 'butterflies'. Bird species are not generally indexed separately if they are included in the bird survey data in Appendix A, but all references to bird species are included in the entry 'birds'. A complete list of birds recorded from Carrifran is on the project website. Names of people are not included, and generally we have not indexed names of visiting groups.

Further Information

Organisations

Borders Forest Trust (www.bordersforesttrust.org) and **Carrifran Wildwood** (www.carrifran.org.uk)

British Association of Nature Conservationists (journal *ECOS*, website www.banc.org.uk)

John Muir Trust (www.jmt.org)

Reforesting Scotland (www.reforestingscotland.org; journal *Reforesting Scotland*)

Society for Ecological Restoration International (www.ser.org)

Trees for Life (www.treesforlife.org.uk and www.restore-earth.org; journal *Caledonia Wild*)

Publications

Aronson, J, Milton, S J & Blignaut, J N (eds) (2007) Restoring Natural Capital. Island Press, Washington.

Ashmole, N P (ed) (1994) *Restoring Borders Woodland*. Peeblesshire Environment Concern, Peebles.

Ashmole, P (2006) The lost mountain woodland of Scotland and its restoration. *Scottish Forestry* 60(1), 9-22.

Deakin, R (2008) *Wildwood. A Journey through Trees.* Penguin Books.

Johnston, J Laughton & Balharry, Dick (2001) *Beinn Eighe: The Mountain above the Wood*. Scottish Natural Heritage.

Kohn, D (ed) (2003) *Restoring Borders Woodland: the vision and the task.* Occasional Paper, Borders Forest Trust, Ancrum, Jedburgh.

Newton, A C & Ashmole, P (eds) (1998) *Native woodland restoration in southern Scotland: principles and practice.* The University of Edinburgh and the Borders Forest Trust.

Peterken, G F (1996) *Natural woodland: Ecology and conservation in Northern Temperate Regions.* Cambridge University Press.

Preston, C D, Pearman, D A & Dines, T D (2002) *New Atlas of the British & Irish Flora*. Oxford University Press.

Ramsay, P (1997) *Revival of the land: Creag Meagaidh National Nature Reserve.* Scottish Natural Heritage.

Ratcliffe, D (2007) *Galloway and the Borders*. Collins (New Naturalist).

Rodwell, J S (ed) (1991) *British Plant Communities. Volume 1. Woodlands and scrub*. Cambridge University Press.

Rodwell, J & Patterson, G (1994) *Creating New Native Woodlands*. Forestry Commission Bulletin 112.

Smout, T C, MacDonald, A R & Watson, F (2005) *A history of the native woodlands of Scotland, 1500-1920*. Edinburgh University Press.

Stace, C (1997) New *Flora of the British Isles,* 2nd ed. Cambridge University Press.

Tipping, R (1997) Vegetational history of southern Scotland. *Botanical Journal of Scotland* 49(2), 151-162.

Warren, C (2009) Managing Scotland's Environment, 2nd ed. Edinburgh University Press.

Looking to the future
Photo: Pamela Ross

I would like to support the Carrifran Wildwood by (please tick preferred options):-

☐ **establishing a Stewardship with a gift of £250** ☐ **£500** ☐ **or more £** ....
in the name of ....
I wish ☐ (or) I do not wish ☐ the Steward's name to be published on the website and in lists
of donors. Dedication for the website (if any) ....
....

or ☐ **making a donation of £** ....

or ☐ **making a regular donation of £** .... **per** *month / year* (please delete one, and complete Standing
Order form below)

☐ **considering a legacy to the Wildwood.** If you tick this option we will send you some notes about
legacy arrangements. Funds would be used only for the Wildwood project.

Your details (if you have designated another person as a Steward, please enclose their details separately)

Name .... Title ....
(please print)
Address ....
.... Postcode ....

☐ **I enclose a cheque payable to Borders Forest Trust (Wildwood) for the sum of £** ....

or ☐ **Please debit my credit card with the sum of £** .... (minimum credit card donation £25)

Credit Card Number (Visa, Master, Euro, Delta, CAF) _ _ _ _ _ _ _ _ _ _ _ _ _ _ _ _

Name (as on card) .... Expiry date __ / __

Signature .... Date ....

or ☐ **I authorise you to send the following standing order request to my bank:**

To (bank) .... (address) ....
.... Postcode ....

Sort code _ _ - _ _ - _ _ A/C No. _ _ _ _ _ _ _ _ A/C Name ....

Please pay to: Borders Forest Trust (Wildwood), Bank of Scotland, High Street, Jedburgh,

Sort Code 80-16-48, Account No. 00105529, **the sum of £.....** *monthly / annually* (delete one)

Starting on (date) _ _ / _ _ / _ _ Signature .... Date _ _ / _ _ / _ _

GIFT AID. If you are a UK taxpayer, we can recover from HM Revenue & Customs the tax you have paid
on any donation, greatly increasing its value. **Please sign the declaration below:-**

**"I want the Borders Forest Trust to treat all donations I make from the date of this declaration
(until I notify you otherwise) as Gift Aid donations. I am a UK taxpayer."**

Signature .... Date _ _ / _ _ / _ _

Please return to: The Borders Forest Trust, FREEPOST SCO2459, JEDBURGH, TD8 0BR

cut